WISDOM TAKES WORK

WISDOM
TAKES WORK

LEARN. APPLY. REPEAT.

RYAN HOLIDAY

Profile Books

First published in Great Britain in 2025 by
Profile Books Ltd
29 Cloth Fair
London
EC1A 7JQ

www.profilebooks.com

First published in the United States by Portfolio,
an imprint of Penguin Random House LLC

1 3 5 7 9 10 8 6 4 2

Printed and bound in India by
Manipal Technologies Limited

A CIP catalogue record for this book is available from the British Library.

Our product safety representative in the EU is Authorised
Rep Compliance Ltd., Ground Floor, 71 Lower Baggot Street,
Dublin, D02 P593, Ireland. www.arccompliance.com

ISBN 978 1 78816 629 4
eISBN 978 1 78283 756 5

CONTENTS

Part II: THE SIRENS
(THE PERILOUS ROCKS YOU MUST BEWARE)

Part III: THE APOTHEOSIS
(TOUCHING THE DIVINE)

Let no one be slow to seek wisdom when they are young nor weary in the search when they have grown old. For no age is too early or too late for the health of the soul. And to say that the season for studying philosophy has not yet come, or that it is past and gone, is like saying that the season for happiness is not yet or that it is now no more.

—EPICURUS

The Four Virtues

~

It was long ago now that Hercules came to the crossroads.

At a quiet intersection in the hills of Greece, in the shade of knobby pine trees, the great hero of Greek myth first met his destiny.

Where exactly it was or when, no one knows. We hear of this moment in the stories of Socrates. We can see it captured in the most beautiful art of the Renaissance. We can feel his budding energy, his strapping muscles, and his anguish in the classic Bach cantata. If John Adams had had his way, Hercules at the crossroads would have been immortalized on the official seal of the newly founded United States.

Because there, before his undying fame, before the twelve labors, before he changed the world, Hercules faced a crisis, one as life-changing and real as any of us have ever faced.

Where was he headed? Where was he trying to go? That's the point of the story. Alone, unknown, unsure, Hercules, like so many, did not know.

Where the road diverged lay a beautiful goddess who offered

him every temptation he could imagine. Adorned in finery, she promised him a life of ease. She swore he'd never taste want or unhappiness or fear or pain. Follow her, she said, and every desire would be fulfilled.

On the other path stood a sterner goddess in a pure white robe. She made a quieter call. She promised no rewards except those that came as a result of hard work. It would be a long journey, she said. There would be sacrifice. There would be scary moments. But it was a journey fit for a god, the way of his ancestors. It would make him the man he was meant to be.

Was this real? Did it really happen?

If it's only a legend, does it matter?

Yes, because this is a story about us.

About our dilemma. About our own crossroads.

For Hercules the choice was between vice and virtue, the easy way and the hard way, the well-trod path and the road less traveled. The same goes for us.

Hesitating only for a second, Hercules chose the one that made all the difference.

He chose virtue.

"Virtue" can seem old-fashioned. In fact, virtue—*arete*—translates to something very simple and very timeless: Excellence. Moral. Physical. Mental.

In the ancient world, virtue was comprised of four key components.

Courage.

Temperance.

Justice.

Wisdom.

The "touchstones of goodness," the philosopher king Marcus Aurelius called them. To millions, they're known as the "cardinal virtues," four near-universal ideals adopted by Christianity and most of Western philosophy, but equally valued in Buddhism, Hinduism, and just about every other philosophy you can imagine. They're called "cardinal," C. S. Lewis pointed out, not because they come down from church authorities, but because they originate from the Latin *cardo*, or hinge.

It's *pivotal* stuff. It's the stuff that the door to the good life hangs on.

They are also our topic for this book, and for this series.

Four books.* Four virtues.

One aim: to help you choose . . .

Courage, bravery, endurance, fortitude, honor, sacrifice . . .

Temperance, self-control, moderation, composure, balance . . .

Justice, fairness, service, fellowship, goodness, kindness . . .

Wisdom, knowledge, education, truth, self-reflection, peace . . .

* This is book 4.

These are the key to the good life, a life of honor, of glory, of *excellence* in every sense. Character traits, which John Steinbeck perfectly described as "pleasant and desirable to [their] owner and makes him perform acts of which he can be proud and which he can be pleased." But the *he* must be taken to mean all of humankind. There was no feminine version of the word *virtus* in Rome. Virtue wasn't male or female, it just *was*.

It still is. It doesn't matter if you're a man or a woman. It doesn't matter if you're physically strong or painfully shy, a genius or of average intelligence. Virtue is universal. The imperative remains universal.

The virtues are interrelated and inseparable, yet each is distinct from the others. Doing the right thing almost always takes courage, just as moderation is impossible without the wisdom to know what is worth choosing. What good is courage if not applied to justice? What good is wisdom if it doesn't make us more modest?

North, south, east, west—the four virtues are a kind of compass (there's a reason that the four points on a compass are called the "cardinal directions"). They guide us. They show us where we are and what is true.

Aristotle described virtue as a kind of craft, something to pursue just as one pursues the mastery of any profession or skill. "We become builders by building and we become harpists by playing the harp," he writes. "Similarly, then, we become just by doing just actions, temperate by doing temperate actions, brave by doing brave actions."

Virtue is something we do.

It's something we choose.

Not once, for Hercules's crossroads was not a singular event. It's a daily challenge, one we face not once but constantly, repeatedly. Will we be selfish or selfless? Brave or afraid? Strong or weak? Wise or stupid? Will we cultivate a good habit or a bad one? Courage or cowardice? The bliss of ignorance or the challenge of a new idea?

Stay the same . . . or grow?

The easy way or the right way?

Introduction

The end of being is to know; and if you say the end of knowledge is action—why yes, but the end of that action again, is knowledge.

—RALPH WALDO EMERSON

Of all the virtues, wisdom is the most elusive. It is something to which you aspire, something that we are always trying to acquire.

Yet we understand that we will almost certainly never arrive, not fully anyway, that at best, true wisdom is something we can only *approach*. Despite a lifetime of work, it exceeds our grasp each time, slipping with each step further into the distance, like the horizon that can never be reached.

The same elusiveness holds when we try to define wisdom. It's obviously more than being smart, more than the possession of knowledge and facts, more even than insight. It's intelligence, intuition, experience and education, philosophy and practical understanding, awareness and wit, perspective, perspicacity, and, yes, the "prudence" that the ancients sometimes called wisdom.

It's all these things yet still, somehow, so much more.

So you're telling me you can't tell me what wisdom is or how to get it?

Yes. Welcome to life. It's complicated. Only a fool believes in simple step-by-step formulas.

Wisdom takes *work*. Like love and happiness and everything worthwhile, wisdom can't be accessed through hacks or shortcuts. Anyone who claims to have an easy way to get it is a liar, and anyone who claims to have it probably doesn't.

One thing we can say clearly about wisdom is that it isn't something you're born with.

And yet, certainly the other virtues are born from it—wisdom is called the mother of all virtues for precisely this reason. Can a person who doesn't understand risk be genuinely courageous? Without wisdom, how would they even know what to be courageous about? Does it not waste self-discipline to direct it at the wrong thing incorrectly or to do so inefficiently? You can have a good heart, but without competence, without savvy and perspective, your attempts at justice will surely fail.

Wisdom, then, we might say, is knowing . . .

. . . *what* to do,

. . . *when* to do it,

. . . and *how* to do it.

Wisdom is *knowing what's what.*

It's the ability to see what's in front of you with clarity. It's approaching an understanding of the way things work, why things happen, where things stand now, and what might happen next. It's not an encyclopedic knowledge of facts and figures but something both profound and applied—for it was not Gandhi's sharp legal mind that made him the mahatma.

If wisdom is hard to define, its opposite is not. Just as courage is complicated but cowardice is simple, so it goes with wisdom, a virtue whose elusiveness is in stark contrast to folly. We know a fool when we see one. We know we don't want to be that.

Just as no one is born wise, no one is born dumb—ignorant, sure, but remaining so is a choice. What will we choose?

Both wisdom and foolishness are a kind of asymptote. Some of us are further from the axis than others—some are smarter, some are more educated—but because the function is infinite, the possibilities are endless. There is always more to learn, more to know, more to understand about the world and yourself. The converse is also true: No matter how dumb someone seems to be, there is always room for surprise, for human stupidity is also infinite.

We pursue wisdom for one essential reason: We need it. Later and right now. Life is a thinking person's game. A decision about our future appears before us one day, a moral dilemma the next. Complex problems. Complicated people. Confusing situations. Hidden opportunities.

In these moments, big and small, the wisdom you need will either be there or it won't. The experience and knowledge and understanding will have been accumulated or not. We've either done the study necessary or we haven't. It is in that moment that we discover the reason that you can't spell *learned* without *earned*.

Wisdom, then, is a lagging indicator of work done long ago, the fruit nurtured from seed planted long ago. And, as the ancients taught us, we can only reap what has been sown.

THIS IS THE WAY

Seneca tells the story of a pretentious but lazy Roman. He wanted to be able to impress his educated friends, so instead of reading for hundreds of hours, he purchased a set of well-read slaves. One knew Homer by heart. Another knew Hesiod. He had a slave for Sappho, another for Pindar, and one for Simonides, one for each of the ancient Greek poets that an upperclass Roman was supposed to know inside and out.

He thought he was getting away with it, having these men feed him lines at dinner parties, on hand whenever he needed to look something up, until a friend suggested that he take wrestling lessons. "But I am weak and frail," the man replied. "Don't say that," his friend teased. "Consider how many perfectly healthy slaves you have!"

We all wish there was a way to get something for nothing, that we could fast forward to the part where we "have" it. We look for tricks and cheat codes, as if wisdom were possible without incredible amounts of effort, without a lifetime of study. This matter, Seneca reminds us, cannot be delegated to someone else.

There is no technology that can do it for you. There is no app. No teacher who can simply download everything into your brain. No guru who can lead you to enlightenment or shaman who can give it to you in a dose. It's not about what you're born with. It's about what you *do* with it.

The path of wisdom is not just rocky, it is guarded by bridge trolls and beset by obstacles. There are dead ends. There are pits of despair. There are staggering peaks and terrifying wonders. There is so much ground to cover. You will meet unfriendly people and unpleasant ideas along the way. Are you tough enough to handle that? Are you prepared for a long journey? Or do you want everything to be nice, neat, and easy?

Even if you are naturally gifted, even if you've already graduated from the best schools, wisdom is not yours. Still, Seneca writes, "much toil remains; to confront it, you must yourself lavish all your waking hours, and all your efforts, if you wish the result to be accomplished."

This book, then, is not a book *of* wisdom but rather a book about that work. It aims to explain the methods of some of the wisest people who have ever lived as well as the traps that trip up the foolish. These aren't always methods our subjects articulated themselves. Wise people don't often talk about their wisdom, fools don't know they're foolish, but both have given us something better: their example.

Wisdom has been the work of great men and women for millennia, long before Socrates supposedly brought philosophy down from the heavens. We'll look at the ideas of Montaigne and Emerson—our guides in the book—alongside the hubris and stupidity of people who should have known better. We'll look at the patient, practical wisdom of Lincoln, and contrast it with the impulsive immaturity of so-called geniuses who, for all their brainpower, fail to understand so much.

Most of all, we'll look at the work they did—because nobody got their wisdom for free.

Like the other virtues, wisdom is a by-product of doing the right thing in the right way at the right time, not just once but consistently over the course of a life. It is the result of a method, and yet it is never actually possessed.

That's because *it is the method.*

Not a groundbreaking one either, but the same practices, the same questions people have posed and actions they've taken since they started roaming the earth. It's mentors and apprenticeships. It's studying history. It's reading, so much reading. It's seeking out experiences. It's delving, discovering, disassembling, discussing, debating, and demanding answers. It's focus and observation. It's avoiding error—and learning from mistakes. It's self-evaluation. It's questioning our assumptions. It's remaining a student, no matter how old or accomplished we are.

The methods might be simple, but committing to them for a lifetime? The returns might be modest day to day, but over the course of a lifetime . . .

We can get wiser, but never wise.

Smarter but never smart.

Closer but never *there*.

Wisdom is available to anyone willing to earn it.

Wisdom is not comfortable.

Wisdom is a battle to be won.

Wisdom takes work.

Wisdom is worth it.

PART I
THE AGOGE
(YOUR TRAINING GROUND)

No man was ever wise by chance.

—SENECA

We must get it ourselves. No one can give us an education. The most important decision a person makes in their life is to become a student and to remain one not just in school or in their profession, but for life. There's a reason that wise people speak so little of wisdom. They are still too busy looking for it, still identifying as students themselves. A good education instills us with good morals, good ideas, good habits—the skillset that allows us to learn everything that the world is able to teach. What we put in our brain, especially early on but also on a daily basis, forms a kind of bank balance that we will draw on in the future. The practice we form now will sustain us . . . or betray us. We must become students of history, of humanity. We must cultivate the ability to listen, to look, to learn. We must hone a powerful sense of curiosity, an insatiable desire to acquire knowledge. Charting our own course of study will require immense discipline and considerable courage. Let us begin.

A Most Unusual Education . . .

~

As the scion of a noble family, Michel de Montaigne should have spent his early days surrounded by servants and coddled in luxury. Instead, his parents sent their boy to live with a local peasant family—not out of neglect, but to give him something he couldn't get at home. Most wealthy children in the sixteenth century were handed over to wet nurses and nannies, but Montaigne, within sight of but a world away from the enormous estate that bore his name, was, in his words, "formed by fortune under the laws of the common people and of nature."

It was an unusual beginning to an unusual education, one that would continue until Montaigne took his last breath, at age fifty-nine.

After those early days in the bosom of his surrogate family, Montaigne was brought home, where his father decreed that no one would speak any language around his son but Latin. Instead of their local dialect of French, Montaigne lived in the world of Horace and Cato, coming naturally to the language the same way the ancients had.

Even residents of the village went along with the plan, and years later, Montaigne was surprised to hear one of them casually refer to a tool by its Latin name, so ingrained had the habit become for his sake. With no other languages allowed within earshot—his Latin tutor was German and didn't even know French—the mother tongue of philosophy came to the boy quickly and painlessly. The Romans had first come to Bordeaux around 60 BC, and Rome had fallen in the centuries since, but for Montaigne, Urbs Aeterna still stood eternal.

Soon enough, Montaigne was more fluent than his parents and more proficient than his tutor. "As for me," Montaigne would later recall, "I was over six before I understood any more French . . . than Arabic."

One might expect that an education this strict and directed—not to mention strange—would be joyless. Montaigne was lucky, for he was formed as much by love and tenderness as he was by these experiments. He would be taught Greek later, a bit more traditionally, but his father envisioned it as a game. Montaigne would recall the fun of volleying "conjugations back and forth" with his instructors, not even aware that he was learning. Montaigne recalled that in his father's travels abroad, educational experts advised him to shape his son's soul "entirely through gentleness and freedom," that his choices should be respected and that he should *love* to learn. Is it any surprise that Montaigne would go to his deathbed believing that he had the best father there ever was?

Only twice in his life was Montaigne ever physically disciplined—gently, he noted—something that many children today could not say and few could have said in the sixteenth century. Most mornings, he was awakened not by a nagging parent or a stern schoolmaster, but by beautiful songs of the musicians whom his father had hired. It was a way to teach his son music, but it was also a way to address a rather touching concern—startling the "tender brains of children" awake with a shake or a shout, his father believed, was borderline cruel.

At seven, Montaigne was reading Ovid for fun, already tired of patronizing kids' stories. But he wasn't just a bookworm. In the Montaigne household, everything was an opportunity to learn—even pranks or mistakes were material for discussions or lessons. Everything was designed to "serve as an excellent book," every situation provided a takeaway, even "some cheating by a page, some stupidity on the part of a lackey, something said at table," was a chance to discuss, to debate, to analyze. Everything was to be questioned. Every idea to be traced back to its original source. Great thinkers were turned to for advice and for answers, but they were not exempt from challenges. "Pass everything through a sieve," Montaigne would later say about how to educate a child, "and lodge nothing in his head on mere authority or trust."

He was taught not to be precious about mistakes, even encouraged to admit he'd made them. The important thing to teach kids, he said of the real lesson he'd learned in his youth, was "that confessing an error which he discovers in his own argument even when he alone has noticed it is an act of justice and integrity, which are the main qualities he pursues." In Montaigne's family, stubbornness was a vice, belief in one's infallibility or superiority the only screwup to be ashamed of.

It must have been shocking the first time Montaigne stepped into a classroom, at the Collège de Guyenne, which his father had helped start. To suddenly be surrounded by other students, doing this thing called "school." As Montaigne would have known, the root of that word is the Greek word meaning "leisure." Then, as now, how distant the etymology is from reality.

Montaigne did not love how often he and his fellow students were "left to the melancholy humor of a furious schoolmaster." There was so much schoolwork, the days were interminable; he and his fellow students found it excruciating "slaving away for fourteen and fifteen hours a day like a porter." They were forced to memorize and recite and translate passages as if these noises and sounds and symbols were a replacement for understanding. It is tragic, Montaigne felt, but not a surprise, how many kids hate going to school and, sadder still, how many teachers hate their students.

Just as birds carry food in their beaks "without tasting it to stuff it down the beaks of their young," Montaigne said, "our schoolmasters go foraging for learning in their books and merely lodge it on the tip of their lips, only to spew it out and scatter it on the wind." His fellow students who could repeat

5

what they'd learned from their teachers? They were no more than parrots. "To know by heart is not to know," Montaigne would say later, "it is to keep what they have given you and store it in your memory."

School taught him the basics: math, logic, poetry. But he dreamed of gaining control over his own studies, and later was envious to learn that Socrates would let his pupils do most of the talking.

Unlike his schooling, the rest of his early education was *active*. Dancing, horseback riding, handling a pike, playing an instrument, he took instruction in it all. Montaigne and his brothers both learned the French game of tennis, which was unusual, for athletics were not considered important. Montaigne joked that many of his fellow students would have been better off if they had *only* received tennis lessons, because they would have been spared the school and at least gotten in shape. They would have also been spared, he noted, the ego that came along with the sense that they were educated. In any case, he was raised to be not some effete intellectual, but an active and vigorous young man.

The saving grace of any institution of learning is its teachers. For all the flaws and frustrations of his traditional education, Montaigne was blessed with several great teachers. One, George Buchanan, was in Bordeaux fleeing religious persecution. The future tutor of kings was a long way from home, and he was able to give the young Montaigne a worldly perspective.

Buchanan loved theater and staged many plays at school, dragging this unusual boy into performing in them.

Perhaps Buchanan was the teacher Montaigne later credited for encouraging his reading habit. In a time when books were expensive and censorship commonplace, this teacher understood that Montaigne's curiosity could not be satisfied by the school syllabus. They came to an agreement: As long as Montaigne could keep up with the school's assignments, he was free to explore on his own. We can imagine Buchanan nudging Montaigne this way and that, even lending him copies from his own library. "Pretending to see nothing," Montaigne said gratefully, "he whetted my appetite, letting me gorge myself with these books only in secret."

It was a brilliant stroke too, for Montaigne watched as so many of his fellow students came away from school hating to read.

One of the books he found was a beautiful folio copy of the works of Terence, edited by the scholar Erasmus, which Montaigne bought for himself in 1549, at age sixteen. He was still reading and rereading it late in life, finding it impossible, each time he picked Terence up, "not to find in him some new beauty and grace."

He finished school several years ahead of schedule. He had done well. He had had a better experience than most. "But for all that," he said, summarizing his college experience, "it was still school." What did he have to show for his years there?

Nothing compared to what he'd gotten at home, where he'd learned to love to learn.

The aim of education has always been to spark curiosity, the desire to understand the world and one's place in it. Often, this is precisely what is later snuffed out.

Of all the inheritances the boy would get—which would include enormous tracts of land, a winery, and a castle—this was his greatest blessing. "He grew up constrained by some of the most bizarre limits ever imposed on a child," Montaigne's biographer Sarah Bakewell observed, "and at the same time had almost unlimited freedom. He was a world unto himself."

Yet eventually, like all graduates, Montaigne had to enter the actual world. His father had always understood that his son's education was not merely for its own sake but to prepare the boy to run the family business, to hold office, to be a leader, to contribute to society by being a torchbearer for values that not long ago had been lost in a "dark age." Perhaps Montaigne would have loved to remain a scholar, but life—and his father—had other plans.

"To school-learning he owes but the first fifteen or sixteen years of his life," Montaigne wrote later; "the rest is owed to action." We all face this transition, from school to experience, from the classroom to the school of life. All the things that Montaigne had read about—Greek democracy, the Roman Empire, the law cases of Cicero, the power of the medieval church—he would now come face-to-face with, not in the glow of the golden age but in the messy, muddy present moment.

After his legal studies, Montaigne found himself working as a magistrate in the Bordeaux Parlement, a job that involved assessing complex legal cases and liaising with different courts. In those days, magistrates were considered and interviewed along two very different lines. One approach, which is used to this day, was to evaluate an applicant's academic performance and ability by testing them on their knowledge. A simpler approach was to give a future magistrate a case to judge and see how they performed, which would reveal how their mind worked.

The latter was a superior procedure, Montaigne noted, "even though both those are necessary and both needed together, nevertheless the talent for knowledge is less to be prized than that for judging. Judgment can do without knowledge, but not knowledge without judgment."

Montaigne almost certainly got his job through the connections of his father, but over the fifteen years he held the job, he came to understand that knowing the law and *understanding* it were very different things. He would have learned, as great legal minds have all learned, that theory has to be made to fit reality and not the other way around, and that only real, painful experience can teach someone how to master their profession.

Much had been left out of the books, Montaigne quickly

realized when he encountered the complexities of the human heart or considered the ambiguity of outcomes. Not that his colleagues approached their profession with much thought. Montaigne would recall with horror watching a judge he knew to be unfaithful to his wife sentence a defendant for the very same crime, just before writing his mistress a love note.

Year after year on the job, Montaigne developed this judgment—about what makes people tick, how to spot a liar, how to get to the truth of the matter. It was for this reason that he was recruited to serve at the court of King Charles IX and why, at the end of his legal career, he was awarded the Order of Saint Michael, effectively French knighthood.

To enter the real world is a shock to all young people. The transition from the realm of ideas to the realm of kings and criminal courts was always going to be a messy and disappointing one, but the France that Montaigne navigated and inhabited must have seemed like it was unraveling.

A generation earlier, Michelangelo had painted the Sistine Chapel. Magellan had circumnavigated the globe. Copernicus had displaced the earth from the center of the universe. The Renaissance had flowered, bringing with it beautiful art and earth-shattering awakenings. A new world was discovered across the Atlantic. As word of different cultures trickled back, even man's sense of the size and shape of the globe had to be reconsidered.

Alongside discovery and invention, however, came destabilization. The church, which had long been a unifying force, had been undermined by these new forms of thought, by the new technologies that spread new ideas. There was, in Montaigne's expression, a common belief that "the world is turned upside down." For the first time, people began to question the oppressive role that priests played in society, and even more generally, they began to ask, *Why are things this way?* and *Should they continue this way?*

Martin Luther tacked his theses to the door of the church. Reformation and Counter-Reformation followed. Riots and unrest ensued. New faiths emerged, and they battled not just for their right to exist but for the power to crush all others as heresies. Inquisitions and persecution raged. The flower of the Renaissance withered up there on the scaffold. The tolerance and acceptance of the Enlightenment lay *centuries* in the future. It was, and remained, as one scholar said, a world still lit only by fire.

In 1562, Montaigne, then serving Charles IX, witnessed the carnage from the siege of Rouen, a violent Catholic insurrection in which more than a thousand people were killed in a bloody clash over religious tensions dividing France. Just a few months earlier, the Duke of Guise had massacred dozens of French Huguenots attending a church service in the town of Vassey. A year later, the duke himself would be gunned down by the side of the road by another French nobleman who lay in wait. When the assassin was caught, he was drawn and quartered—except the sentence was botched, and when the man's limbs failed to be ripped from their sockets after multiple attempts, he was finally put out of his misery by the executioner's sword.

Reprisal followed reprisal, culminating in the St. Bartholomew's Day massacre, when tens of thousands were killed, the dead dumped into the Seine.

All this must have seemed particularly horrifying to a man who had been taught intellectual humility, who believed that ideas should be questioned and that humans were prone to error. "It is to take one's conjectures rather seriously," Montaigne would say, "to roast someone alive for them." Yet this was common practice over the course of his life; thousands of people were burned at the stake for mostly imagined crimes. In the Inquisition, multiple relatives of Montaigne had been burned to death, including a great-great-great-grandfather.

The French Wars of Religion lasted for decades, claiming the lives of over a million people, many in almost indescribably heinous ways.

How far this was from the idyllic and sheltered days of his youth, when his father had protected him from the carnage and its fallout all around him, when his teachers smiled upon him, encouraging all his curiosity and eccentricity.

In a world still medieval in practice, defined by fear and persecution, being a free or unconventional thinker was a risky proposition. So was standing out. As new-money merchants, the Montaigne family could not help it. Montaigne's mother's side of the family were Marranos, Spanish Jews who during the Inquisition converted to Christianity under the threat of death. His paternal uncles were Protestant.

When Montaigne read about people different from himself, especially observations about the just-discovered peoples living in the "New World," he was curious rather than judgmental. "So many humors, sects, judgments, opinions, laws, and customs teach us to judge sanely of our own," he said. Did the people of the Amazon draw and quarter one another, burn one another at the stake, accuse one another of black magic? Who was actually the barbarian?

Later, he would strike a coin for himself to carry as a reminder. "I reserve judgment," it said. He would not be sucked into fanaticism and fundamentalism. He would not take part in quarrels and conflict. He would not chase what everyone else chased or strive to beat or surpass anyone. He would keep a cool head while the rest of the world lost theirs.

This discipline, this tolerance, did not win him the friends it should have. He sensed that he was a man without a country. He knew he had a target on his back. "I was belabored from every quarter," Montaigne lamented; "to the Ghibelline I was a Guelph, to the Guelph, a Ghibelline." Those who refuse to pick sides . . . make twice as many enemies.

He must have sensed he was reaching the end of the road of public service—how could a person attend to the affairs of state when murder and persecution were publicly accepted? When had extremism become commonplace? When had the future felt so uncertain?

"Only he knows," the novelist Stefan Zweig would write, as he turned to Montaigne's works during the early days of the rise of Nazism, "that no task on earth is more burdensome and difficult than to maintain one's intellectual and moral independence and preserve it unsullied through a mass cataclysm." To not be made crazy by the craziness around you demands courage and discipline and justice and wisdom.

The cataclysm came for Montaigne at the end of the 1560s, in an unexpected way. Out for a ride on his estate, Montaigne smashed into another rider at full speed and was thrown to the ground. As his friends carried his broken, dying body to the house, Montaigne felt his life escaping him, his soul all but dancing on the tip of his lips.

Just as suddenly, life returned, and Montaigne was given a second chance. "Imagine that you have died," Marcus Aurelius writes in *Meditations*. "Now take what's left of your life and live it properly."

Marcus is one of the few Stoics Montaigne never quotes, but he got the idea. In the light of this near-death experience, the law didn't seem so important. The affairs and rituals of court must have seemed almost painfully stupid, even grotesque.

So he walked away.

"In the year of Christ 1571," he wrote in an inscription in

the Latin he had learned by his father's methods, "Michel Montaigne, aged 38, on his birthday, the day preceding the Calends of March, already long wearied of the servitude of the law courts, and of public offices, has retired, with faculties still entire, to the arms of the learned virgins, there to pass in all quiet and security such length of days as remain to him, of his already more than half-spent years, if the fates permit him to finish this abode and these sweet ancestral retreats consecrated to his freedom and tranquility and leisure."

Here, then, in this library, the man whose education had so long been directed or supervised was taking the reins fully in his hands. His father was dead, his career lifeless. He himself had nearly died. His life was now half over or more, having been dedicated to studying other people, working on other people's problems.

Now he said, *Enough*, and put himself to following that ancient command from the great Oracle at Delphi: *Know thyself.*

For the first few years after the accident, it seemed all Montaigne did was read. In a tower on the estate his father had left him, he arranged his books on long, wraparound shelves that hugged the walls of the circular building. He could take in his entire library in a glance, thousands of books, a life of learning arrayed before him. Montaigne turned the room his father had used as a chapel into a temple of wisdom. "Books are my kingdom," he said. "And here I seek to reign as absolute lord."

When he wasn't reading he was thinking, luxuriating in his

own company and the freedom to nurture his own thoughts, to exercise his mind.

"He wanders about the room," one biographer portrays Montaigne in his element, "taking from his shelves one book after another, opening them at random, reading a scrap, and then talking about it. On he goes, talking wisely, wittily, kindly, while the flickering firelight plays over his sensitive, intelligent face, and the Fascon moon shines in patches on the floor, till the world we are used to dissolves under his talk and its constituent parts wave and flicker with the firelight."

On the shelves was his copy of Terence from school. There were the Stoics. There was Lucretius, Horace, Virgil, and Diogenes Laertius. There was his beloved Plutarch. "What profit will he not get out of reading the *Lives* of our favorite Plutarch!" Montaigne would say rapturously, celebrating this ancient biographer not for the way he recorded the "date of the fall of Carthage . . . as the behavior of Hannibal and Scipio; less . . . the name of the place where Marcellus died as to how his death there showed him unworthy of the task."

Montaigne had taken pains to carve some of his favorite quotes into the beams of the ceiling of his study, right above the books. Many were from Sextus Empiricus, the Greek philosopher. ΟΥ ΚΑΤΑΛΑΜΒΑΝΩ (I do not understand). ΕΠΕΧΩ (I stop.) ΣΚΕΠΤΟΜΑΙ (I examine). From Terence, "I am a man and nothing human is foreign to me." From Socrates, "Impiety follows pride like a dog." From Pliny, "The only certainty is that nothing is certain." And of course, from Epictetus, "That which worries men is not things but that which they think about them."

Is it any wonder, then, that when Montaigne sat down to write, he began with a question and not a statement? *"Que sais-je?" What do I know?* What did Montaigne know about himself? What had he learned from his unique education? From his books? From his peasant godparents? From his father? From his teachers? What did he *really*, truly know?

Stepping back from the deranged violence of his time, he decided to explore the human condition in the form of rambling meditations, some no more than a page, some almost the length of a short book. An essay, it would be called, or, in French, *an attempt.*

Montaigne wrote on many topics—fear, idleness, affection we feel for our children, cruelty, experience. He also wrote about his favorite authors, and the cannibals he'd heard about in the New World. But the topics of these essays were, at most, a jumping-off point—an excuse to explore and consider *anything* that struck him as interesting. And in the end, they all came back to the main character in his search, himself. "I would rather be an authority on myself than on Cicero," he said.

"He follows his subject as a young dog follows a carriage hounding off the road a hundred times to investigate the neighborhood," one biographer writes. "His loose-limbed mind is easy, light, yet serious. He pares away the rind of things, smelling the fruit joyously. . . . He is a considerer, an examiner, a skeptic. He prowls about the beliefs, the opinions and usage, of men, and, taking up a thought, lifts from it, one by one, as if he were peeling an artichoke, the envelopes of custom, of prejudices, of time, of place. He holds up the opinion of one school, praising and admiring it, and then the contradictory opinion of another school, praising and admiring that. In his scales he balances notion against notion, man against man, usage against usage."

Being born into a world that was so chaotic had presented Montaigne with an opportunity. For too long, the church had been the authority on everything. Still, too much knowledge lay cloistered in monasteries, inaccessible and impractical. For centuries, the individual had been told they were insignificant. Truths long held as irrefutable were proved laughably incorrect by Columbus and Copernicus. Basic questions that had long gone unasked, and certainly remained unanswered, were now bubbling to the surface. Simply the fact that no one had ever really written an essay before is case in point!

Staring at his cat one day, entertaining it with a toy, he stopped and wondered, "Who is toying with whom?" His essays abound with animal stories, intended to illustrate that there is a vast, beautiful world out there that we hardly experience, in some cases that we can't even begin to imagine. What was his cat thinking when he played with it? Who was he to that cat? He is just as baffled by his own anatomy, his sex drive, his emotions. He just wants to *know* anything and everything.

How fresh this all was. How new and transgressive, even. The idea that learning mattered, that truth mattered, that Montaigne—that the individual—was a topic worth exploring. But just because some of it was simple, just because it was fun, doesn't mean the answers were easy. It is a "thorny enterprise," he said, "of following a path as wandering as that of the mind and penetrating the dark depths of its inner folds." It was, he wanted the reader to know, *more difficult than it looked.*

For nearly a decade Montaigne noodled on these essays, which came to fill more than a thousand pages in all—writing them primarily for his own benefit, and in the process creating a very different kind of "self-improvement." Would anyone care? As civil war tore through France, as people fought over scraps of religious doctrine, he waged a war against his own ignorance, exploring the things that make human beings strange and wonderful. This would be his lasting contribution to humanity—he pulled at the thread that artists and journalists and social scientists and psychologists and memoirists have been weaving with since.

In 1580, he published his first essays, which quickly made their way to the homes of nearly every literate gentleman in

France. King Henry III read a copy. Francis Bacon read and loved them. In 1603, when Montaigne was translated into English, a self-taught playwright (and fellow lover of Plutarch) named William Shakespeare bought a copy—indeed, a passage from Montaigne appears deftly cribbed in *The Tempest* and may well have inspired one of his most famous lines, "This above all: To thine own self be true." The books Montaigne had written solely for himself turned out to be for everyone, and became what we would call bestsellers (and remain so to this day).

Montaigne celebrated the completion of his work and its success by doing something he had not gotten to do for many years: travel. Ostensibly, he had to get from France to Italy for business, but mostly he was using the trip as a chance to see new places and have new experiences, and all the while, he kept learning and writing and taking stuff in.

Here he is exploring some old ruin. Here he is under a tree, reading a book. Here he is in the streets of Rome speaking aloud to Caesar and Cicero, "mutter[ing] their great names between my teeth and mak[ing] them resound in my ears." Here he is in an inn, his essays laid out before him, delighted by something he'd written or, when he was embarrassed by it, not hesitating to change it. Here he is struck by a bit of inspiration, dictating a few sentences to his page as they trot along. Here he is with some new book he's purchased, adding yet another heavy volume into his saddlebags. "Books are," he said, "the best provisions a man can take with him on life's journey."

Ultimately, he could not completely withdraw from public life. No wise man can. He consulted on fortifications for Parlement. He was named Gentleman of the Chamber by Henri de Navarre, the next king of France. He hosted important guests for dinner. He went on diplomatic missions. He corresponded with the leading minds of his time. He was elected mayor of Bordeaux, now a large and important city, and then reelected. At one point, the persecution he had dreaded came, and he was thrown in the Bastille, but now his fame saved him, and he was freed by Catherine de' Medici. Through it all though, he was still reading, still writing, still revising his essays. Even in the last months of his life, he was consulting King Henry III, trying to make him into a philosopher-king.

He had asked in Rome to be made an honorary citizen, but in fact, he was a citizen of the world. A friend to himself and to all, he lived outside time and place—residing and conversing with "the worthiest minds, who lived in the best ages"—and had since boyhood.

He made his mark not in the political arena, not on the battlefield, not even in the form of scientific breakthroughs or some work of scholarship. Instead, he persisted in the educational experiment that dated back to his childhood, his father's vision for his son, and the son's effort to prove himself worthy of all the expectation and effort that his teachers had put on him. He had explored an unknown and unprecedented new continent—himself.

He had asked more questions than he had answered, read more than he wrote, saw more than he understood. He tried to put himself and his times in perspective. "It will be a lot," he wrote, "if a hundred years from now people remember in a general way that in our time there were civil wars in France." He knew he would be largely forgotten. He refused to despair. He declined to write humanity off. And in this, he was a truly wise man.

What can we say we know, what can we say we have learned from the life of Montaigne? First, that education is something that does not end. We know that an education, even if directed by someone else at the beginning, eventually reverts into our own hands—we must teach ourselves if we are to learn anything. We know from Montaigne that ego is the enemy of wisdom, that conceit is the impediment to knowledge. We take from his example the need to be always curious, always questioning, always open, always ready to learn something new. And finally, we understand that we learn in order to live, that all accomplishments pale in comparison to that rarest of rare things, *self-awareness*.

His education began with a fresh vision and relied on unconventional methods, the most unique being that it never stopped. As a young man, he explained, "I studied in order to show off; later, a little, to make myself wiser; now I do it for amusement, never for profit."

He kept learning until the day he died, and indeed, the questions that he asked, the inner journey he so eloquently described, continues on through each of us today.

If we are brave and disciplined enough to pick up the task he lays before us.

Talk to the Dead

~

He had come from Phoenicia. It had been a long journey, traveling from port to port across the Mediterranean, trading in purple dye, the color of the cloaks worn by the wealthiest Greeks.

But today, young Zeno was not traveling on business.

As he wound along the Sacred Way, toward the Temple of Apollo, home of the Oracle at Delphi, he began the sacred rituals, washing his hands in the holy spring. He lit a stick of incense. The flickering light of torches lined his path to the inner sanctum, where the priestess waited for his question.

What is the secret to a good life?

"You will become wise," the priestess told Zeno, "when you begin to have conversations with the dead."

It took many years and a terrible accident for him to understand what she meant. At thirty, Zeno found himself in Athens, shipwrecked and penniless. He passed a bookseller in the agora and listened to a story from the life of Socrates. Suddenly, the meaning of the priestess's words revealed itself.*

Socrates had been in the grave for many years. Yet Zeno was listening to him as though he lived. *Conversations with the dead.* That's what books are!

In that bookshop, Zeno was surrounded by the dead—poets and philosophers, playwrights and storytellers. From the pages of these books, they were speaking forth their wisdom and experiences, their ideas and insights. When he picked up Plato or Xenophon, Euripides or Homer, Aristotle or Sappho, he could hear them; with his own hand, he could reply in the margins.

Indeed, today we refer to the reading and studying of these books, many of which now make up the so-called Western Canon, as *the great conversation.*

Yet most people choose not to participate. Or do so only occasionally. The average person watches something like twenty hours of television a week and spends nearly five hours a day on their phone. Almost nobody reads that much.

Meanwhile, while Charles de Gaulle was president of France, he read two to three books a week and was famous for reading all the annual winners of the literary prizes. In office,

---

* As it happens, the story Zeno heard was the story of the choice of Hercules, the one that opens each of the books in this series.

German Chancellor Angela Merkel read fifteen-hundred-page history books on the 1800s and took deep dives into Shakespeare. As secretary of defense, General James Mattis blocked out an hour each day for "lunch/reading time," having previously managed to read the Stoics and hundreds of other books while actively fighting in a war. Napoleon took 125 books with him during his invasion of Egypt. Franklin Delano Roosevelt managed to read *Mein Kampf* in *German* in 1933, shortly after becoming president, in the midst of a ceaseless and overwhelming economic crisis.

We all have time to read.

We just don't do it enough.

It's about the craziest thing in the world. Imagine having a superpower—being able to talk to the dead—and not using it! Imagine being able to talk with the wisest people who ever lived, as Tolstoy said, and not doing it!

When you think of the sheer price paid for the painful personal and historical lessons contained in so many biographies and memoirs and literature, it's almost insulting how cheap books are. You can't afford them? They're free at the library!

It doesn't matter that we can read. If we don't, as General Mattis has said, we are choosing to be *functionally illiterate.*

There are many paths to wisdom, but nearly every one of them runs through books.

Can you think of any truly wise person who does not read? Can you think of anyone you know who reads a lot and does not wish they read even more?

Growing up in a small town of a few thousand people, Harry Truman found in books not just knowledge, but an escape, an ability to travel to different worlds and back and forth in time. He estimated that as a boy he'd read nearly every book in the town's two-room library, starting with the kids' section. By fifteen, he'd read the King James Bible from cover to cover three times, as well as "all the histories of world leaders and histories I could find."

What is *your* reading age? Not what age level are you reading at, but how many years of life and experience have you gained through reading? Truman might have been the oldest teenager to ever come out of Missouri. His reading habits not only changed him but opened him up to *live* multiple lives, to absorb, in his mind, the experiences of *generations* of people. And that's not even getting into fiction, which allows us to explore whole other worlds, species, and fantasies!

Truman, like Montaigne, was also a lifelong reader of Plutarch. As a boy he had saved his money for a copy and begged his father to read it to him. It was the first of many times that Truman would explore Plutarch's biographies of the great men and women of the ancient world. A practice that began as entertainment continued as career development. "When I was in politics," he reflected, "there would be times when I tried to figure somebody out, and I could always turn to Plutarch, and nine times out of ten I'd be able to find a parallel in there."*

Sadly, too many people are not taught *how* to read, how to actually extract something usable from the books available to us. Nor are they empowered as readers to quit books that suck, to disagree with a book, or to dive into the rabbit hole of knowledge to master a topic.

Because reading is a conversation, great readers are not passive. They put books through the wringer, they put the author on trial. They ask questions. They talk back. And they don't just read occasionally, but constantly, devouring fiction and nonfiction alike, philosophy and history, memoir and biography, poetry and prose.

Like Montaigne, whose beloved copy of Lucretius survives with all his notes, Founding Father John Adams was a lifelong producer of what is called "marginalia." The pages of his books show that he was no passive reader, nor was he easily convinced of anything. "Fool! Fool!" he would write. "Nonsense!" But when he liked something, he'd note his agreement, sometimes giving an author a well-earned "Excellent!" In a book on the

---

*Not only Plutarch. One reporter, tracking down something Truman had said, found a book in the Library of Congress that had not been checked out in many years. The last person to read it? Senator Harry Truman in 1939.

French Revolution, John Adams wrote something like twelve thousand words of notes and comments.

Reading may be a shortcut, but it's still a lot of work.

Work that's worth it.

The wisdom Zeno gained through reading, experience, and personal loss twenty-five centuries ago not only saved his life but formed the foundation of Stoicism, a tradition which continues to this day. That's what books allow us to do—to gain cheaply knowledge that someone else gained through pain and suffering.

Think about how many people have lived before you; think of the immensity of their lives, what they said, what they heard, what they did. Think of them sitting at their desk, struggling to articulate this experience for others. Think of the historians and philosophers and wise people who dedicated their whole careers to figuring out how and why certain events unfolded, why and how individuals made fateful decisions. Think of all the books they had read just to create a single, distilled volume they published.

They are all long dead and buried, yet they continue to reach out, collapsing centuries and shattering barriers, traveling across time and space and the vast range of perspectives. They are offering you their hand along your own life path.

Will you take it? Will you listen to them?

This great stream of civilization and experience is there. Will we enter it? Will we drink from it?

Each of us is unique, with our own perspectives, our own

taste and experiences. This means that each book we read is unique in its impact on us. It also means that connections and wisdom are lost each time we fail to pick up a book. The river passes us by if we are not careful, never to return or be possible again.

You must read.

Read something new.

Read something old.

Reread something you've already read.

Read a few pages of this one or that one. Linger when a passage strikes you.

Read something critical.

Read something beautiful.

Read something dark.

Read something you disagree with.

Reflect.

Read more.

Repeat.

Talk to the dead until you die.

Be Curious

~

They were just two curious kids, that's how it began.

Their father had brought home a little toy from one of his trips. A stick with some rubber bands and two propellers, *but it flew.*

How?

Orville and Wilbur watched in wonder, played for hours with this flying machine, their curiosity whetted in a way they'd be chasing for the rest of their lives.

"It isn't true to say we have no special advantages," Orville would say after he and his brother had changed the world and taken man into the air. "The greatest thing in our favor was growing up in a family where there was always much encouragement to intellectual curiosity."

The Wright house was filled with books. Thucydides. *The Decline and Fall of the Roman Empire.* Milton. Plutarch's *Lives.* Darwin. Dickens. Twain. The shelves burst with classics and cutting-edge science for the time. Everyone in the family was expected to be a reader.

Doing well in school? It mattered, but their parents always understood if the boys had a project they'd rather do instead. What was most important was following one's curiosity to its natural end. Even if that was inconvenient or even if it made a mess. "She would never destroy one thing the boys were trying to make," their sister, Katharine Wright, said of their mother. "Any little thing they left around in her way she picked up and put on a shelf in the kitchen."

How did the Wright brothers, with less than one thousand dollars of their own money—and no college education—manage to solve the problem of manned flight before world governments? How did their plane beat a US project that cost some seventy thousand dollars (*millions* in today's dollars)?

It wasn't money that motivated them, although ultimately their inventions would make them quite rich. "If my father had not been the kind who encouraged his children to pursue intellectual interests without any thought of profit," Orville explained, "our early curiosity about flying would have been nipped too early to bear fruit."

At the beginning, most ventures, especially risky or experimental ones, are horribly *unprofitable*. The odds are stacked against you. All sorts of drudgery and dead ends loom ahead. A genuine fascination, a desire to *know*, is the only force powerful enough to drive someone to real discovery.

There wasn't any profit in the early days of the Wrights' experiments at Kitty Hawk and then back in Ohio. Quite the opposite: The Wright brothers would do a short season of flying and then return home and work very hard at their bicycle factory to put together the funds to support another round of flights. "Instead of thinking about getting money out of an airplane," Orville said, "our chief concern was always to get money to put into it. We were at it for the sport. It was something to spend money on, because it interested us, just as a man spends money on golf if that interests him, with no thought of making it pay."

A wise general said that the secret to success in life was wanting to learn what was on the other side of the hill. It wasn't just that toy that had piqued their interest, it wasn't just flight that they hungered to figure out—but indeed, just about every machine and contraption and phenomenon they ever witnessed lit those boys up. It got them going. It started a process for them that not always but usually ended up with some kind of insight or project or understanding.

It's magic—being interested in something. It's powerful—that driver that is curiosity.

Why does it work like that?
Is it possible to . . . ?
I wonder if . . .
Tell me more!
What if we tried . . . ?

It was questions like this that had helped them build a printing press as children and a bicycle repair and manufacturing business after that. "Making it pay came as an after-thought," they said. People will almost work harder for what they're interested in than what they have a *financial* interest in.

When it came to airplanes, other people may have been smarter and better educated—while countless others *knew* that flying was impossible—but it was the Wrights who asked the Smithsonian for every book ever written on flight. It was the Wrights who stood spellbound, watching birds and trying to figure out what their secret was. "Curiosity, like gravity, is accelerative," the brothers' biographer David McCullough once said. "The more you know, the more you want to know."

What about you? How curious are you? How much are you tinkering? What are you figuring out?

Seneca said that we ought to read like a scout in the enemy's camp—exploring ideas we disagree with or schools of thought we know nothing about. The playwright Ben Jonson loved this idea and inscribed each of his books—a little bit of marginalia—with the Latin version of Seneca's phrase *tanquam explorator.* "Like an explorer."

Are you one?

As a schoolgirl, Anne Frank was asked to do a report on the Roman Empire, which she knew nothing about. When she asked her father for help, he responded by saying, "Well, let's see what we can find," and off they went to the library. What a wonderful gift to give a child! The idea that everything is figure-out-able—

that the information you seek is out there, you just have to go look for it.

It was simple curiosity that brought Theodore Roosevelt down to the slums on the Lower East Side. Other lawmakers were content with what a report said, or the position their patrons gave them. He wanted to know more. It was curiosity that sent Beatrice Webb to live with a working family in 1883, opening her up to social activism and economics as a result. You have to *want to know* how the other half lives; you have to be interested in what it is like to be someone other than yourself, or to live somewhere else.

Kids are curious. It's natural. But it's not enough to have *once been* curious. You must keep the fire going. You must *stay* curious.

Curiosity is not something you cure. It's not something that is sated. It takes us to the other side of the hill . . . and to the next hill after that, as long as there is horizon in front of us. It takes us to the next question, the next project, and as a result, without fail, to a little more knowledge.

This is why it is so powerful, such a self-actualizing force.

If you are curious, you can't *not* learn.

But conversely, the opposite is also true.

Not being curious?

We know for certain that that leads to nothing.

It takes you nowhere but where you've already been.

Ask the Question

~

Like every parent, she wanted to make sure her son was learning. She wanted him to behave, to make sure he was following the rules. She wanted him to do well in school so that he might be able to get ahead, for the next generation of this immigrant family to find its footing.

Yet when Isidor Rabi came home from Manual Training High School each day, his mother didn't ask about grades. She didn't ask how he scored on his test or if he had stayed out of trouble. She didn't even ask, as all the other Jewish mothers in Brooklyn at the turn of the twentieth century liked to ask, whether her son had learned anything.

"Izzy," she would say, "did you ask a good question today?"

This doesn't seem like much, and yet it is everything. After all, questions drive discovery; they are curiosity embodied. Questions about everything, from ideas to people, were the key to Socrates's wisdom.

"That is the essence of science," another Jewish immigrant

scientist of the same era, Jacob Bronowski, explained; "ask an impertinent question, and you are on the way to the pertinent answer."

Not that all questions must be probing or incisive. They can be simple: "What do you mean?" They can be inquisitive: "How does that work?" They can aim for clarity: "Sorry, I didn't understand, can you explain it another way?"

For young Isidor, this emphasis on asking questions translated into stellar academic performance. He raided the local library for books about science. He published his first scientific paper in elementary school. His grades got him into Cornell, then Columbia, and then all the great institutes of Europe. He consulted on the Manhattan Project and advised Eisenhower. His group at MIT helped in the development of radar. He collaborated with some of the most renowned scientific minds, including Niels Bohr and J. Robert Oppenheimer. The drive to ask, to inquire, to figure stuff out, turned him into one of the greatest physicists of his time—earning him a Nobel nomination by Albert Einstein in 1940 and the Nobel Prize in 1944. His work led to the invention of the MRI.

Questions are the key not just to knowledge but to success, discovery, and mastery. They're how we learn and how we get better.

We are born full of questions. We want to know the names of things. We want to know how they work. Most of all, we want to know *why, why, why.* But too many people lose this impulse as they grow into adults. "I think physicists are the Peter Pans of the human race," Isidor once said. "They never grow up, and they keep their curiosity."

Too many kids are robbed of this curiosity, however, having it stamped out by adults who, frustrated by the demands of their own lives, dismiss them with "Because I said so." Eventually, children stop asking.

We must fight to preserve the part of us that dares to inquire.

Richard Feynman was another great scientist, of the same era as Jacob Bronowski and Isidor Rabi. From a young age, his father didn't just encourage him to ask questions, he *showed* him the art of questioning. He never told his son to leave subjects alone, and didn't say "I don't know" unless it was a way for them to explore something together.

He liked to take his son for long walks in the woods. "See that bird?" his father would say. "What kind of bird is that?" It wasn't really a quiz, because oftentimes Feynman's father liked to just make up names. You could know the name of every bird in every language in the world, he said, but that would tell you absolutely nothing. What he really wanted to figure out with his son was *why* that bird was pecking at its own feathers. They sat back together to watch. Was it to straighten out its feathers after flying? Was it mating behavior? Neither seemed right. After some observation and research, they got it. Ah, the bird was picking at lice. Cool!

What Richard learned was to notice little things and to pursue what he noticed, and that interesting discoveries were the result of that process. Questions led to questions, and that was a good thing. His father wanted him to notice the *big* things too, those you might easily miss if you were too focused on what was in front of you.

"What makes the toy go?" his father asked.

"The toy goes because I wound it up."

"How did the spring get wound up?"

"I wound it up."

"And how did you get moving?"

"From eating."

"And food only grows because the sun is shining."

Richard Feynman would go on to win a Nobel Prize, but as a child, it was his father who had been the one bringing questions to *him*.

He even prompted his son to question titles and prizes. Pointing to a picture of the pope in the newspaper, his father asked Richard, "Here's one human standing here and all these others are bowing in front of him. Now, what's the difference?" When Richard couldn't answer, his father—a uniform salesman—joked that the only difference was the hat that the pope was allowed to wear.

Eventually, this habit took root. "Say, Pop," Feynman said one day, dragging a toy behind him, "I noticed something. When I pull the wagon, the ball rolls to the back of the wagon. And when I'm pulling it along and I suddenly stop, the ball rolls to the front of the wagon. Why is that?"

Nobody knows exactly *why*, his father explained, giving his son his first physics lesson, but "the general principle is that things which are moving tend to keep moving, and things which are standing still tend to stand still, unless you push them hard. This tendency is called 'inertia,' but nobody knows why it's true." What stuck with Feynman about this was that his father didn't just answer, he didn't just give him the *name* for the phenomenon, but he helped his son *understand* it. Even better, he gave him a tease of the mystery of the subject, one his son would be chasing all his life.

Asking leads to answers, and answers lead to more questions. From not knowing, we get to knowing, and eventually to the truth. This is why we must understand that there is no such thing as a dumb question. In fact, a person becomes smart *only* by asking questions. The more impertinent and relentless the better.

We must ask questions when we are young, and we must also remain humble enough to ask them when we are old, powerful, and well-informed. Marcus Aurelius noted the way that Antoninus, his predecessor as emperor and mentor of some twenty years, asked "searching questions at meetings" and was "almost never content with first impressions or breaking off the discussion prematurely."

The guy who was supposed to have all the answers, to make all the big decisions, still had plenty of questions himself—as we all must.

We ask. We are asked. In an endless loop of learning and exploration.

Years later, when Feynman was home from school at MIT, his father had a question for him. "Now that you've become educated about these things," he said, "there's one question I've always had that I've never understood very well. I understand that when an atom makes a transition from one state to another, it emits a particle of light called a photon. Is the photon in the atom ahead of time?"

"No," Feynman replied, "there is no photon beforehand."

"Well," his father said, not at all satisfied, "where does it come from, then? How does it come out?"

And with this, the genius's university education proved insufficient, and he had to go off and think of a better way to explain advanced physics to his still-curious father.

Focus, Focus, Focus

W hen Samuel Scudder interviewed for a position under the great Harvard biologist Louis Agassiz in 1864, he probably expected to be quizzed on what he knew or be given a difficult problem to solve.

During the first part of his examination Agassiz confirmed Scudder knew enough Greek and Latin to be comfortable with classification. He asked some questions about the latest research and inquired about how much reading he had done. He was pleased to learn that Scudder had trained in fencing.

But then the interview took a strange turn. Agassiz reached behind him and removed a dead fish from a jar of alcohol, placing it on a tin tray in front of Scudder. "Look at the fish," was his only instruction before he left the room.

How long can you stare at a fish? The hours passed while Scudder fought boredom. He picked it up, turned it over, stuck his fingers down its throat. Still no sign of Agassiz. He began to count the scales. Then he drew the fish.

When he returned Agassiz was not impressed. "You have

not looked very carefully," he said. "You haven't even seen one of the most conspicuous features of the animal, which is as plainly before your eyes as the fish itself; look again, look again!" Then he left.

The next afternoon, the exchange repeated itself. "Do you see it yet?" Agassiz asked. "No," Scudder replied. "I am certain I do not, but I see how little I saw before." Another day, and a few long walks later, Scudder thought perhaps he had seen something. "Do you perhaps mean," he asked Agassiz, "that the fish has symmetrical sides with paired organs?"

"That is good, that is good!" Scudder recalled Agassiz telling him; "but that is not all; go on." In all he spent three days with that fish, forbidden from looking at anything else. His only instructions were "Look, look, look."

So what did Scudder ultimately discover?

Nothing at all. As Scudder explained, it was a deeper lesson, perhaps the most important one he ever got in his career as a scientist: the power of focus. The importance of intensely looking, with dedication and without interruption, at something as simple and ordinary as a fish in order to truly see it. It was "a lesson whose influence has extended to the details of every subsequent study; a legacy the Professor had left to me, as he has left it to many others, of inestimable value, which we could not buy, with which we cannot part."

Focus is the skill that wisdom depends on. Not just for a few minutes but for days and months and even years. Looking at a fish for that long without distraction takes a certain kind of patience and determination, which helps if you want to dedicate your life to being a biologist.

Concentration and time commitment are essential to any work. "To do real good physics work," Feynman explains, "you do need absolute solid lengths of time . . . it needs lots of concentration."'

It's not just true for physics. Some said that the great Jim Brown was sometimes aloof or distant on the football field, as if he wasn't paying attention. It was the exact opposite, he later explained to the author Alex Haley. "I was focused mentally."

Focus is hard work. It's as tough as any feat of physical prowess and especially challenging to maintain in our algorithmic world. But it can also be a source of joy and comfort and beauty.

Focus is a ritual. Machiavelli, who lived in times as violent and disruptive as Montaigne's, wrote about his daily ritual. At a particularly dark time in his life, when he had lost his important position in the Florentine court, he was exiled to the countryside, far from the seat of power and the luxuries of city life. Returning home from the fields or work at the local inn, Machiavelli removed his mud-spattered clothes and boots before entering his study. Only when he was clean and well-dressed would he be ready to dive into his books. "Fitted out appropriately," he explained, "I step inside the venerable courts of the ancients, where, solicitously received by them, I nourish myself on that food that alone is mine and for which I was born; where I am unashamed to converse with them and to question them about the motives for their actions, and they, out of their human kindness, answer me. And for four hours at a time I feel no boredom, I forget all my troubles, I do not dread poverty, and I am not terrified by death. I absorb myself into them completely."

Again, four hours of uninterrupted focus and study?

Yes.

Four hours of freedom. Four hours of time travel. Four hours of conversing with the dead.

Indeed, imagine what you might be able to do if you could manage that level of dedication and concentration.

"If you want to hit a bird on the wing, you must have all your will in focus," Supreme Court Justice Oliver Wendell Holmes Jr. once explained of hunting. You can't be thinking about yourself. You can't be thinking of ten other things. You can't be only half paying attention. You have to be tracking, aiming, and firing in one quick, fluid movement—a perfect coordination of mind and body. "Every achievement," he said, "is a bird on the wing."

To discover something new. To make some surprise connection. To get the words in the exact right order. To find the right note. To see the whole picture. To solve that vexing problem. To really *see* what is before you. These are birds on the wing.

Without focus, they will escape you.

But this is not a skill you are born with. It's something you have to train.

The famed artist Marina Abramović is essentially an athlete. The feats of strength behind her most famous performance pieces are as much mental as they are physical. To sit across from total strangers for hours and hours without being distracted by them demands incredible focus. In one of her pieces, she lived, for twelve days, in what was effectively a diorama raised six feet off the floor. All the while, the sound of a metronome beat methodically in the background. Imagine how excruciatingly slowly the time passed, and being unable to eat or speak or even write. The only exit was down a ladder... made of butcher knives. She had to focus through the boredom as well as the pain, with nothing but her own thoughts and inner life to keep her occupied. On top of simply enduring and surviving these experiences, one must also think of the creativity that it took to conceive them in the first place!

Again, she was not simply born this way. This was a skill she trained in herself and in her students. This technique is different from that of Agassiz. Instead of having her students look directly at an object, she might have an aspiring artist walk backward for an extended period while holding a mirror, so that they can begin to observe reality as a reflection. Or she might walk them to a forest, blindfold them, and tell them to find their way home. "Like a blind person," she said, "an artist needs to learn to see with his or her whole body." She might have them do something very slowly, forcing them to perceive every painstaking moment of drinking or showering or even going to the bathroom. After three hours of slowly opening a door, she said, "the door is not a door anymore."

That's the thing about focus. Sometimes it helps you see what's there. Other times it can help you see what *isn't* there.

A chaotic existence, an undisciplined mind, a short attention span—these are the enemies of wisdom. They prevent us from doing all we can do. Leonardo da Vinci was brilliant, and when he wanted to, he focused, but he also left much of his best work only partially completed, because he would flitter onto the next thing. In the centuries since, one shudders to think how many discoveries were interrupted by a phone call from a creditor, how many connections lost because the paper was buried on a desk, how many details went unnoticed, ideas went unexpressed.

We are lost without focus and presence.

So look.

Look, look, look.

Look again.

Focus!

Learn to Listen

~

Z eno talked with the dead. He studied under Crates.

And then, eventually, he set up his own school in the center of the Athenian agora, on a little porch where he and his pupils would sit and talk.

There, on the *stoa poikile*, he taught two very different students.*

Aristo was a brilliant and brash student, a once-in-a-generation talent. He was a true believer in Stoicism, but what he loved more than anything was to argue. He argued with his fellow students. He argued with his teacher. He was often right and he often won, but even more than winning, what Aristo loved was *talking*, period. He was known for long discourses and endless tangents. Almost naturally at odds with Zeno's dictum that each of us is given two ears and only one mouth for a reason, Aristo talked far more than he ever cared to listen.

Meanwhile, Zeno had another student who often seemed

* The Greek word for porch, *stoa*, is the root of *Stoic*.

LEARN TO LISTEN ❧ *WISDOM TAKES WORK*

less promising. Cleanthes came to philosophy later in life. He was not a brilliant kid, but a manual laborer who carried water to the gardens of wealthy Athenians. He didn't make much of a presence on the *stoa,* and he certainly didn't interrupt with obnoxious disagreements. What Cleanthes did was sit and listen . . . for twenty years.

He took it all in, over thousands of lectures, thousands of long walks, thousands of interactions. We sometimes call a great listener like this a "sponge," but Zeno had a more precise analogy. Cleanthes, he once said, was like a hard waxen tablet— hard to write on, but once imprinted, the writing was there for good.

Some of Cleanthes's fellow students, on the other hand, made the same mistake that ignorant college students make with older peers today, judging him for being old and out of place. His nickname was "the donkey," because he was such a slow learner. Of course, anyone who has spent time around donkeys knows that they are incredibly attuned to what's happening around them—they're also strong-willed and independent minded. Cleanthes's reply was always something like, *Sure, it's good that I'm a donkey, that means I'm strong enough to carry the load.*

Which is what he did after two decades of study and learning, because it was Cleanthes, not Aristo, whom Zeno entrusted with the future of Stoicism.

What's the point of going to school or finding a mentor if

you're not going to listen? When you're talking, what you're doing is not hearing. When we open our mouths, we shut our ears.

Really, what we're doing is closing doors. We could have learned something. We could have gotten someone else's perspective. We could have heard their experience. We could have gotten their advice.

When we're not talking, we can't get ourselves into trouble. When we're listening, we cede that foolhardy opportunity to someone else.

It's out of insecurity, though, that we babble. We're sitting across from someone smart, someone we admire, and suddenly we're telling them all about ourselves. We might not even notice the deftness with which they, more disciplined and more curious, are asking us questions, even though we're far less interesting or accomplished. It's only on the walk back to the car that it hits us: *We dominated the conversation. We didn't learn anything new. We missed out.*

What could we have learned had we been more receptive, more interested in them than in the sound of our own voice?

Remember the Spartan who was asked if he was stupid because he hadn't said a word at dinner: "A stupid person wouldn't have been able to be silent," he said, and then went back to listening. "Be a listener only," Jefferson advised his grandson. "Keep within yourself and endeavor to establish with yourself the habit of silences, especially in politics." This is what Gandhi did when he left South Africa and returned to India as a celebrated activist. At the request of one of his closest political advisers, Gandhi gave no speeches and embarked on no new campaigns for nearly a year. Instead, he traveled the country—one he had not lived in since law school—with his "ears open but his mouth shut." It was the equivalent of a listening tour or a fact-finding mission. It's a shame that those phrases have become political clichés, because they're essential and all too rare in practice.

How can you lead if you haven't listened to the people you'll be leading? Why are you trying to solve a problem before you've asked what others have already tried? What information are you crowding out with all your chatter?

Cleanthes loved a quote from Sophocles, "Silence, silence, light be thy step."

This is the approach of a great listener. It is a conduit to learning.

We're not just talking about nodding your head along. To be a listener is not to be passive. "Practice really hearing what people say," Marcus Aurelius wrote to himself in *Meditations*. We can see in that book, especially the first chapter, just how much Marcus got from his teachers and mentors over the years. He didn't just nod along. No, he took what they said and thought about it. He wrote it down. Years later, he was still tossing it around, trying to put it into practice and add his own spin on it.

There are a lot of great talkers in this world.

There are not nearly enough listeners.

As a young girl, Maya Angelou became, in her words, "a giant ear which could just absorb all sound." Her childhood was a scary and dark one, but the solace was the time she spent in her room, inhaling poetry, listening to the voices in her house, on the street, on the radio. "I would listen to the accents," she recounted, "and I still love the way human beings sound. There is no human voice which is unbeautiful to me. I love them, and so I'm able to learn languages, because I really love the way people talk. I still get excited about any human being speaking or singing."

All around us are people who know better, who know more. All around us are experience and hard-earned lessons. Feedback permeates everything. To every action we take, there is a reaction.

But most of this is subtle.

The world speaks to us always, but often in no more than a whisper. Most teachers do not repeat themselves, do not beg for us to sit and be quiet and listen.

We have to take that upon ourselves.

We have to open ourselves up to it.

Don't be a big mouth. Be a giant ear.

Talk less. Listen.

Create a Second Brain

~

It began when Joan Didion's mother gave her a small notebook, hoping to keep this precocious five-year-old girl busy.

She would still be filling notebooks eighty-two years later. She used them as a reporter and a novelist. She turned to her notebooks when she was reeling from grief. She used them on her travels. She used them to process her thoughts after sessions with her therapist. Over the years, she filled too many to count. When she died of Parkinson's disease, her estate had to figure out what to do with dozens of blank notebooks leftover— clearly Didion had planned to keep going, believing there was so much more to observe and record and write.

Didion relied on these notebooks, as well as index cards, to record enough observations and insights to produce five novels, thirteen nonfiction books, screenplays like *A Star Is Born*, and countless articles. As for every creative, the observations in these notebooks were her raw material, or, to use a more modern term, *a second brain*, which she could rely on for her work and life.

In a famous essay, she referred to the notebooks as a kind of rainy-day fund that she'd been contributing to since her mother had given her that first Big 5 tablet in 1939. "Some morning when the world seems drained of wonder," she explained, "some day when I am only going through the motions of doing what I am supposed to do, which is write—on that bankrupt morning I will simply open my notebook and there it will all be, a forgotten account with accumulated interest, paid passage back to the world out there."

For hundreds of years, lovers of books and ideas have kept what was called a "commonplace book," where they collected observations, quotes, ideas, diary entries, and anecdotes that they wanted to preserve. As far back as the Greeks and Romans, *ars excerpendi*—the art of excerpting—was a skill to be taught. "Never read," Pliny the Elder advised in the first century AD, "without taking extracts."

Whether they learned it in school or not, the tradition continues. Anne Frank filled her diary with passages from the biographies and history books she was reading, celebrating sentences she liked and anecdotes that meant something to her. As a young man, future General James Mattis hitchhiked to listen to a talk by the philosopher Eric Hoffer. Afterward, Hoffer—possibly the only philosopher to also work *as a longshoreman*—gave Mattis a piece of life-changing advice: "Make sure you write down everything interesting you find." The result was a series of three-ring binders Mattis called his "Book of Wisdom," which he drew on as he created battle plans, weighed difficult decisions, wrote speeches, or drafted orders.

Montaigne started the same habit around the same age, and his early essays, so filled with quotes, read as if they might have been torn directly from his commonplace book. Emerson referred to his journals as his "savings bank," and it's true, many of his best talks and writings, from free-form musings on quotes he liked or things he was curious about, first appeared there. But as the habit developed over the years, he ran into the same problem that any avid commonplace-booker will experience: How do you keep track of where all the stuff is? Emerson's journaling spanned hundreds of notebooks that filled multiple shelves, so in the late 1830s, he began a separate notebook that served as a sort of index for all the others. A decade later, it was a four-hundred-page list of topics and themes, citing the exact location in his journals where the best material could be found.

John Adams's commonplace books represented his search to "examine how men think." It was in these pages that he found secrets and insights about greatness that he would apply to his work and effort to form a government built on ideas that would bring peace and prosperity to countless millions.

It's not enough to read. One should engage in a practice of capturing information and recording it so it can be drawn on later. Like reading, travel provides abundant material for future use, but how much of what we experience on our travels is immediately forgotten? The same goes for conversations and mentorship and experience. If you don't write it down, did it even happen?

"A collection of anecdotes and maxims is the greatest treasure for a man of the world," Goethe explained, because we can draw on it in conversation and in moments of personal crisis. That little epiphany we had on a hike. That piece of advice we got from our grandmother before she passed. That mistake we made and want to never make again. That fleeting moment of serene happiness and peace. That beautiful passage in the novel we read on vacation.

Write it down. Write it down. Trust nothing to memory. Capture it before it passes.

Do it in whatever form works best for you. Mattis used three-ring binders. Emerson had his journals and his index. Some people use apps or computer programs. The Florentines pioneered their *zibaldone*—probably the first thing we'd recognize as similar to a modern notebook—starting in the fourteenth century; these were designed to be passed down and continued by each generation of a family.

There is a German system of the 1500s, called *zettelkasten*, that uses index cards, which are usually stored in little boxes. The biologist Carl Linnaeus used his own version of this. So did Ronald Reagan, who maintained a system throughout his political life of using little photo binders to collect anecdotes and quotes that he would use in his speeches. Didion once advised a young writer working on a big story to put all the pieces down on index cards, and "then spread them on the floor and see how you can fit them together, with space breaks in between. Like arranging a patchwork quilt." When the comedian Joan Rivers died, she had over *one million* typed three-by-five index cards. And Eric Hoffer, who had pushed Mattis to record what he read, filled well over a hundred notebooks with ideas, along with multiple metal file cabinets that contained quotation-covered notecards he thought he might someday need.

Study all systems but make your own—one you'll actually use.

Because that's the point. Whether we're beginning some creative work or we're trying to solve some complex problem, we should never be starting from zero. Invariably, at some point in our lives, we have seen or read or heard something that would be of use in this situation. But will we remember it? Will we have access to it?

Montaigne's copy of Lucretius, which he read multiple times, shows his evolution as a thinker and as a person. Anne Frank, had she not been murdered, would have grown up to be a wonderful writer. Those pages that had offered her such solace in the moment would have also given her much to remember years later.

We keep the notebooks, sure, but in the end, they keep us.

Each event, each exchange, each moment we think is important enough to record is an insight into who we are in an instant that will never happen again. By taking the note, we are preserving ourselves for our future selves . . . and perhaps future generations too.

Find Your Classroom

~

Claude Monet wanted to be an artist. From an early age, his caricatures brought him attention and no small amount of pocket money. A talented painter took the young boy aside and told him he was obviously gifted. "I hope you are not going to stop there," he said to Monet. "Study, learn to see and to paint, draw, make landscapes."

But the boy had always been rebellious, and with his natural talent, he was not taken with the idea of study, especially in the way that so many of the great painters of the past had learned, under the direction of a strict master. His parents, to their credit, offered to send their son to train at the École des Beaux-Arts, the most prestigious art school in the world, but the thought filled Monet with dread and boredom. From his earliest days, he had liked nothing more than to be outside in the open air, running along the cliff tops of Normandy and paddling in the water. School and studio seemed to him like prisons.

The course of his life was decided when, at age twenty, Monet was drafted for a seven-year term in the French army. His wealthy parents, who worried their son was frittering away his life, saw their chance to intervene. Give up this silly, bohemian fantasy, they said, and we'll pay to get you out of the service. Get serious. Go to *real* school.

If he didn't, came the ultimatum, they would disinherit him.

But to Monet, the army was the classroom he wanted to be in. "A friend who was in the 'Chasseurs d'Afrique' and who adored military life had communicated his enthusiasm and inspired me with his love for adventure," he recounted in his memoirs. "Nothing seemed more attractive to me than the endless treks under a great sun, the raids, the crackling of gunpowder, saber-rattling, nights in the desert under canvas ..."

He dismissed his parents' threat and requested to be drafted into an African regiment, precisely the kind of dangerous posting everyone else was trying to avoid.

"In Algeria," he explained, "I spent two really charming years. I incessantly saw something new; in my moments of leisure I attempted to render what I saw. You cannot imagine to what an extent I increased my knowledge, and how much my vision gained thereby." Even though his intuition had drawn him to Africa, he could not have predicted the education he would get. "The impressions of light and color that I received there were not to classify themselves until later," he said; "they contained the germ of my future researches."

It's not surprising that generations past have used physical force to get children to submit to school, as boring and ill-suited as it is for many of us. The whole thing is tinged with tyranny: Sit down. Shut up. Read that. Watch this. Blend in. Behave. Pay attention. Perform. Here's a test. Here's some homework. Here's another lecture. *Hey, stop looking out the window. Hey, stop messing around. Hey, look at these grades, you're a failure. Hey, next year, you've got to come back and do this all over again.*

Monet's art—the painting of landscapes—by definition was something you did outside . . . . Yet his parents wanted to ship him off to spend years in stuffy old buildings!

The credit belongs to Monet, then, who even at a young age seemed to understand not just what he needed to learn but where and how to learn it. He didn't just reject what he didn't like, he found what he did like, what did light him up, literally and figuratively. He had always loved Delacroix's paintings of Algeria, and there, on the ground, even though much of his day was taken up by drilling and chores, he was actually *living* inside them. He was bathing in that light. He was developing his approaches, his perceptions, even his stamina and strength. It was here that he was learning, not so much how to do the landscapes he would later become famous for, but something more essential. He was learning how to *see* what he would paint in those landscapes for the rest of his career.

This is the key to life: finding the classroom that works for you, that allows you to take over your own education.

Because an education is not something you "get," it's something you take. It's something you *make*.

It's there, if we want it badly enough.

Leonardo da Vinci was an illegitimate son, which meant he could not attend university in fifteenth-century Italy. So he had to teach himself. The world became his classroom. The philosopher Eric Hoffer did not go to college either. Instead, he spent the Great Depression working in migrant camps and mining towns. He spent twenty-five years as a longshoreman. All the while, he was reading a lot, but mostly his education came from the people he met, and from scraping around on the fringes of society, struggling to survive.

For some of us, our classroom may be in the ranks of the army or on a work crew. For others, it's dropping out of college and starting a company. For some it's an apprenticeship with someone in the profession we want. For others it's academia all the way, for every advanced degree imaginable. There is no party line. There is no best way.

You have to find the school that works for you, and you've got to show up.

Even if your parents or the experts try to stop you. Even if it goes against society's expectations.

Think about the people who read through the prison library. Think about how many were born in unfavorable circumstances, how many were deprived of access to schools or teachers, who experienced discrimination or depravation through slavery, who pushed through learning disabilities or poverty, yet managed to claw their way to learning, to books, to mentors, to knowledge.

They were certainly disadvantaged in one sense, but in another they had it better: More time. More freedom. More urgency. Fewer expectations. Fewer standard operating procedures.

The demonstrable truth is that you can learn anywhere and everywhere. You can learn about yourself in the woods. You can learn about people in small towns. You can learn to paint outside. You can learn to dance from instructors or through hours and hours of videos that you hunt down. You can learn math from textbooks you saved from the trash. You can even get an education on a college campus!

We cast our bucket down where we are. We make the most of what is available to us.

The world is our classroom. If we choose to make it so.

Find Your Teacher

~

Musonius Rufus was not an easy teacher.

He didn't suffer fools. He expected his students to be silent. He expected them to pay attention.

He knew firsthand that life was hard—he had been exiled *three*, possibly four times by cruel emperors—and he didn't coddle anyone who came to learn from him. Musonius taught many students, including kings, but it didn't matter to him if they were important or the children of someone important. It didn't matter if they were sensitive or brilliant. He held them all to incredibly high standards.

Epictetus, studying under Musonius, once made a small grammatical mistake on an assignment that he did not think was very important. "It's not like I set fire to the capitol," Epictetus said, minimizing the error. It did not go over well. "In this case, the thing you missed *is* the capitol," Musonius told him, following the correction with a stern lecture. Because his student hadn't just messed up—he'd been lazy and then tried to make excuses for it.

It might be nice if every teacher was friendly and fun and every classroom was self-directed and met outdoors. It would be nice if every idea was comforting and inspiring. But that wouldn't prepare students to face challenges.

Not every student could handle Musonius, but Musonius survived exile and Epictetus endured slavery, and their trials made them a good match for each other. Besides, for all his strictness, Musonius was clearly an openhearted man who loved to teach. There was, even in his harshness, a profound compassion—after all, he was expecting excellence from this man others considered less than human. Furthermore, he was an open advocate for inclusion, arguing, in the first century, no less, that women deserved to be taught philosophy too.

Under Musonius's instruction, Epictetus would become one of the great minds of antiquity and ultimately an inspiration to Marcus Aurelius. Could Epictetus have done this on his own? Just by reading books?

Maybe.

But Zeno didn't. After that life-changing encounter in the bookstore, he asked the bookseller where he could meet a man like Socrates. As it happened, at that very moment, a great philosophy teacher named Crates was walking by. The bookseller pointed, and Zeno's education began.

Crates's nickname in Athens was "the door-opener," because that's what great teachers do: They open doors to worlds and possibilities we didn't even know existed. They penetrate, as Musonius said, "the very intellect of his hearer." They reach them at their core.

Through a single student a teacher can change the world.

Would Helen Keller have become what she was without her lifelong teacher and friend Anne Sullivan? Would Plato be Plato without Socrates? And Aristotle without Plato? What about Alexander without Aristotle? What if Rusticus had not turned Marcus Aurelius on to Epictetus? What if, centuries later, Professor Rhinelander, a World War II veteran, had not turned James Stockdale on to the same text?

We must find the great teachers . . . and avoid the bad ones.

Because a teacher can also deprive the world, steal from us curiosity and innovation and even goodness. Imagine how differently Malcolm X's early years might have gone had his English teacher, Mr. Ostrowski, not crushed his dreams. "We all here like you, you know that," the teacher had told him. "But you've got to be realistic about being a nigger. A lawyer—that's no realistic goal for a nigger." Mr. Ostrowski told him to think of something where he could use his hands. Malcolm became a street criminal.

Some teachers open doors, some close them.

John Adams's father wanted nothing but for his son to go to college. John Adams wanted to do anything but go to school. He often skipped class to go fishing or hunting or to fly his kite. He didn't like his teachers or think he was learning anything useful.

When he declared that he wanted to be a farmer, his father

took him down to the salt marsh to cut thatch and wade through muck, showing him what that work would actually be like. The next day, John went back to school. But still, the junior Adams struggled. "I don't like my schoolmaster," he told his father. "He is so negligent and cross that I can never learn anything under him." The next day, Adams's father enrolled him in the private school down the road. There, under a schoolmaster named Joseph Marsh, Adams made a dramatic turn. He was studying. He was reading. He saved up to buy Cicero's *Orations*. In less than a year, the fifteen-year-old was pronounced "fitted for college." The following fall, he enrolled at Harvard.

You may be dyslexic. You may think you're bad at math, or not creative. You may have always hated school. But have you considered that perhaps you just haven't found the right teacher?

There is someone out there who is the perfect instructor for you. There is someone out there who *gets* you. It's your job to find them. They say that when the student is ready the teacher will appear. That can be true . . . but we also can't just sit around waiting for a miracle. We must seek out teachers and schools that are right for us. As parents and guardians we must help to find the right learning environments for our children, within and outside of educational institutions.

Musonius understood the necessity of making the student an active participant in their education as a vehicle for transformation. In fact, he would sometimes turn away particularly promising students just to see what they were made of. "A stone, because of its makeup, will return to earth if you throw it up in the air," he said. "The more one pushes the intelligent person away from the life he was born for, the more he inclines toward it."

He didn't just want students to be smart, he wanted them to *want* to learn.

But as much as we're driven to learn, we must rein in our impatience.

There is a story about a samurai warrior named Banzo, who sought an education in a hurry, so that he could impress his father. Told by a great teacher that mastery would take ten years, he was aghast.

"I can't wait that long. What if I work extra hard?"

"OK," the master said. "Thirty years."

"But I will do whatever it takes to make it go faster," Banzo pleaded.

"In that case," the master said, "it shall take seventy years. A student in a hurry learns the slowest."

The lessons we need will take time. Some may be painful. As Epictetus would tell his own students, having modeled himself on Musonius, "The philosopher's lecture hall is a hospital. You shouldn't walk out of it feeling pleasure, but pain, for you weren't well when you entered."

Valuable things are rarely free. Education is one of them.

It's never too late to find a great teacher, but sooner is always better. Because the process will not be a quick one.

Become an Apprentice

U nlike most of John F. Kennedy's administration, Lyndon Johnson did not get an Ivy League education. He rode to elementary school—a one-room schoolhouse—on a donkey. The only college he could get into was Southwest Texas State Teachers College, in rural Texas.

And yet, if he was deprived of great teachers and even adequate classrooms, it is improbable that anyone was ever so meticulously and methodically educated for the job of president. Certainly, no one had more mentors on the path to power than LBJ.

He paid for college by working as a kind of assistant to the head of the school, Dr. C. E. Evans. How close was the student to his boss? How big of a suck-up was he? The inscription in the college yearbook says of Johnson, "Believe It Or Not—Bull Johnson has never taken a course in suction."

After school, Johnson became friendly with a state senator in Austin named Alvin Wirtz. When he was a congressional aide, he used his position within the Little Congress, an association of staffers, to meet every powerful person he possibly could, including Congressman Sam Rayburn, who would be his lifelong patron. When Johnson won his first congressional seat, at age twenty-eight, he developed a close relationship with President Roosevelt. "You know," FDR would say to Secretary of the Interior Harold Ickes, "that's the kind of uninhibited young pro I might have been as a young man—if I hadn't gone to Harvard." When Johnson entered the Senate, he went to work under Senator Richard Russell, a multiterm Southern institution.

These were not Johnson's teachers in the traditional sense— there were no lessons, no homework—yet it was at their feet that he learned the art of power.

For years, he was their shadow. Running errands. Whipping votes. Campaigning. Raising money. Handling unpleasant tasks. Solving problems. All the while, he was always watching and listening. Listening to them bullshit. Asking them questions. Seeing how they worked. Inviting them over or inviting himself along. Mimicking their techniques. Cultivating their support. "With men who had power, men who could help him," one observer who knew him said, "Lyndon Johnson was a *professional son*."

It was more than just mentorship. He attached himself so firmly to people he wanted to learn from that they became almost like family. He could not have gone from small-town Texas to the "Master of the Senate," could not have gone from an obscure elected official to the Oval Office—where he signed the Clean Air Act and the Civil Rights Act of 1964, and created Medicaid, Medicare, and the Department of Housing—had he not absorbed so much from them, nor could he have achieved anything without the doors they opened along the way. "You get close to the people at the center of things," Johnson would later explain the secret to getting things done in politics and life. It's elemental to justice, and also the best way to learn *how* things get done.

Is there anyone who is able to reach their potential totally alone? Who can learn everything they need to learn by trial and error?

Sure, Johnson had some natural acumen for politics. All of us have gifts and skills—and these are precisely the assets best shaped under the supervision of a master. As the great Jack London writes in his novel *Martin Eden*, "no matter how peculiarly constituted a man may be for blacksmithing, I never heard of one becoming a blacksmith without first serving his apprenticeship."

For thousands of years, this is how trades—and life skills— were taught. Not in a classroom with hundreds of other students, but attached to a professional, who taught, largely by example, until the student was ready to head out on their own. There are some things, the tennis great Billie Jean King would say of her time training under Alice Marble, an eighteen-time Grand Slam Champion, "you can only learn from someone who's been the best in the world."

Or at least, someone who is world-class.

While formal apprenticeships (which, sadly, were also often abusive and exploitative) are largely a thing of the past, learning from someone is still essential. A true mentor is not someone you ask for advice every once in a while. They are someone you attach yourself to and they to you.

In the *Odyssey*, the goddess Athena embodies the role of a mentor, guiding and protecting both Odysseus and his teenage son Telemachus—one struggling to return home, the other struggling to come of age in an equally treacherous world. It is not mere wordplay that she takes on the identity of Odysseus's old friend who was named *Mentor*, to instruct Telemachus directly, helping him find his courage. Odysseus could not have survived his ten years of trials and tribulations without her support, and Telemachus could not have grown from a timid, helpless boy into a brave and capable man without her guidance.

Michelle Howard, the first female four-star admiral in US Navy history, calls mentorship "the transference of wisdom." We each have a choice, she explains. "You can either figure it out on your own and stumble . . . or you can talk to someone who has the same shared experiences."

This process is not always fun. It will often be painful. Your master is not your friend. They are your *master*.

In the *Odyssey*, Athena picks Odysseus to mentor, but in real life, we have to be more like Lyndon Johnson, seeking out and cultivating this relationship. As his biographer Robert Caro wrote, Johnson understood that the old possess a "sagacity" that can be of use . . . if only the young would ask.

We have to find the people who can teach us and open ourselves to learning from them. This is something most people who want mentors often miss. They either think that mentorships are some sort of pro bono obligation that successful people must endure, or they despair of getting one because "What do I have to offer anyone?" No, you gotta work for it—you have to show you are worth working on.

A person's coaching tree* says a lot about them—we admire those who open doors for others—but it also says something about the students.

Whether we're at the Odysseus stage of life or at the Telemachus stage, there is someone who knows more than us, who has been through more than us, who can open doors for us. How do we attract their attention? How do we make ourselves worth their while?

In the early days of his career, Bill Belichick often volunteered as a driver for the older coaches, knowing it meant twenty or thirty minutes in the car together. He took his first job working for the Baltimore Colts, making twenty-five dollars a *week* before taxes because it was his way into the game, his

---

* See chapter in *Right Thing, Right Now.*

chance to learn the game from people who knew it. Eisenhower, stuck in a boring posting in Panama, started getting book recommendations from General Fox Conner, who, appreciating Eisenhower's diligence, began to shape this Kansas farm boy for greatness.

You have to show yourself as somebody with the hunger to learn and excel. You have to show yourself as somebody who listens. Somebody curious. Somebody who is worth teaching. Somebody who is coachable.

They give us books to read. They give us problems to solve. They give us riddles to chew on. They provide an example that inspires or even shames . . . and sometimes cautions.

Even as president, Lyndon Johnson was still the dutiful professional son, looking for guidance from whomever he could get it from. His first move was to ask Kennedy's cabinet members to stay on and to continue to advise him.

You will get to lead one day. But first you must figure out how to obey. First you must learn how to serve.

Join a Scene

~

They met at houses across the empire: Panaetius, the Stoic philosopher; Publius Rutilius Rufus, a Roman politician who defied Rome's culture of corruption; Polybius, the great historian. Scipio Aemilianus, the famed general, brought these men and many other thinkers, writers, and leaders together, and it was after him that historians named their group the Scipionic Circle.

Scipio was not some ordinary soldier. He was a philosopher warrior who loved to be surrounded by great minds. An ancient historian said that Scipio was equally committed to his "pursuit of arms [and] his studies, he was either training his body by exposing it to dangers or his mind by learning."

There were plenty of opportunities to learn how to train his body, but the meetings of the Scipionic Circle were the best place for him to train his mind.

There, he and his friends debated the qualities of leadership. They argued over Rome's growing challenges. They talked about justice. They shared books and recited poetry. They theorized about forms of government and which offered the best chance of stability and progress. They found moments to laugh too—at the cyclical nature of history and human error, at one an other's contradictions, and at the odd theories of the day, like the one about people seeing two suns up in the sky.

What a scene it must have been. Even a fly on the wall would have been enchanted.

Exceptional people have always cultivated such scenes.

In 1764, a small group of artists, writers, and philosophers formed "the Club." They met once every other week at various places around London. Samuel Johnson was there. James Boswell, Edmund Burke, Edward Gibbon, and Adam Smith were there too. Even if those names don't land with you today, know that we live in the world that they helped create through their literary criticism, biographies, political theories, economic discoveries, and histories.

"For years, the group met," the author Leo Damrosch writes in his fascinating book about the Club. "They gave each other ideas. They inspired each other. They challenged each other. They grieved with each other and had grievances with each other."

Like the Scipionic Circle, the friends at the Club had long-running, wide-ranging conversations on every topic imaginable. They argued, teased, and critiqued one another's work. They competed with one another. "He that wrestles with us strengthens our nerves and sharpens our skill," Burke said, echoing a metaphor from the Stoics. "Our antagonist is our helper." They also supported and opened doors for one another.

And at nearly the exact same time, across the Atlantic, the up-and-coming printer Benjamin Franklin started a little club of twelve friends he called the Junto, which was dedicated to mutual improvement of all involved. It was the first of many such clubs he would start, from lending libraries to the American Philosophical Society. He was trying to make his world bigger and better.

The tradition continued into Emerson's time, with the Transcendental Club, coalescing into the scene around Emerson, who also funded it, in Concord in 1836. It included Thoreau, Nathaniel Hawthorne, Margaret Fuller, Louisa May Alcott, and Elizabeth Peabody. After World War I, the so-called Lost Generation came together in a social cohort of expat writers—Ernest Hemingway, Gertrude Stein, F. Scott Fitzgerald, T. S. Eliot, Ezra Pound, among others—in Paris. Earlier, in twentieth-century London, the influential Bloomsbury Group emerged, including such luminaries as Virginia Woolf, E. M. Forster, and John Maynard Keynes. In the fifties, the Beats transformed literature, just as, in later decades, punk and grunge and rap scenes transformed music. Today, there's the so-called PayPal Mafia—Peter Thiel, Reid Hoffman, and Elon Musk—which came out of a single start-up in the late nineties.

It's not a stretch to say that most of these people were extraordinarily talented on their own. Many were out-and-out geniuses. Yet even they needed a community.

We all do.

The musician Brian Eno coined the word "scenius" to explain how we get better by being part of a group or a culture or an ecosystem of influences. Are there some lone, solitary geniuses out there? Sure. But there are a lot *more* sceniuses.

The sooner we find our scene, the better.

You gotta find your people, then you'll find yourself.

Think of all the people who never get so lucky. Who limp along, alone. Who wither, alone. Think of all the flowers not pollinated, hybrid vigor left un-vigorated. Think of the wasted years, art not made, breakthroughs delayed because people have been delayed in finding their people.

But the most devastating alternative for not finding your scene is the graveyard of talented people with potential who ended up in the *wrong* scene. It's a story as old as the Scipionic Circle. A talented young mind falls in with some bad influences. An athlete is surrounded by yes-people and gets complacent or entitled. A scientist gets sucked into a vortex of conspiracy theorists or whack jobs.

It's very rare that someone does not become better by surrounding themselves by great people. Socially. Professionally. Spiritually. It's also very common that a potentially great person is ruined by not-so-great influences.

"Tell me who you consort with," Goethe said, "and I will tell you who you are."

We need to find a scene that challenges, inspires, and understands us, exposes us to new ideas, holds us accountable, and pushes us to go beyond our limits. "Associate with people who are likely to improve you," Seneca advised. "Welcome those who you are capable of improving."

Your scene can get together once a year for a long weekend. It can meet for dinner and conversation at the same restaurant once a month. It can gather at the same conferences. It can be a group text. It can be formal. It can be self-organized and sporadic. But it needs to be something that promotes your growth and makes you better than you were before.

Today, there are so many options for how you create and sustain your group. With so many opportunities online and in person your net is much wider than what the Scipionic Circle, the Lost Generation, or the Bloomsbury Group could imagine. You can make yours however you like, just make sure the group will make you better.

And wiser.

Study the Past

~

Major George Patton had been there before. He was sure of it.

"I was at this battle as a boy," Patton said, as he stood surveying the now-grassed-over field where thousands of men had died in the Civil War, decades before his birth.

He would often tell friends about flashes of memories: Being carried on the shield of a Viking. Fighting in Poland in the fourteenth century with John the Blind. Marching in the Napoleonic Wars. Leading a Roman legion in Gaul.

In the midst of his reveries in 1933 about the events of the Battle of the Wilderness, Patton and the military historian he was speaking with were interrupted by a much older man. "The gentleman is quite right," the veteran explained. "I was in the battle, and gentlemen, we ran like hell."

Patton insisted this déjà vu was authentic, that within him was reincarnated spirit of generations of warriors. Maybe there's something to that, for his success on the battlefields in Africa and Italy and France and Germany in World War I and World

War II were so dashing, so daring, that they seemed like a continuation of the mythic campaigns of the past.

But there is also a simpler explanation that hardly dampens the magic: Patton was such a student of history, he was so deeply read—consuming not just countless books but poems and novels and firsthand accounts at the knees of old soldiers—that the memories of what he had studied merged fluidly into his own sense of self until there was no longer any difference between the two.

He wasn't just *talking* to the dead, as Zeno would have observed; he had come to live with them.

Indeed, he all but admitted it in a manuscript he began writing for future officers. "The road to high command leads through a long path called 'The History of War,'" he wrote. "To be useful in battle, military knowledge, like discipline, must be subconscious. The memorizing of concrete examples is futile for in battle the mind does not work well enough to make memory trustworthy. The officer must be so soaked in military lore that he does the military thing automatically."

History is not just something that happened. It is not theory. It did not happen in black and white. It was *alive*. It was *new*. It was touch and go at every second, and so easily could have turned out some way other than it did.

That's why we study it. We study history because it's ...

... biography.

... psychology.

... philosophy.

... human greatness.

... human evil.

It's the splendid and the vile, the possible and the impossible.

Historia est magistra vitae. History is the teacher of life, and *Clio,* the ancient muse of history, is our teacher.

Many don't know this, but Patton was dyslexic, and as a child reading was incredibly difficult for him. Words on the page made little sense and books filled him with dread. His family overcame this obstacle by reading *to* him, constantly. Shakespeare, the *Odyssey,* the *Iliad,* the Bible, Xenophon, Kipling, the stories of Plutarch and the Civil War—the glory of war and all its horrors went into his ears over and over and over until it was imprinted deeply into his mind.

By his early teens, Patton was reading on his own, and reading like a man on a mission.

One biographer estimates that by the time World War I broke out, Patton had read nearly every book on mobile warfare that had ever been written. He had read the memoirs of the great American generals—Sherman, Grant, Lee—enough times to have them memorized.* This is the empowering part of history

---

*After a tough meeting, he noted, "I worried a little but I feel I was right. I thought of Grant and Nelson and felt OK. That is the value of history."

that puts the reader there alongside the greats, bringing close the awareness that they were just human beings and if they could do it, maybe you can as well.

Patton's diary notes multiple times when he stayed up till midnight, reading by lamplight. And when he finished a book, he'd put an *R* on the flyleaf and add it to his library. His studies weren't limited to military history. He read novels and plays—fiction written in the past and fiction *about* the past. In 1942, knowing that he was about to fight in Morocco, he read the Koran. A European priest observed Patton at a cathedral sketching copies of stained-glass windows in his notebook. Photojournalists captured Patton in museums. He toured battlefields and castles and the scenes of world events.

The Stoics said that by studying philosophy, we annex every age into our own. Each era, epoch, and event that we study is a way to live through those times. "By means of history," Montaigne said, we "frequent these great souls of former years." They become our companions, our enemies, our Cassandras, our inspirations, our cautionary tales. We absorb their lifetimes— and their life lessons—in our own. We get a wider perspective, a bigger view, while turning down the volume on the frivolous opinions and biases of the moment.

Too many people think history is supposed to be entertaining—perfect for a Father's Day gift. But history is not all high-water marks. It's not only the big names and big events. It's filled with ordinary people. It's filled with suffering. It's filled with hypocrisy and failure. It's long centuries and cycles. It's the same things happening over and over.

You don't have to like what happened in the past to learn from it. You do have to engage with it.

The Greek word *historia* means inquiry, investigation. History isn't something that is presented to you, it's something you unearth, piece by piece, book by book, visit by visit, question by question. As we read and study, we become a pioneer, a refugee, a Union soldier and a slave owner, a colonizer and a native, a Greek and a Roman and a barbarian. We must inhabit their world to understand it, see things through their eyes, feel the heat of battle, the fear of persecution, the hope of a better future.

"The crimes and misfortunes of history cannot be too frequently pondered on, for whatever people say, it is possible to prevent both," Voltaire reminds us. The study of history inspires, but it also disabuses us of our illusions. A close study shows us that heroism is not the norm, that progress is not inevitable, that right does not always triumph, and that change takes a long time. "That men do not learn very much from the lessons of history is the most important of the lessons that history has to teach us," Aldous Huxley once said.

We can choose to be different.

Patton did. Whether his déjà vu was theatrical flourish or not, it was based on something real and it produced something real. He knew what to do on the battlefield because he under-stood what generations and generations of men had done there. He knew their mistakes. He could put himself in their shoes. He felt their gifts. He had acted out their greatness, mulled over their decisions a thousand times from a thousand directions.

History, you must understand, is not about the past. It's a lens for understanding the present (that's why we fight over what gets taught). It's a way of predicting, even determining, the future.

Patton grew up reading about battles on horseback and even elephant . . . but it prepared him for wars of tanks and airplanes and unimaginable new technologies. How did the past prepare him for such uncharted territory? Because it wasn't uncharted at all. War and leadership and politics were different in the twentieth century because of technological advances and other factors, but they were also as familiar as they had been before and will be in the future. "The only thing new in the world," Truman liked to say, "is the history you do not know."

Very little changes over time. Very little wisdom is new.

What prepared Patton for all the innovation and disruption the future would bring? The history that he knew.

History shows us that change is constant, and for every-thing that changes, much remains the same.

There is always history you do not yet know. Each historical event, each era, is defined by what preceded it, all the way back to the very beginning of time. There is no limit to the number of alleys and parallel tracks that one can go down, a truly infinite number of perspectives to consider for each moment. There is always something new being discovered, an inexhaustible amount of information to take in.

Let us begin then, overjoyed, knowing that we'll never get to the end.

Hit the Road

~

Herodotus did not become the world's first great historian by sitting at home with his books. No, he hit the road.

From Persia to Athens to Italy, Libya, Babylonia, Byzantium, and the Black Sea, he traveled thousands of miles over the course of his life. He traveled the Nile by boat. He visited Phoenicia, the birthplace of Zeno, a century before the philosopher was born.

The Greeks had always been travelers, as Herodotus noted. Some traveled for trade, some for war, and others, he said, speaking almost certainly of himself, "out of mere curiosity, to see what they could see." Then, and now, travel was a source of wisdom, a means to discover new places and understand yourself.

He inspected temples. He ate the food. He made conversation. He visited big cities and little ones. He saw the flora and the fauna—from crocodiles to camels. He walked dusty roads and along beautiful beaches. He crossed deserts and entered bustling ports. He watched their ceremonies. He loved monuments and public works. "I have myself seen it," he says of a great labyrinth in Egypt at which he gazed for hours, "and indeed no words can tell of its wonders."

Before Herodotus, there was no "history" as a subject, so he wasn't able to just read it. There was no travel writing either—it would be another seventeen centuries before Marco Polo came along. If he wanted to learn about the Far East or even the culture in a neighboring country, the Persian wars or the deeds of the great Spartans, who gave everything at Thermopylae, he had to see the places and the people for himself.

Herodotus wanted to get the *aitie*—the root causes of things. He was fascinated by the *nomos*, the people's customs, and the ways they differed from his own. He wanted to hear their stories. He wanted to know *why* they did things the way they did.

His famous book, *The Histories*, is full of delightful asides. Here's how the Persians collected taxes. Here's how the Babylonians irrigated their crops. Here's how the Scythians fought on horseback.

Delighted, he watched the river trade on the Euphrates, observing circular boats made of watertight skins. Herodotus notes where the boats were made (Armenia), what goods they carried (mostly wine), their tonnage (up to 130) and besides the crew, the special passengers who rode aboard (live donkeys!). When boats arrived, they were broken down and sold for parts, and then the donkeys carried money and goods back home to start the process over again. "This," he said, "I find the greatest wonder of all things there, except for [Babylon] itself."

How many questions did he ask to learn all this? How curious he must have been!

Every culture thinks its norms are, well, normal. Only travel can fully shake us from this ethnocentrism. In his travels, Herodotus met Persians, Indians, Phoenicians, Scythians, Babylonians, Egyptians, Lydians, Syrians, Thracians, Phrygians. They all worshipped different gods, wore different clothes, told different stories, spoke different languages. They were all so different, yet the same in their parochialism—as humans remain to this day. With his trademark perceptiveness, Herodotus notes that the Egyptians also referred to people who didn't speak their language as "barbarians." (The Greeks did it because to them it sounded like the Persians were saying "bar bar bar" when they talked.)

Herodotus loved to point out that there was a small sect in India that ate a small piece of their dead as part of a religious ritual. Obscene! Disgusting! But how did these people react when told that Greeks burned their dead on a funeral pyre? An outrage! A sacrilege!

The world is very big. Our culture is but one of many. There is wisdom in geography, wisdom in the generations of people who have lived in one place, adapting to the land and the environment around them. If only we are curious enough to learn it.

So hit the road! Travel to the well-known places and the little seen. Travel by boat and by car and by train and by plane and by foot—do as much as you can on foot. Read the signs. Struggle with the language barrier. See things from the other side of the road. Eat the food. Go to the museums. Hike the mountains. Sit at sidewalk cafés. Watch a concert. See the ancient hieroglyphs and notice graffiti on city streets. Listen to people chatter. See the cemeteries. Visit the battlefields. Tarry for a while.

Bring your notebook. Write down everything you see and feel and think.

See your own country as a tourist. Live abroad like a local.

Every building, every tree has a story. Think of what they witnessed. Think of who stood where you are standing. Think of what people used to think here, what they were afraid of, what they hoped for, what they believed.

What do I care about a bunch of old buildings? I don't want to get sick. Is it safe? But it's so expensive. I'll do it when I'm older, when things settle down.

There are a million excuses *not* to travel, but that's what they are, excuses. Whether it's a European trip paid for by your parents or a backpacking trip funded by summers washing dishes, exploration is an important step in growing up. It will change you for the better. You don't have to spend a fortune traveling to become a worldly person . . . but you do have to check out what's on the other side of the hill a couple of times.

When he traveled, Montaigne sucked up everything he saw like a vacuum, planning little, leaving himself open to chance encounters and experiences. Like the time he came across men leading two ostriches on leashes as a present for a duke. He stopped in at every church he could find, taking in their various practices like an anthropologist. Here he is at a Jewish circumcision. Here he is at a Protestant church, then at the Vatican, speaking to the pope. Here he is talking to a woman dressed as a man. Here he is chatting with a poor farmer. Here he is talking to Tupinambá people from Brazil, who had made it to France after a journey of some forty-five hundred miles across the ocean. Here he is waylaid by highway robbers, chatting their heads off, cleverly persuading them to let him go.

The only thing that disappointed Montaigne when he traveled was meeting another Frenchman. It seemed a waste to have gone so far to meet someone from home.

"I was never a fan of people who don't leave home," the well-traveled Joan Didion once wrote. "It just seems like part of your duty in life." It's your duty to shed your exceptionalism. It's your duty to learn, to explore, to expose.

New lands generate new thoughts, make us into new people.

Who would Gandhi have become without his time in England? What if he'd returned home to his province in India and never gone to South Africa? Indeed, what he would refer to as "the most creative experience of my life" happened in a train station in Maritzburg, South Africa, when he was discriminated against for the color of his skin. It wasn't a *fun* interaction, but far from his comfortable law office and even farther from his native home, it awakened in him the activism that would change the world.

It was in England, not in India, that Gandhi's vegetarianism became part of his identity. It was in England that Gandhi met suffragettes and saw firsthand how nonviolence could work as a political strategy. It's where he was introduced to the Bible and learned the Christian teachings he would then use to shame the British for their hypocrisies. It was his experiences in South Africa that awakened him to the plight of the Untouchables in India. As a friend observed, Gandhi left England a lawyer and left Natal the mahatma.

Like so many of us, he met many people on his travels, he discovered many things, but most of all, he found himself. The outer voyage facilitates the inner journey.

This is what the wide world and the road promises us— a route to wisdom. It can show us what's out there, who we were meant to be, what we are capable of being.

Go forth.

Not later.

Now.

Acquire Experience

~

Plutarch was more than just some writer.

Although his essays on power and greatness would shape the lives of Montaigne and Truman and Patton and so many other leaders and thinkers, Plutarch's neighbors knew him as something slightly less glamorous: a local official.

It was said that his fellow citizens were often surprised to see this famous writer and philosopher out supervising the delivery of a load of stones for a new road or checking on a sewer system.

But that was a magistrate's job, which Plutarch held for decades in his hometown of Chaeronea, near the Temple of Apollo, where he also served as a priest. Sure, he wrote lofty and inspirational stories about the great men and women of history, but his day job required tending to the masonry work, listening to citizen complaints, passing budgets, enforcing laws. He traveled as a diplomat on important missions. He mingled with consuls and emperors. He cultivated a scene of philosophers and politicians.

Life in politics became a critical part of his practice as a writer, and his love of books and ideas and history were an essential part of what made him a good leader. "The process may seem strange," Plutarch would explain. "It was not so much that by means of words I came to a complete understanding of things as that from things I somehow had an experience which enabled me to follow the meaning of words."

He spent years studying Cicero and Demosthenes. In the process, he became a better public speaker, but in giving countless speeches at home and abroad as his job required, Plutarch understood these men at a level that few other writers have accomplished. This is the reason his biographies resonate some twenty centuries later.

Plutarch saw much of Greece and Rome. He got married. He sat in on legal proceedings. He had unpleasant colleagues and bosses to persuade. He buried a beloved child. People bothered him with petty problems and he had to put up with assholes and egomaniacs. He navigated bureaucracy, figured out how to get things done. He would have seen how power corrupts, felt the pull of it himself. He felt the burden and the loneliness of leadership.*

He wasn't the emperor, but he racked up enough experiences, high and low, that he could understand both an Alexander

---

* The word *idiot* comes from a Greek word that referred to a person who did not hold public office and had no experience in the public eye.

the Great and a Diogenes the Cynic. He lived life, he knew people, he saw things—ordinary and extraordinary—and it was from all this that he drew his wisdom.

That's why Truman could find an answer to nine out of ten modern political problems in the pages of Plutarch's books. Plutarch imbued each passage with his direct personal experience of similar, timeless human issues. And in turn Truman took his own experiences in war and in politics to Plutarch, coming to a complete understanding of the words as a result of the life he had led, for Truman had met a Demosthenes (Churchill) and a Pericles (FDR) and a Caesar (MacArthur), and faced off against more than one Xerxes (Stalin and Hitler).

We put street smarts up against book smarts as if it is some binary choice. We must have *both*. Education and experience are a loop—a mutually reinforcing process. You go to school. You listen to teachers. You read. You try things. You journal. You watch a mentor. You ask a question. You make mistakes. You explore new territory. You study things up close. You get out into the field. You come back to your books. Over and over and over again.

Both take work. We do both as *part* of our work.

Da Vinci, as an illegitimate son, was not given much formal instruction. Like Monet, he didn't love the classroom and preferred to be outdoors whenever possible. Yet he was clearly one of the most brilliant minds to ever live. Who taught him? Was he simply a natural genius? No, he was, as he often signed his own letters, *disscepolo della sperientia*—a disciple of experience. That's Italian and not Latin, for da Vinci was not great with languages. "Though I have no power to quote from authors as they have," he said, comparing himself with his better-schooled peers, "I shall rely on a far more worthy thing, on experience."

It was, he liked to say, his mistress.

Everything he knew came from going out and seeing for himself. From dissecting bodies. From buying birds and watching them flutter about. He wandered the streets of Florence. He visited workshops and observed artists at work. He apprenticed under Andrea del Verrocchio. He analyzed shapes and shadows. He designed and conducted experiments in various forms—in his imagination, through detailed sketches, and with tangible models. He worked on military and civil engineering projects with Machiavelli (himself, like Plutarch, a student not just of books but of life experience). Da Vinci was methodical about processing and recording the information he came across and the insights it spurred—jotting them down in a notepad he often tied to his belt. He was a sponge, always looking, always meeting new people, always trying new things.

Da Vinci was an artist, but he was also a *doer*, and it was what he learned by doing that not only made him better, but gave his work the character and the depth that made it what it was.

You have to figure out how to get your reps in. The author takes a gig writing ad copy. The comedian accepts the hosting job. The doctor volunteers at the free clinic or in the developing world. The lawyer does pro bono work.

You have to get practice *doing the thing*. Not once but hundreds and hundreds of times. Get your hours. Get stronger, smarter, wiser with each turn.

"I have hunted wild boars and watched wild lions, sailed the Aegean (and sailed ships), bent bows, lived with pastoral peoples, woven textiles, built boats and killed many men," T. E. Lawrence said in the introduction to his groundbreaking translation of the *Odyssey*. What best qualified him to take on this mammoth literary task? His years of studying ancient Greek? His classes at Oxford? Or his own odyssey in World War I, where he battled and sacrificed and traveled great distances far from home?

The answer is all of the above!

Knowledge and experience are not at odds; the latter is simply another form of the former. Still, the Stoics had an abhorrence of so-called pen-and-ink philosophers, the types who never lift their eyes from their books as they study and, worse, never use their knowledge out in the world, where it would be of benefit to real people. (Though, to be fair, perhaps it's better that these academics keep their naïveté a closed loop.) The idea was that you need to be a person of action—because no study is complete without an interplay with the people and places around you. That was Plato's biggest fear, that he would turn out to be nothing more than a theorist, "unwilling to take in hand any practical task."

We should be afraid of that too! For the purpose of knowledge is *action*.

Do you want to invest in an entrepreneur who's never had a job or been in charge of people? What kind of insights can a psychologist offer if they have not spent much time with humans? Would you want to be operated on by a surgeon who had watched a lot of surgeries but had never actually performed one?

Too much study and not enough doing creates a paucity of knowledge, a shelter of naïveté, no matter how smart you are.

There are some things you just can't understand until you experience them up close. There are things that make sense on the page but do not survive contact with events.

Or other people.

Mens Sana in Corpore Sano . . .

~

The mind and the body are the same thing, only expressed
in two ways.

—SPINOZA

Today, when we think about Socrates, we think of him as a
thinker—a man with a great mind.

But his friends admired him for so much more. They admired him for his bravery in battle. They were impressed by his
ability to withstand cold and discomfort. It seems almost unbelievable that Socrates—a *philosopher*—was a kind of macho figure, but he was.

"No citizen has any right to be an amateur in the matter of
physical training," Socrates said at one point. "What a disgrace
it is for a man to grow old without ever seeing the beauty and
the strength of which his body is capable."

It's not just a disgrace, it's a failure of curiosity. Don't you
want to know what you can do? Wisdom need not condemn a

person to a life of scrawny weakness or a nerdy lack of coordination.

A strong mind needs a strong body and vice versa. In fact, to the Romans, a poorly educated person was someone who hadn't learned to read *or swim*.

You need both the mental and the physical. A person is incomplete and unbalanced if they neglect one in favor of the other.

Intelligence comes in many forms. A person who can do brilliant things with their mind is wise . . . but so is the person who can make their body do incredible things. Is music not a fusing of both physical and cognitive ability? With creativity thrown on top? The same goes for the quarterback methodically breaking down a defense, or an explorer conquering the elements, not just with stamina but also savvy.

There is a reason so many creative people have a physical practice. There's a reason that philosophers are famous for taking lots of walks (Aristotle's school was called the Peripatetic, which literally means *walking*). So are scientists (Madame Curie and Einstein loved to hike together). Getting the body moving unlocks something in the mind. It also gets you outside into the real world, filled with nature and people and history, enlarging your perspective, bringing you down from the heavens and into humanity. Socrates used his physical training to walk around Athens, talking and learning.

We must be strong mentally, physically. Brains and courage. Brawn and kindness.

Only a fool neglects the body in favor of the mind, or the mind in favor of the body.

Virtue—*excellence*—is the cultivation of all these traits, the aspiration to be a complete and well-rounded person. Smart and strong. Strong and smart.

PART II
THE SIRENS
(THE PERILOUS ROCKS
YOU MUST BEWARE)

We swim, day by day, on a river of delusions, and are effectually amused with houses and towns in the air, of which the men about us are dupes. . . . In lucid intervals we say, "Let there be an entrance opened for me into realities; I have worn the fool's cap too long."

—RALPH WALDO EMERSON

The purpose of nearly every philosophical and spiritual tradition is to not just reach enlightenment, but first to shake off the foolishness endemic to our species. Human history is a catalog of human stupidity. We all have this in us—and it's something we must be on guard against always. Ignorance, the Vedic tradition tells us, is the chief cause of suffering. The Greeks had a word, *amathia*, that described a kind of intelligent stupidity. The Bible tells us that fools are gullible. Fools are easily upset. A fool seeks out quarrels. Each of us is prone to certainty, smugness, fanaticism, contradiction, chaos, bias, impulsiveness, sensitivity, groupthink, and laziness. Wisdom is a constant battle against these forces, insight impossible without the temporary triumph over them. Foolishness is contagious, stupidity seeks converts. Each of us must be at war with the fool within and outside of us. We must seek calm and contemplation and clarity, always. None of us can rest content that just because we're smart or educated, we're not also capable of being an idiot.

The Storm Within Us...

~

Elon Musk is a smart man.

To say he is not smart would be like saying he is not rich.

In fact, he is both one of the richest and one of the smartest men in the world—sometimes the richest and perhaps, in some areas, the smartest.

This was someone who at age thirteen designed his own video game. He got his first computer in 1981. By the age of twenty-four, he'd started his first technology company, and he sold it four years later for $307 million. Next came PayPal, which revolutionized the banking industry and sold for $1.5 billion.

There are many smart entrepreneurs and many successful people. Elon Musk separated himself from them when he took the money from his first two companies and dumped almost all of it into *rockets*, the physics of which are rivaled only by the complexity and bureaucracy of the industry.

Who was he to think he could just waltz in and do it better than Northrop Grumman, Raytheon, Lockheed Martin . . . or NASA?

Plenty of richer and more qualified people had already tried and failed. In fact, there was a graveyard of space companies filled with physics PhDs and ambitious billionaires. Sovereign nations have tried and failed to build viable space programs!

"When I met Elon it was apparent to me that although he had a scientific mind and he understood scientific principles, he did not know anything about rockets," the aerospace engineer Dr. Robert Zubrin said of the Musk he met in 2001. *"Nothing."*

It's not quite fair to say Musk knew *nothing* when he started SpaceX, because he had always been curious about rockets. He and his cousins began experimenting as kids, just like most rocket scientists do. "I'm lucky I have all my fingers," Musk reflected on his childhood experiments with gunpowder and chemicals. "It is remarkable how many things you can get to explode."

The good thing about not being an expert about something is that it's a solvable problem. Ignorance, if you choose, can be a temporary state. Expertise is a function of interest, teachers, and drive.

It seems unlikely that somebody could learn to launch rockets from a self-assembled reading list, but Elon did. Friends recall watching this newly minted multimillionaire carrying around obscure Soviet rocket manuals. He borrowed biographies of Wernher von Braun and Sergei Korolev, pioneers in the field. He borrowed copies of *Aerothermodynamics of Gas Turbine and Rocket Propulsion* and *Fundamentals of Astrodynamics.* More surprisingly, he read them.

"It's true," explained one of SpaceX's earliest employees and the person whose library Musk raided. "He *devoured* those books. . . . He's the smartest guy I've ever met, and he'd been planning to build a rocket all along."

Elon had been reading science fiction since he was a boy, dreaming of space and a better, nearly unimaginable future. He had read Richard Feynman's lectures and writings by Isaac Asimov and Douglas Adams. His nickname was Encyclopedia, so prodigious was his memory, so tenacious was his determination to read the family set from cover to cover. When his parents couldn't find their son, they knew to look for him at the local bookstore, which he usually headed to after school, spending three or four hours a day there, or until the owners kicked him out. And this was only after he had, like Truman, read everything in the school and town library. "I was raised by books," Musk said, "books and then my parents."

"When Elon gets into something, he develops just this different level of interest in it than other people," his college roommate recalled. "That is what differentiates Elon from the rest of humanity." But it was more than just the level of interest, it was the way he locked on to something he cared about, tuning out every distraction, everything and everyone else. "Ever since I was a kid," Musk explained, "if I start to think about something hard, then all of my sensory systems turn off. I can't see or hear anything. I'm using my brain to compute, not for incoming information."

But his curiosity could not be sated simply by reading. He

went directly to the source. He flew around the world meeting experts and asking them questions. He joined the Mars Society, a group that included NASA scientists and even the director James Cameron. He rented out hotel conference rooms and hosted salons about space, inviting the most interesting people in the industry, whom he then peppered with questions. He hired the best and the brightest. "I thought at first that he was challenging me to see if I knew my stuff," one early SpaceX employee said. "Then I realized he was trying to learn things. He would quiz you until he would learn 90 percent of what you know."

We are quick to throw the word *genius* around, but in many cases this label is unfair to the person it intends to compliment. It implies that they were born that way, that they're just freaks of nature. As late as high school Elon was not much more than a slightly above-average student—usually only getting good grades in subjects he liked—who scored a respectable 1400 on his SATs. He was a promising but by no means extraordinary student at Penn and later at Stanford, where he did postgraduate work.

One of the signs of a great mind, it has been said, is the ability to understand the exponential function—to be able to wrap one's head around compounding numbers. No one achieves a net worth in the hundreds of billions of dollars without this understanding, but in Musk's case, his education was itself an example of it. His immersion into various scientific fields was slow going at first, but his focus and determination multiplied by the sheer amount of *time* he dedicated to various enterprises, and it became something incredible. "By 2007," Zubrin says with amazement, "[Elon] knew everything about rockets—he really knew everything, in detail."

Knowledge, it turns out, is also a demonstration of the exponential function.

Musk's original plan for the company that became SpaceX was to contract out the building of rockets, as pretty much all space companies do—including, now, NASA. The problem with doing what everyone else does is that you tend to get the same results as everyone else. "Though most of our life we get through it by reasoning through analogy, which essentially means copying what other people do with slight variations," Musk would explain. "But if you are trying to break new ground and be really innovative, that's where you have to apply first-principle thinking and try to identify the most fundamental truths in any particular arena and you reason up from there."

Aristotle taught that one must go to the origins of things, go all the way to the primary truth of the matter, instead of just accepting common observation or belief. Musk urged his team to explore what it would cost to actually make rockets themselves, to question the basic processes of the industry. *Take it down to the physics*, he would say. When the SpaceX team did this, they found that the material costs were roughly 2 percent of the market price of the expensive rockets they hoped to buy.

Two percent! Not twenty. Not twelve. *Two.*

Nobody had been curious enough to find this out. Elon Musk asked, "What would it take to make them ourselves?" And then he did it.

Nor was this the only conventional wisdom that Musk would end up challenging in the space industry. Every part of the industry had become swallowed up by bureaucracy and conservative thinking. The country that had sent people to the moon in 1969 had literally forgotten how to do it. By 2002, it had been three decades since an American left low Earth orbit. Everything cost a fortune. Everything took forever.

It took a newcomer, strapped for resources, to figure out how to make reusable rockets and to deliver multimillion-dollar avionics systems for a fraction of the cost. Musk did things that the smartest people in the industry said, repeatedly, *were just not possible*. Because he had to. He did not have the luxury of doing things the way they had always been done … or not done.

It was partly these experiences that led Musk to articulate the idea he came to call the "idiot index." The difference between the quoted price of something—a rocket or a battery or a contract to build a new facility—minus the cost of the raw materials is the idiot index. The bigger the index, the bigger the chances that waste, inefficiency, or outright stupidity is involved.

Over the years, Musk developed what he has come to call his "algorithm," a process for thinking unconventionally yet logically that breaks through bureaucracy and limited beliefs while solving complex problems.

The algorithm, which his employees have heard him repeat thousands of times, begins, naturally, with *questioning everything*. All requirements, all assumptions, all regulations and constraints must be scrutinized. Only the laws of physics are binding. Next, *delete, delete, delete*. Try to eliminate every unnecessary part or process wherever you see them—err on the side of deleting, Musk says, because you can always add back in. *Simplify*—just make sure you're not simplifying something that should be deleted. *Operate with a sense of urgency*. Most things take too long, most people operate too slowly. *Automate* everything that can be automated. Again, just make sure not to automate something that should be deleted.

Walter Isaacson, Musk's most recent biographer, adds in a few corollaries based on the many hours he spent observing how Elon works: Hands-on experience is key. Lead from the front. Attitude is more important than intelligence or skills. "It's OK to be wrong," he paraphrases Musk as saying. "Just don't be confident and wrong."

"One of Elon's rules," one engineer would say, "is 'Go as close to the source as possible for information.'" In his factories, he asks the line workers how the process actually works. He pushes back on bureaucracy. *Why do we have to do that?* He trusts the people with hands-on experience to see what's necessary and what is the best way to do something. To the intelligent questioner go the spoils and the profits.

SpaceX would go on to have more than three hundred successful launches, deploy thousands of satellites, send people to the International Space Station, and build the world's tallest and most powerful rocket, among countless other innovations. It's almost unbelievable to watch the company's rockets land on drone ships in the middle of the ocean or the "Mechazilla"—mechanical chopsticks—successfully catch a rocket's booster as it returns to its original launch site.

Like a true visionary, Musk dreamed of a future that didn't exist and he *made* it real. He did this through sheer willpower and technical persistence, through many failed launches, near bankruptcy, intractable and vexing problems. He did it despite the state of the American space program, which was, when he started, essentially stalled out.

There is also the fact that while Musk was teaching himself aerospace, he was also making himself a fast study of automobile manufacturing and electrical engineering.* After an introduction to a team that was attempting to build an electric car, Musk became involved in Tesla, which he would fund, and ultimately lead. It would become the first viable new American car company in nearly a hundred years—since Chrysler's founding in 1925—and the first mass-market electric car company.

Success makes things look easy, but this too was a near-impossible task. Tesla began as a high-end sports car, and even to

---

* Though again, these interests go way back. "Do you ever think about electric cars?" he asked a woman on a first date in college.

make that work required massive innovation in battery, transmission, and charging technology. To make the company viable, Tesla had to make affordable and accessible cars; it had to build enormous factories and a direct sales operation and survive the Great Recession and the ensuing financial crisis.

Even the large touch screens that Tesla popularized were, at the time, totally unprecedented and incredibly difficult to source. "There's nothing like that in the automotive supply chain," Musk was told. "That's because it's never been put in a fucking car before," Musk replied. As with rockets, he and his team went and figured it out.

They figured out gull-wing doors, they figured out engines that could do zero to sixty mph in 1.99 seconds, they figured out autopilot and self-driving technology, and they figured out how to develop batteries that allow vehicles to drive over 350 miles on a single charge.

Not since Henry Ford had any one person more fully revolutionized transportation or manufacturing. Musk managed not only to make the electric car possible, but *cool*—and he managed to build, from scratch, the supply chains and facilities to produce millions of them and then sales channels to move them.

As with SpaceX, Tesla looked like it would fail many times. It was widely seen as a money pit, a bankruptcy waiting to happen. The same could be said about SolarCity, his enormous solar-panel and battery company. But he pulled these companies through . . . and while he was building/saving them, he also became an original founder of OpenAI, the breakthrough AI company. SpaceX launched Starlink. Musk would start the Boring Company and Neuralink.

The combined value of these companies is easily more than a *trillion* dollars.

To achieve just one of these things might qualify as an extreme feat of intelligence, business acumen, creativity, ambition, and determination. To do it all in a two-decade period is nearly unbelievable!

"What's really remarkable to me is the breadth of his knowledge," the astronaut Garrett Reisman, who has a PhD from Caltech, would explain. "I mean, I've met a lot of super, super smart people, but they're usually super, super smart on one thing, and he's able to have conversations with our top engineers about the software, and the most arcane aspects of that, and then he'll turn to our manufacturing engineers and have discussions about some really esoteric welding process for some crazy alloy, and he'll just go back and forth, and his ability to do that across the different technologies that go into rockets, cars, and everything else he does."

Elon Musk is a man straight from the pages of Plutarch. Someone who bestrides the world like a colossus. Someone who can actually claim to have made a dent in the universe.

And yet, Plutarch would have also spotted that beneath the greatness has always been an epic, tragic flaw—a narcissism as profound as his brilliance, a destructive, delusional impulse that has often made this very smart man very, very foolish.

"One of Elon's greatest skills is the ability to pass off his vision as a mandate from heaven," one of Musk's cofounders at PayPal once said. He convinced his employees that PayPal was the future of banking, that Tesla was on a crusade to reduce carbon emissions, that SpaceX would bring humanity to Mars.

But this superpower is also a kind of insanity—close cousin to a messiah complex.

It's a timeless story. As Elon has succeeded, as his billions piled up and his fame grew, he slowly, steadily became unmoored from reality. Inseparable from his drive are emotional instability, dark currents of paranoia and prejudice, and an endless need for attention. It makes for a compelling spectacle, but it is also torture for him. "My mind is a storm," he admitted in an interview. "I don't think most people would want to be me. They may think they would want to be me, but they don't. They don't know, they don't understand."

"He is a drama magnet," Elon's brother, Kimbal, explained. "That's his compulsion, the theme of his life." Imagine, this is a man with fourteen children, effectively running nearly as many companies with a combined employee roll in the tens of thousands, whose goal was to "make humanity interplanetary," who has nevertheless tweeted *over twenty thousand times* since joining Twitter/X in 2010 (sometimes as many as five hundred times in a single day).

And so many of them have been so, so, so dumb.

Like, objectively dumb. One study by *The New York Times* found that roughly 30 percent of the 171 tweets (171 tweets in one week!) that Musk had recently posted were either "false, misleading, or missing vital context."

It's OK to be wrong, Musk once said, just don't be *confidently wrong*.

It might even be OK to be confidently wrong . . . in private. But to do it in front of hundreds of millions of followers who worship you? It's dangerous.

When Elon was asked by a reporter why he isn't more careful with his words, Musk said he just didn't care. "I'll say what I want to say," he said with a shrug, "and if the consequence of that is losing money, so be it." A strange thing for the CEO of a *public* company and the steward of large government contracts to say, but what about the consequences for *people other than him*? Or for the society he's helped to build?

"Based on current trends, probably close to zero new cases in US too by end of April," Musk—not an epidemiologist—tweeted in mid-March 2020 in reference to a pandemic that would go on to infect more than three hundred million Americans, killing over 1.2 million of them in the process. Here he is telling investors that Teslas will be fully autonomous within a year. "I am certain of that," he said in 2019. "That is not a question mark." Here he is "confidently" predicting humans would be colonizing Mars by 2022. "Funding secured," he announced, claiming that he had financing lined up to take Tesla private at $420 a share. Funding was not secured, and the price was a lame weed joke that he thought would make his girlfriend laugh. As a result, Musk was fined forty million dollars by the SEC for this tweet and threatened with a ban *from ever running a public company for life.* He was forced to step down as chairman and banned from the position for three years—and he's lucky the funding didn't go through, because if Tesla had gone private, it would have cost him billions of dollars.

Here he is—not a doctor—telling people they shouldn't get vaccinated. Here he is, again not a doctor, telling people that taking antidepressants might kill them. Here he is telling investors he thinks his own stock is overvalued. Here he is hawking dodgy cryptocurrencies. Here he is making fun of Bill Gates's body (not that his own is so great). Here he is telling the SEC to "suck my cock." Here he is complaining about government spending—when his own companies were saved by enormous government loans and contracts (estimated to be cumulatively fifteen billion dollars). Here he is calling a noted cave explorer who had just rescued twelve children from certain death a "pedo guy." And then after apologizing, at the advice of his lawyers, he tweeted, "You don't think it's strange he hasn't sued me?" and thus ensuring a two-hundred-million-dollar lawsuit. Here he is posting the home address of a journalist he disagreed with.

Here he is, a billionaire, accusing people who work in foreign aid of being criminals. Here he is, once an environmentalist, calling climate change activists "communists." Here he is calling one of the founders of Facebook a "retard" . . . and a SpaceX astronaut "fully retarded." Here he is challenging the other Facebook founder to a *literal cage match* (before backing out like a coward). Here he is smoking pot on camera, despite being a defense contractor, subjected to strict drug standards. Here he is on a fake account, under the name of his toddler, insulting his ex—the mother of the child he's pretending to be. Here he is ranting about immigrants (despite immigrating first to Canada and then to America, as an "illegal," according to his own family).

What do all these erratic, seemingly contradictory views have in common?

Well, him. Not just manic energy or immaturity and impulsiveness or the sheer amount of time they wasted, but Musk's insistence on making so many different complicated problems and hot-button issues about *himself*. It's always: "Let *me* tell you *my* opinion about this. *I* know best. *I* have to weigh in. *I* know how to fix this. *I* think you're an idiot. *I* think this is very simple. *I* have feelings about this (and they matter more than anyone's facts). The rules don't apply to *me*."

Musk loves to consider himself a technologist, which he surely is. But he is also a malignant narcissist, and as is true for so many of us, his irrational side often wins over his rational, scientific side.

Why has it gotten so bad? Well, influences matter. Habits matter. The man who used to rely on his algorithm for going to first principles has been worked on by the algorithms of social media. The guy who used to approach every topic like a physicist, reading every book he could find, now outsources major business moves to polls on Twitter, speaks via emojis, and gets his political opinions from accounts like Catturd2 and EndofWokeness! The guy who once held salons to learn about space now lives in a bubble where nearly everyone he meets or speaks to either wants something from him or fears him.

With extreme success the air becomes thinner. Real feedback, rarer. Truth, scarcer.

It cannot be easy running this many companies at the same time, but his own decisions have compounded the difficulty. A decade back, Musk fired his longtime assistant, saying she was unnecessary after twelve years of service and that he could do her job better himself. "Elon's worst trait by far, in my opinion, is a complete lack of loyalty or human connection," Tesla's former CTO explained. "Many of us worked tirelessly for him for years and were tossed to the curb like a piece of litter without a second thought." Firing these people wasn't just insensitive, though—it was stupid. He was punishing himself. Inexplicably, he never replaced his assistant, even as his schedule got busier and busier and he took on more and more tasks and had more and more children.

No wonder his decision-making became more and more erratic.

It's too much stress for one person. It's a crushing daily burden. One gets to a dark place quite quickly . . .

"You have said the actual truth," Musk tweeted in response to a rabid anti-Semite who had posted about the "Great Replacement Theory." Here he is un-banning the loathsome Alex Jones (and then siding with Jones in a legal case involving the *parents of the Sandy Hook victims*). Here he is spreading Russian propaganda and literally taking calls from Vladimir Putin. Here he is tweeting with a neo-Nazi, and endorsing the party associated with neo-Nazis in Germany, and chiding the country for "too much of a focus on past guilt" . . . a few days after making what sure looks like a Nazi salute. Here he is mocking the use of pronouns even as his own sixteen-year-old transitioned. Here he is wrongly accusing a twentysomething Jewish man of being a federal agent participating in a "false flag" operation, subjecting him to so many far-right trolls that the man and his family had to flee their home. "What advantages does . . . the color of my skin give me?" the man born and raised in *apartheid South Africa* would say dismissively in an interview with a Black journalist.

Instead of owning these mistakes or taking a long, hard look in the mirror, or just shutting up, Musk decided instead to *sue the Anti-Defamation League*, one of the oldest and more venerable nonprofits in the world, one that has long been dedicated to stopping exactly the kind of anti-Semitic hate that his policies on Twitter have unleashed.

Now, Musk would obviously deny that he's a racist, but for someone who is not a bigot, he sure says a lot of stuff that the bigots who follow him like. "You don't have to read between the lines with me," Musk once told a journalist. "I'm saying the lines." *Mm-hmm.* It doesn't take much reading between the lines, then, to conclude that our century's Henry Ford seems to be turning into . . . well, also this century's Henry Ford.*

Of course, the dumbest thing Elon Musk did on Twitter was to buy Twitter. In 2022, he began accumulating shares in the social network—violating securities law, it's worth noting, when he failed to disclose his ownership position in a timely fashion. After being offered and accepting a board seat, he changed his mind in the course of a single, five-minute, angry text conversation with Twitter's then-CEO (which had occurred because the CEO had asked him to stop saying on Twitter that Twitter was "dying"). It was an impulsive, emotional decision that was shortly followed by an offer to buy the whole company for $54.20 a share, or $44 billion, a massive overbid. "What Twit-

---

*Or perhaps embracing his family's legacy. Musk's maternal grandfather, J. N. Haldeman, was, as *The New Yorker* captured it succinctly, "a pro-apartheid, antisemitic conspiracy theorist who blamed much of what bothered him about the world on Jewish financiers."

ter needs is a fire-breathing dragon," Musk said, believing that the current leadership was not aggressive enough.

It would take several months and many millions in legal fees before he could be that fire-breathing dragon. Getting what he wished, he promptly burned one of the world's largest social networks to the ground.

Within months, the network he bought for nearly $50 billion would be worth much less than $10 billion. Buying Twitter wasn't a "mistake," not an error in the way that we make them. Every business has failed ventures. Every leader makes bad bets. Every quarterback makes a bad throw or two. No, buying Twitter was more like running the field from end to end and scoring on your own goal, despite every single one of your teammates and the crowd and even the referee trying to stop you. Indeed, as the deal closed, Musk reportedly screamed "FUCK ZUCK," in celebration—a taunt to Mark Zuckerberg, who was certainly not about to interrupt his rival making perhaps the biggest unforced error in business history.

"How do you make a small fortune in social media?" Musk would later joke. "Start with a large one." It was a twinge of self-awareness before he continued with the very same kind of decisions that had destroyed something like 80 percent of the company's market cap.*

---

*It's actually worse when you consider he sold valuable Tesla shares to pay for the acquisition.

The purchase of Twitter was actually dozens, maybe hundreds, of blunders, not just an error but the repeated, dogged determination to remain in error and compounding it with a series of stupid and reckless subsequent decisions. The purchase was impulsive to begin with, with Musk claiming he wanted to buy Twitter in part to "defeat the bots" . . . only to try to back out of the deal because, as he then claimed, the service had too many bots. Musk had rushed to sign the purchase agreement, signing away any rights to due diligence, trusting his gut instead of digging into the company's books. When he tried to back out, Twitter sued and pointed to the contract terms he had proposed. "I don't know why I did it," Musk would admit. "The judge basically said that I have to buy Twitter or else, and now I'm like, okay, shit."

But no one forced him to immediately lay off more than six thousand employees (80 percent of the workforce), gambling on a complicated technology and ad-services business to operate on a skeleton crew. No one forced him to make these layoffs so quickly and haphazardly that he had to ask many of the critical employees to come back. No one told him to get rid of Twitter's PR team and autoreply to all media inquiries with the poop emoji—antagonizing the media and effectively guaranteeing negative coverage. No one forced him to ban numerous journalists on the platform or to block the word *cisgender*, making a mockery of the argument that he'd bought the platform to "protect free speech."

No one forced him to stop paying rent on the company's offices or stop paying for janitorial service, so that the bathrooms stank and the remaining employees had to bring toilet paper from home. No one asked him to pick fights with Disney and Apple, two advertisers that spent hundreds of millions of dollars on his platform. No one but the very worst fringes of the extreme right wanted him to un-ban noxious trolls and whackos. No one but them was hoping to see hate speech and racial slurs spike on the platform, as they immediately did. No one thought it was a good idea to change the seventeen-year-old name of one of the most well-known brands in the world from "Twitter" to "X."

And certainly no one at his other companies—Tesla and SpaceX—or their sensitive customers asked for this enormous distraction . . . or the negative brand association with this dumpster fire.

Here he is getting rid of the verified check mark system that advertisers and businesses used to prevent fakes and imposters on the site. Here he is, two days before a set of critical meetings intended to reassure skittish brands, posting a link to a conspiracy site to speculate that Nancy Pelosi's husband had not actually been attacked by a deranged person (who was ultimately sentenced to life in prison) but by his gay lover. "It's really such obvious partisan misinformation and it makes me worry about you and what kind of friends you're getting information from," one employee would tell Musk to his face in response. "It's only really like the tenth percentile of the adult population who'd be gullible enough to fall for this."

Musk fired them on the spot.

"I'm a fucking idiot," he'd tell a crisis PR consultant after another needless scandal. "I'm guilty of many self-inflicted wounds," he would say in a deposition in a lawsuit over one of his many irresponsible tweets.

Yup.

His critics say that the last few years are proof that the emperor had no clothes all along. They point to the fact that Musk had many cofounders at PayPal and was not an original founder of Tesla. They point to the enormous government subsidies his companies have received. In Rian Johnson's murder-mystery movie *Glass Onion*, the main character, loosely based on Elon Musk, is revealed to be not an evil genius but a bumbling, over-confident clown—a hype man whose greatest accomplishment is not his companies but making people think he is a genius.

This is, in a way, both too simple and too generous. Because if Musk were a true fool, it would excuse him of responsibility for the horrible things he has said and the reckless decisions he has made. The most curious and alarming thing you can say about Elon Musk is that *he is smart enough to know better.*

He certainly didn't get where he was by behaving and thinking like this.

For many years, it didn't just look like Musk had the Midas touch, he *did.* He created billions of dollars of wealth. He did things that were supposed to be impossible. He was on the cover of bestselling books and magazines. He was the recipient of fawning press coverage and made cameos in superhero movies. He accumulated one of the largest social media followings in history. Everything he did, every time his critics questioned him or the market doubted him, he proved them wrong. If he had listened to them, where would he be? Where would we be?

Elon Musk *was* Midas. Everything he touched did turn to gold.

Yet it's all too easy to forget that the timeless story of King Midas is a tragedy, that power corrupts, that success breeds bad habits, that pride goes before the fall. "People have said that my entire life," he said of all the people who told him something was impossible, not to do this or that, to be careful, to slow down, to accept reality. "What else is new? They also said we couldn't land rockets." His friends, he cannot forget, had literally held an intervention when he considered starting SpaceX—"Elon, you cannot start a launch company. This is stupid," they told him.

Why should he listen to anyone? About anything?

One of Musk's more admiring biographers, Ashlee Vance, would note that Musk's against-the-odds successes displayed "a trademark style of entering an ultracomplex business and not letting the fact that he knew very little about the industry's nuances bother him in the slightest." It's not a surprise, then, that he started to think he could learn anything, do anything, that he was smarter than *everyone*.

Domain expertise is tricky. Sometimes it is transferable. Sometimes it is not. Wisdom and humility and self-awareness are key to knowing the difference.

Elon Musk developed the habit of viewing people who disagreed with him as "idiots"—it's right there in the "*idiot* index." So common were his rages at mistakes or differences of opinion that employees came to call it "the idiot bit." You know, where Musk, one of the richest and most powerful men in the world, gets in the face of a factory worker or a manager or a publicist or a government employee and yells, "You're an idiot. Get the hell out and don't come back."

This intense, combative environment does weed out the weak. It keeps people on their toes. Over time, it also almost exclusively selects for sycophants and psychos. Over and over again in the Musk universe, employees who have challenged him, advised him not to do or say something controversial, told him the unvarnished truth, or urged caution or consideration have found themselves suddenly out of a job. The kiss of death, another engineer would explain, is "proving Elon wrong about something." It's well-known in the culture of Musk's companies that people who raise concerns about safety or regulations or question whether something is possible are excluded from meetings and eventually pushed out of the company.

No wonder he's gone the direction he has. Who wouldn't?

Musk's second wife, the actress Talulah Riley, once explained that her role was to keep her husband from going "king-crazy"—

from being corrupted by power and stress and wealth. Musk, resisting all forms of constraint—from the SEC to the social responsibilities of a high-profile CEO—and Riley divorced, not once but twice, and Musk subsequently went quite king-crazy.

The most dangerous thing that can happen to the smartest person in the world is to start to believe that they are the smartest person in the world.

It turns them into a very dangerous fool.

Because they start to think everything they do is smart, even when it's dumb.

Friends and admirers have long spoken of Musk's "demon mode"—where he would turn himself into a beast or a machine to fix whatever seemingly impossible problem or meet whatever inhuman deadline was necessary to succeed. The months he spent sleeping at the factory. The last-minute fundraising rounds that staved off bankruptcy. The supply chain and logistics miracles he pulls off.

Musk would spend the Christmas of 2022 away from his family, ignoring his other companies, with a small team of dedicated employees personally manically unplugging and loading hundreds of Twitter's servers into trucks to reduce the company's computing costs. He would later admit the whole thing was actually a mistake, because Twitter had had hard-coded references to the servers he was ripping out, thus breaking important parts of the service.

Why hadn't anyone told him? They'd probably already been fired . . . or were worried they'd be called an idiot if they tried to interject.

The point of wisdom is to get *out* of demon mode, which the author Robert Greene has better described as "tactical hell." A leader's job is not to lead their company into a ditch and then rally everyone out of it. No, the leader's job is to be strategic and proactive, calm, controlled, to prevent drama, not seek it out.

Even if Musk manages to turn Twitter around—and he has pulled many rabbits out of his hat over the years—it's indisputable that the crisis was one of his own making and any financial success will be the most pyrrhic victory.* Because in the process, he destroyed his once pristine reputation. He allowed himself to become a globally divisive partisan figure (a dangerous thing for a capitalist and a government contractor to be). He broke his brain.

He wasted so, so much time and energy.

That's the problem with allowing your mind to be a storm, as Musk described his own. You invite chaos. You ignore warnings. You career from crisis to crisis, conflict to conflict; you

---

* Some have now tried to claim that the purchase was genius because Twitter influenced the 2024 election. Spending forty-four billion dollars to influence an election where both candidates themselves only raised two billion dollars would, in itself, make this one of the worst business decisions ever. He also almost immediately fell out with Trump.

expend incredible amounts of energy that could have been better deployed elsewhere.

The cult of Elon celebrates his heroic, company-saving moments, but most of them were avoidable. Most of the messes he got himself into in the first place!

Musk has always had an immense appetite for pushing his chips onto the table—in fact, his friends would say his tendency to do that on every hand made him a terrible poker player. Still, the decisions to put his Zip2 money into PayPal, then his PayPal money into SpaceX and Tesla, were brilliant gambles that paid off many, many times over. Yet Peter Thiel, one of Musk's cofounders, whom Musk nearly killed in a car accident in 2000 while recklessly driving a McLaren F1—"Watch this!"—has come to fear that "Elon wants risk for its own sake. He seems to enjoy it, indeed at times be addicted to it." If you were writing a book about risk, Thiel later said, you would title the chapter about Elon, "The Man Who Knew Nothing About Risk."

It doesn't take that much wisdom—or a degree in statistics— to see that the problem with going all-in all the time is that eventually, inevitably, you go bust.

There is a scene in Isaacson's book that shows Musk in his new element, revealing the rot that has set in. Isaacson is observing as Musk watches a group of Tesla solar workers install panels on the roof of a house. But Musk no longer goes to the source of things to learn; apparently, he's there to teach, angrily lecturing the crew for using too much hardware to secure the solar panels, telling them to reduce the number of nails by 50 percent. "If the house has a hurricane, the whole neighborhood is fucked up, so who cares?" Musk explains. "Don't worry about making it as waterproof as a submarine. My house in California used to leak," Musk tells them, perhaps referring to one of his Bel Air mansions, the group of which he sold for $130 million. "Somewhere between science and submarine should be OK."

Things do not end well for dictators and tycoons who live in a bubble. They don't end well for the egotistical, the incurious, or those devoid of empathy. If someone can't see that, how smart are they really?

Few have done more in less time in the history of humanity than Elon Musk. His accomplishments cannot be measured against entrepreneurial peers but against entire *industries*; in some cases, they can be compared only with whole countries.

Perhaps it's to be expected, then, that the same maniacal urgency could also be destructive, that the desire for attention that made him a cult hero could also turn him into a cartoon villain. He's done *great* things. This does not exempt him from the responsibility for his words and his deeds; this does not give him a pass for the harm he's done and seems hell-bent on continuing to do.

Because that is the most dangerous and foolish and tragic part of his whole story. He didn't just blunder his Twitter acquisition; he learned the absolute opposite lesson and tried to repeat the disaster inside the federal government! Doubling down despite the evidence, it has been said, is the definition of insanity.

Whether karma catches up to him—whether gravity will bring him back to earth—is a matter for a higher power. What's more pressing and personal is how what happened to Elon Musk can happen to each of us.

Intelligence can so easily veer into stupidity. Hubris and delusion tempt us all. We are all in a war against radicalization, rigidity, rage. The algorithm can lead anyone astray.

Wisdom is not work you do once. It's work you must *continue* to do. The mind battles against itself—against its prejudices, its simplifications, its conceits, its patterns, its demons.

Every scientist has their madness. Every genius is touched with insanity. Each of us has a fool inside us.

We have a rational and irrational side. A part of us that builds and a part of us that destroys.

Who will rule?

It's the fight of a lifetime to beat these forces.

Who will win?

Empty the Cup

~

There is an old Zen story about a master who receives a student for tea. As the visitor extends their cup, the master pours . . . and pours, and pours. The cup begins to overflow.

Finally, the student says something: "Stop! The cup is full. It can hold no more."

"Yes," the master replies. "And your mind is like this cup, full of opinions and speculations. How am I to show you Zen unless you empty your cup?"

This is a message about the perils of ego, obviously. It's a message about keeping an open mind.

Because the cup also does not have to be *full* to cause problems. "If this vessel is not clean," the Roman poet Horace said in the first century BC, "then whatever you pour in goes sour."

The human mind is a spectacular thing, the most exquisite and advanced cognitive engine to ever exist. And yet it is also preposterously vulnerable and weak. We are supposedly rational creatures, capable of thinking our way through every problem. Yet scientists have discerned close to *two hundred* cognitive biases that make our mind work against us and our desire to see the truth.

We create patterns and stories where there aren't any.

We jump to conclusions and trust first impressions.

We engage in wishful and magical thinking.

We assume everyone sees the world the same way we do.

We latch on to bits of information; we overvalue the information that's available to us or what's most recent.

We get caught up in the energy of a moment or the mood of the room.

We find it easier to double down on preposterous beliefs than to face the embarrassment of admitting a foolish belief.

We defer to authority.

We are snobbish or condescending.

We think we are immune to these biases—itself a wicked bias!

It would be amusing if these errors didn't come with such serious consequences. If people didn't lose their lives because people misled them. If soldiers weren't fed into an unwinnable war because leaders just can't admit they are wrong, because escalating is easier than changing course.

"Every misconception is a poison," Tolstoy said, paraphrasing Schopenhauer; "there are no harmless misconceptions."

We alone among all species have been given a powerful mind and the gift of reason—but how do we use it? To make up reasons for what we already want to do. To keep us comfortable and unchallenged. To work against our own improvement, to push wisdom away.

We have to watch and filter what we pour into our cups. We have to make sure the cup is empty. We have to wash the cup too.

If we don't, the poison accumulates. We don't just risk making the occasional bad decision or embarrassing error. We turn sour.

This is what happened to Louis Agassiz at Harvard. The man who had taught so many students to *look* at their fishes became, in his old age, incredibly closed-minded and delusional. When Darwin published *On the Origin of Species* in 1859 he sent it to Agassiz with a nice note, expecting that this forward-thinking biologist, whose work he was influenced by, would see the beauty of his new theory.

It was not to be. Agassiz quickly denounced evolution as the "sum of wrong-headedness." In articles and lectures, he ranted against Darwin and his ideas, somehow believing they violated his understanding of nature and the universe. He had never been a rabid creationist, but upon being challenged, he became one, ignoring all the evidence he had seen with his own eyes. In one of his final talks, Agassiz would explain—without the slightest hint of self-awareness—that a scientist "is lost as an observer, who believes that he can, with impunity, affirm for that which he can adduce no evidence. . . . Have the courage to say I do not know. . . ."

Classic projection . . . an insidious psychological device. *I'll accuse others of something so I don't have to face it in myself.* As many people do as they get older, he stopped looking. He stopped being open to new information. Science, Agassiz often told his students, *hates beliefs.* Where he once looked to the evidence for facts, he now denied evidence to support his opinions.

Nowhere was this more egregious than in the scientific racism for which he was a toxic and effective proponent. Agassiz embraced polygenism, a ludicrous and baseless theory that Black people had descended from different ancestors than whites. In private letters he worried about inbreeding between the races, which he considered a "sin against nature." "The brain of the Negro," he said, with zero scientific basis, "is that of the imperfect brain of a seven months' infant in the womb of a White."

It was exactly what slave owners wanted to hear. It was a relief to non–slave owners too, letting them off the hook for the injustices of the time. Indeed, scholars trace some of Agassiz's racial attitudes—he was a Swiss immigrant with a thick accent—to trying to fit into American society. More likely, there was serious cognitive dissonance at play. He was an immigrant in a country with a racial caste system, becoming a citizen during the midst of the Civil War. All around him there were incredible, visible injustices. Like so many Americans, he had a choice: Be outraged by the status quo or come up with an explanation for why it was not all that outrageous.

He was a smart man, but he took the coward's way out.

It is striking, then, to look at the famous picture of a statue of Agassiz that was knocked off a building at Stanford during the 1906 San Francisco earthquake, a few decades after the man's death. The camera catches Agassiz as he spent his last years, upside down, his head buried in dirt up to the shoulders, like the proverbial ostrich, denying what he did not want to see.

It is sad to watch a brilliant mind turn on itself, whether it's the bizarre dysfunctions of Elon Musk or the racism of Agassiz. When someone works for years to master a domain, but then forgets what got them there, their certainty becomes a kind of kryptonite that ultimately destroys them. It's a pathetic, awful sight. As Asa Gray, one of Darwin's great champions, lamented of Agassiz: "This man, who might have been so useful to science and promised so much here, has been for years a delusion, a snare, and a humbug, and is doing us far more harm than he can ever do us good."

The scientific hero lived long enough to become the anti-science villain.

It is tragic but very common.

Oh the things we cut ourselves from seeing!

Imagine a prophet is brought before you. He has drawn enormous crowds. He has earned himself powerful enemies. He is said to be the son of God. Even if you don't believe this, there is something unusual about him, some kind of fire, a new way of thinking and living. He is not like anyone else you have met.

Pontius Pilate, the Roman provincial governor, has this man—Jesus—brought before him. "This is what I was born for," the prisoner says to him. "This is why I came into the world, to bear witness to the truth." Pilate, too busy, too certain, fundamentally uncurious, dismisses him with a flick of the wrist. "What is truth?" And then he leaves the room.

Your preconceptions, your certainties, your biases make you stupid. Pilate didn't have to believe Jesus was the Son of God . . . but to think, he wasn't even interested in finding out what he had to say! Someone claimed to know real truth and he just wanted to move on to his next meeting.

Closemindedness closes us off. It makes us evil.

Our mind, we must understand, is not always our friend.

We can take that metaphor of the cups and illustrate it in many other ways. An open window brings in fresh air and drives out sickness. Stagnant, enclosed water gets dirty, but a fast-moving river is usually much safer to drink from.

We must be empty, we must be open, we must keep moving.

The Stoics knew it was hard work to be on guard against misperceptions. They said we have to take every impression and put it to the test, trusting neither our emotions nor our thoughts. We need to review, to question, to ensure that we aren't falling prey to well-worn patterns or false promises. We need to make sure we aren't fooling ourselves . . . and we have to understand that we are very easy to fool.

"You have a mind?" Marcus Aurelius asked himself, not long after Pilate's time.

Yes.

"Well, why not use it? Isn't that all you want—for it to do its job?"

And that's what he was doing in *Meditations*, in his own notebook. He ran tests against his thinking, making his mind do its job through his pen, instead of defaulting to assumptions or first impressions.

It takes real work to guard against our biases. It takes strength to remain open, especially as the years go by. We get tired. We get entitled. We get used to knowing better.

We accumulate opinions as we move through life.

And as a result, it becomes harder for us to learn; there is less room in our cup.

We must continually empty and clean our vessel if we want to sit down for tea with the masters, if we want to achieve enlightenment.

Write to Think Right

For a Trappist monk, Thomas Merton sure talked a lot. On the page, at least.

After converting to Catholicism in the 1940s, he moved to a monastery of the Order of Cistercians of the Strict Observance (otherwise known as Trappists) in Kentucky. With "strict" in the name, Merton knew he was signing himself up for chastity and obedience and poverty, as well as manual labor and ritual. Trappists are not literally sworn to silence, but solitude and silence are the basis of their religious practice. They have been known for centuries as "the monks who don't talk."

To live at the Abbey of Gethsemani, Merton gave up nearly everything but his love of writing.

"I must also put down on paper who I have become," he wrote in his journal in 1949. "It is not an easy vocation. To be as good a monk as I can and to remain myself, and to write about it: to put myself down on paper ... with the most complete sincerity and integrity, masking nothing. ..."

A supportive superior agreed, assigning Merton a job translating and meditating on various ancient and religious texts, a long-standing tradition for monks.* This was no easy task. At times it was torture, almost a kind of crucifixion, Merton said—a toil anyone who has ever written would immediately understand.

That was the point, though: He did it because it was hard. There is a kind of penance in writing, a willingness to be exposed and to put yourself up for review. Yet writing and editing is also a chore, like any manual labor. Merton turned this into a spiritual process, part of his journey to and through his faith. He published books of poetry and a five-hundred-page memoir that became an instant—and perennial—bestseller, called *The Seven Storey Mountain*. He wrote biographies of saints and mystics. He wrote letters to monks and practitioners of other faiths. He became politically active. His unpublished writings alone amounted to nearly one *million* words.

His writings would reach a generation of seekers and thinkers. His labors supported his church. He was challenging himself, he was getting to know God.

Yet not everyone liked the idea of an outspoken monk.

"Tell this talking Trappist who took a vow of silence to *shut up*!" wrote one angry critic. His editor, the great Robert Giroux, thought the whole criticism absurd. "Writing," he ex-

---

* It is thanks to countless nameless monks that many of the great works of antiquity survive.

plained, "is a form of contemplation." In fact, that would be the title of one of Merton's best books, *Seeds of Contemplation*, a spiritual classic.

In his books, letters, and notepads, Merton was not telling people what he thought. He was *figuring out* what he thought. He was meditating on the page, sharing, generously and courageously, his thoughts with the world.

He wasn't so much writing as he was *thinking with his fingers*.

Peter Burke, one of Montaigne's biographers, believed that Montaigne's essays were precisely that, a man's "attempt to catch himself in the act of thinking." Montaigne said that he wrote as though he was speaking to another person. But that doesn't mean his essays were casual or off the cuff. Montaigne had to sit and really *think*—the act of his thoughts flowing from his brain, down his arm, through his pen, and onto the page was a process by which much reflection was transcribed, and, since he continued to edit his writing until the day he died, refined.

Only a fool goes with their first thought. A wise person takes time to contemplate.

In 1941, just days after the attack on Pearl Harbor, a promising general named Dwight D. Eisenhower was called in to see George Marshall, the chief of staff of the US Army. Japan was going to seize the Philippines and dozens of other islands in the Pacific, Marshall explained. America faced a war in two theaters with supply lines that would stretch thousands of miles.

"What should be our general line of action?" Marshall asked Eisenhower.

A certain type of officer might have started thinking out loud. They might have riffed or brainstormed. Not Eisenhower. He understood that his career and potentially millions of lives hung in the balance.

"Give me a few hours," he said. At a spare desk down the hall in the War Plans Division, Eisenhower requisitioned some paper, a pen, and a typewriter and got to work. What did Marshall want to accomplish? What was possible? What was of the highest priority? What risks were acceptable? What resources did he need?

After a period of reflection, Eisenhower began to write his thoughts out, understanding that what Marshall needed from him was "short, emphatic ... reasoning," and not "oratory, plausible argument, or glittering generality." This exercise helped Eisenhower synthesize all the conversations he'd had with his mentor, General Fox Conner, bringing out ideas from the books he'd read, the courses he'd taken at the Army War College, the work he'd done for the previous chief of staff, and the experiences he'd had in his three decades in uniform. As dusk fell, Eisenhower handed Marshall a three-hundred-word briefing on yellow lined paper titled "Assistance to the Far East/Steps to Be Taken," which he supplemented with an oral briefing.

Almost certainly Marshall had already considered most of what Eisenhower had written. The assignment was, in a way, a test. What kind of a thinker was this young officer? How did he approach problems? How good was he at responding under pressure? Could he see the big picture? Could he effectively communicate what he knew and what he wanted to do?

"I agree with you," Marshall replied about Eisenhower's plan, and then told him to execute it.

Thus began one of the most effective partnerships of the war, leading to victory and propelling Eisenhower to the presidency.

Successful campaigns and careers—whether they involve leading men into battle or saving their souls or selling them things—depends on this kind of thinking.

A few years ago, Amazon executives got tired of their valuable time being wasted by pointless or foolish meetings. So they banned PowerPoint presentations and brainstorming sessions. Instead, they dictated that before any meeting begins, the executive leading it must spend the preceding days writing a six-page structured memo in a narrative form with all the necessary information about the subject—the choices available and the objectives desired.

Memos are written, edited by colleagues, set aside for a few days, Bezos once explained to Amazon's shareholders, and then reviewed again for a final tightening. Each company meeting begins not with chatter but with a thirty-or-so-minute period of quiet, reflective reading—almost like study hall.

Instead of pulling answers out of their ass, Amazon executives, like Eisenhower, are supposed to get their thoughts in order first. And then, as Bezos has said, after this quiet bit of focus and after everyone is on the same page about the basics of the problem or the opportunity, then they can have a *messy* discussion. "I like the memos to be like angels singing from on high," he explained, "so clear and beautiful. And then the meeting can be messy."

Joan Didion described writing as a "hostile act." By that she meant that the writer is trying "to make somebody see something the way you see it, trying to impose your idea, your picture." But Keynes was even closer to the mark when he referred to writing as the "assault of thought on the unthinking."

We are in a battle against our own wild thoughts, against the preconceived assumptions of others, against all the alternative ideas (and tempting facts) out there. Winning out requires contemplation and clarity. We cannot make others see what we first have not properly considered ourselves.

Could you have artificial intelligence do it for you? Or a ghostwriter? Maybe—but it would defeat the purpose.

We think as we write. Indeed, we cannot finish a sentence until we have carried the thought all the way through. We ponder opposing ideas as we pause between keystrokes, the pen becomes our third eye. It doesn't even need to be prose—a drawing can help, a diagram lets you see the problem in a new way.

On the page we see the pattern. Transcribing the passage or

a quote, we get to feel real genius and insight pass through our mind and our fingers, processing each word, weighing and understanding the wisdom.

We see what we didn't see before. And when we take edits and feedback from others, we see even more, because editing is a kind of interrogation, a process by which we are refining and sharpening our thinking, a way to get our story straight.

It doesn't matter if we publish, it doesn't matter what the audience thinks, it was the doing that did the work.

"Every book I write," Merton reflected, "is a mirror of my own character and conscience."

We are writing to think right. To understand what we feel and know . . . and who we are.

Assemble Your Board of Directors

~

C ommodus should have been a great leader.
There had been five good emperors in a row. His father, Marcus Aurelius, was wise and patient and modeled everything you could want in both a predecessor and a parent.

So what happened?

We don't know exactly how the son of a philosopher ended up bungling things so badly that he was assassinated (in real life, by a gladiator) and his statues torn down. Marcus Aurelius knew firsthand how impossible it was to step into a great man's shoes, but he did his best not only to prepare his son, but to bequeath to him the team required to be successful.

"Commodus was nineteen years old when his father died," Cassius Dio, a historian who lived through Commodus's reign, would write, "leaving him many guardians, among whom were numbered the best men of the senate. But their suggestions and counsels Commodus rejected. . . ." Marcus had noted with admiration the way his stepfather, Antoninus, would so willingly "yield the field to experts—in oration, law, psychology"—and the way these advisers helped him fulfill his potential and make better decisions. Commodus could not do this, and it cost him—and the Roman people.

Nero, as it happens, is just another verse in the same sad story.

The first few years of his reign went quite well, advised as he was by Burrus, a great military mind, and Seneca, the philosopher. During what became known as the *quinquennium Neronis*, Nero listened to these teachers, consulting with them on big decisions and accepting the constraints on his power. But as time went on, he became convinced of his specialness, of his brilliance, relying instead on his instincts and emotions more and more.

A famous statue of Seneca shows him giving a version of the daily briefing to the emperor Nero. You can see in Nero's body language, the way he's slouched in the chair with a hood over his head, the sullen, bored expression on his face, that the fact that he's sitting across from one of the wisest people to ever live is totally lost on him. He's no longer a boy, no longer the pupil. He already knows what he thinks he needs to know. He's already decided what he wants to do and what's important. *Why is this guy always so serious, why is he always droning on?*

Of course, Nero failed, spinning off the planet into delusion and paranoia and fantasy.

There is a reason that companies have a board of directors. There is a reason that heads of state have a cabinet. There is a reason that athletes and actors have coaches, managers, agents, advisers.

It's so you don't end up like Nero or Commodus.

Plutarch knew this. Just as a ship captain must rely on their sailors, he wrote, so too must a politician learn to "yield to others with goodwill and kindness, allowing them to govern and be summoned to the speaker's platform . . . having under them assistants who are trustworthy and of good character . . . assign[ing] each one to the task to which they are best suited."

Pericles ran his toughest decisions by his wife, the philosopher Aspasia. American presidents have not only their official cabinet but also often a "kitchen cabinet" they turn to for advice and perspective (and the hard truths that others might be hiding). Even the best of us are not wiser than our group.

By 1953, Eisenhower had long outgrown his mentors. He was now the president, so there weren't many living people equipped to tell him how to do his job or what he needed to understand. Yet it was at precisely this level of power and influence that Eisenhower understood would demand a new kind of relationship to advice and consultation.

Which is why, just a few months after his election, Eisenhower assembled a group of policy experts and cabinet officials in the White House solarium, a private third-story room with sweeping views of the National Mall. Although he knew as much as anyone about foreign policy, he was concerned about the direction of the country's strategy with regards to the Soviet Union. So Eisenhower broke this group into three teams and gave them six weeks to explore different major national security strategies. He instructed them not to collaborate with the other groups; in fact, he wanted them to disagree with each other and present distinct, well-constructed policy recommendations for him to choose from.

Not unlike his own exchange with Marshall a decade and a half earlier, what became known as Project Solarium was an exercise in concentrated, independent thinking. Eisenhower did not want to simply follow mindlessly the assumptions of his predecessors, instead he was rethinking the most important and high-stakes geopolitical issues from the ground up. Ultimately, the decisions were his to make—he was wise enough to want all the advice he could get first.

Each of us needs to cultivate this approach to our own problems in our lives, businesses, and leadership positions. It's one thing to have a mentor. It's also important to have a scene. But at the highest levels, we must develop a board of directors that advises and consults, that at times *checks* and even corrects us.

This isn't a formality but an essential practice to always be learning and improving. Whose collective experiences are you drawing on? Whose network and resources are you bringing to bear on your problems? Who in your life can tell you that you're wrong? Who can tell you that you're being an idiot?

Elon Musk's boards, like far too many corporate boards, are famous for rubber-stamping whatever he asks—even when those requests have been unethical, reckless, or self-interested. Want to acquire a company your cousins started? Want to borrow a bunch of our money to buy a social network? Want to tweet whatever pops into your head? Want to feed whole government agencies into the woodchipper? *Sounds like a great idea, boss!* This might be what Elon wanted, but it's certainly not always what he needed.

Marcus Aurelius knew the dangers of being "Caesarified," or "dyed purple" by the cloak of the emperor. He strove to avoid this, and he hoped to prevent it from happening to his son.

He knew that power was often at odds with wisdom, that never hearing "no" often makes smart people very stupid. Advisers help us see where we are blind. They serve as parents to our inner children, a sounding board for our ideas, a check against our impulses.

Each of us is limited by our own experiences and education. Why would we not want to expand our reach and our resources? We might not have a PhD, but we can have access to someone who does. We may have never been through a negotiation or navigated a crisis like this, but we can call upon people who have. They can expand the history we know, the experiences we've had.

Do groups sometimes encourage timidity and consensus? Sure.

But just as often they stave off catastrophe and chaos.

We need to cultivate the ability to tell the difference. To be able to consult without being cowed. To be singular while not thinking we are superior.

We need other voices around us. We need help. We need to be able to yield.

Only a fool declines this priceless resource.

Don't Be a Know-It-All

～

Harry Belafonte dropped out of high school.

He got a job as a janitor.

But his education started when he joined the navy.

Suddenly, he was surrounded by a group of other Black soldiers who were much smarter than him. They had read widely. They followed politics. Despite their lowly jobs—the navy assigned Black troops the worst duties—this was a scene of intellectuals, and Belafonte pined to be a part of it.

One of them tossed him a book to read by W. E. B. Du Bois, which he tore through. Belafonte, hooked on reading, and, striving to impress his friends, went into a library in Chicago to check out some books from an author he kept noticing in the back matter of the books he read.

"I'll make it easy, ma'am," Belafonte said confidently. "Just give me everything you got by Ibid."

"There's no such writer," she said, looking in the card catalog.

Check again, Belafonte told her. And followed it with, "I'd

like to find out before the war's over," when she took too long. In the end, he stormed out, thinking the librarian was a racist.

Of course, there was no such writer—*ibid.* is short for *ibidem*, a way to reference the same book multiple times in a bibliography—but Belafonte didn't know what he didn't know, much to the amusement of the friends he indignantly told this story to. Thankfully, he learned from this lesson to laugh at himself most of all, and years later, when he was one of the most successful musicians in the world, he would tell the story to W. E. B. Du Bois in person. One of his few regrets in life was that he never got to apologize to that poor librarian who had been on the wrong side of his conceit.

The writer David McCullough had a similar experience when he was in his thirties. Having worked in publishing and government, he had decided to try his hand at writing the story of the Johnstown Flood, which became his first book. As he toiled away at the New York Public Library, making very little progress, he approached the librarian and asked for help. "Have you looked in the *DAB*?" the librarian suggested. "Oh no, I hadn't thought of that," McCullough said with that same cocktail of confidence and insecurity that had held Belafonte up, and then walked back to his table. The truth was that McCullough had absolutely no idea what the "DAB" was.

It took no small amount of courage for this Yale-educated Skull and Bones member, who had studied under Pulitzer Prize winners and then worked at the United States Information Agency, to go back to that librarian and admit he'd been pretending to know something he did not. "The *Dictionary of American Biography*," the librarian said kindly, pointing McCullough to a twenty-plus-volume set that would help unlock many ideas in what would become his first of many bestsellers.

If you believe you are dumb, you'll probably stay that way—it's a self-fulfilling prophecy. Unfortunately, believing that you're smart can also make you stupid.

"Remember," Epictetus told his students—many of whom were not just gifted and bright, but the sons and daughters of the most powerful families in Rome—"it is impossible to learn that which you think you already know."

Or pretend to know.

Or refuse to admit you don't know.

How little we know when we think we know . . . how foolish we can remain for fear of looking foolish.

"Many people could have achieved wisdom," Seneca said, in a famous line, "if they had not imagined they had already achieved it." A young Mark Zuckerberg found a mentor in Donald Graham, the publisher of *The Washington Post*. Graham, knowing that Facebook needed to make inroads in DC, handed him a book recommendation. Zuckerberg didn't like politics or follow the news, so the book sat unread, for lack of time and interest. How did this have anything to do with Zuckerberg's job? Besides, he'd already succeeded in outmaneuvering so many successful people in tech without reading a bunch of books on the topic.

Graham, having dealt with many brash upstarts over the years, refused to accept this. "There are very few things you'll find unanimity about," he explained to Zuckerberg about the world, but "one of those things is that reading books is a good way to learn. There is no dissent on that point."

If you think there is nothing anyone can teach you, you are not just insufferable—you're right. You will not learn anything... except the looming and painful lesson of failure.

This is what happened to Sam Bankman-Fried, another shockingly smart kid. Like Montaigne, he was singled out early as a precocious and generational talent. Everyone knew he would go on to do big things, and he did, working first at a cutthroat hedge fund before starting his own crypto fund and trading platform that would, at its peak, be worth something like twenty-six billion dollars.

But the seeds of his downfall were sown in the arrogance that being a wunderkind can engender. As a kid, he was remarkably uncurious for someone so smart, bored by school field trips to old buildings and historical landmarks he didn't find interesting. At some point in school, he decided he hated books. "I started to associate books with a thing I didn't like," he said of his childhood, and he came to "object to the fundamental reality" of English class. He hated Shakespeare in particular, who he believed was unrealistic and preposterously overrated.

It's one thing to be young and conceited, but Bankman-Fried held on to this petulant *I know better than everyone* view well into adulthood. There's a remarkable 2022 exchange between a journalist and Bankman-Fried, then at the height of his power and influence. The writer tells him that he prefers reading to the trivia and brevity of the internet.

"Oh, yeah?" Bankman-Fried replied. "I would never read a book. . . . I'm very skeptical of books. I don't want to say no book is ever worth reading, but I actually do believe something pretty close to that. I think, if you wrote a book, you fucked up, and it should have been a six-paragraph blog post."*

Know-it-alls are dreadfully boring. They are obnoxious. They are also dangerous to themselves and others.

Anyway, he'll have plenty of time to realize the value of books where he is now.

Putting on airs is not a good look, Zeno said, especially for the young. This is what drove him nuts about Aristo. Conceit and pride have nipped as many promising careers and minds in the bud as racism, external obstacles, and censorship.

---

*Yet even the reporter fell for his shtick, writing in complete seriousness, "Since SBF is obviously a genius, I should simply assume that, compared with me, SBF will always be playing at level N + 1."

It's the reason so many smart people end up doing foolish things.

Sometimes it seems like we're more afraid of looking or feeling stupid than *being* stupid—which is what we are when we refuse to ask questions, when we write off whole subjects as pointless, when we reject mentors and teachers and coaches.

It takes real confidence—and courage—to put yourself out there. To say those magic, humble words: "I don't know." To say instead, "Tell me more." To ask, "What else do I need to know?" To be willing to hear from people less successful, less credentialed than you, people you dislike, people who dislike you, people who have been wrong, people you don't understand. To not just seek out a mentor or a master, but more important, to *hear* what they have to say. Especially when they criticize or challenge you.

We should take learning seriously, but never ourselves.

There are enough obstacles already on the path to wisdom. What no one can afford, no matter how brilliant they are, is to get in their own way.

To shut their ears or close their eyes out of ego. To repel teachers or eliminate avenues of feedback. To pretend to know something.

To become wise in their own eyes . . . and thus able to become no wiser.

Watch Your Information Diet

~

Imagine someone who is glued to their phone from the very moment they wake up. Someone with three TVs in their bedroom, who catches *Fox & Friends* every morning . . . and all the evening Fox shows too. They flip through the newspapers, mostly skimming the headlines. They spend hours on Twitter and other social networks. Their smartphone is filled with texts of articles from blogs, YouTube videos, and viral clips about the latest outrage cycle and the most provocative hot takes. People are constantly calling with gossip. "Did you see what just happened???"

In the background, the TV is always on, usually without sound, because they feel like they can absorb *just the vibes*. Late into the night this gluttony continues, during the week and even on the weekend. Endless outrage. Every breaking story. Nonstop punditry, pouring into their eyeballs and ears.

Is that not a recipe for losing your mind?

Well, this is an average day for Donald Trump: a diet of cable news hacks and clickbait blogs and social media posts instead of direct briefings from intelligence agencies and experts. Disdaining books about history or leadership, he employs a special assistant whose job it is every day to bring him *printed-out positive articles about himself to keep his spirits up*. Friends and sycophants go on television and say things they hope he'll see, performing for an audience of one.*

When President Kennedy's doctor heard that he was taking extremely powerful and dangerous drugs to treat his various ailments, he was aghast. "No president with his finger on the red button has any business taking stuff like that," the doctor said.

Trump's advisers feel the same way about their boss's media diet. "What do you think your brain would be like if you did that?" his chief strategist once asked a reporter about Trump's "executive time," which everyone in the White House knows is hours and hours of hate-watching cable news shows. They have begged him to spend time with his wife or his children, but Trump prefers to spend the mornings (and the evenings) with what he has often claimed is the greatest invention in human history: the TiVo.

But putting aside what are clearly addictions every leader— along with ordinary people just trying to figure out how to

---

* "I was going to tell him I'm going on Laura Ingraham," the musician Kid Rock explained to a reporter as he called Trump on the phone. "He loves to watch when I do Fox hits."

make sense of the world—faces some version of the same problem: What information are we going to let in? What are we going to keep out? How do we stay informed about what's happening without overwhelming ourselves with distractions?

Just as what we put in our bodies matters, what we put—or fail to put—in our minds matters too.

Presidents of the United States face this problem most acutely. Each, depending on their personality, has struggled under the weight of all they need to know . . . and all they can know. One of Jimmy Carter's aides believed that Carter's "biggest problem as president was his willingness to read anything," lamenting an instance where Carter had sat and read a 350-page memo on a minor tax issue. He would return briefings with the typos corrected. This might seem admirable, but it was a bad use of such a busy person's time. "We never should have subjected him to that," the aide recounted, "but he never should have read it."

You can consume too much of a good thing—whether it's food or facts.

This mirrors the problem we all face. We are drowning in information—much of which is fascinating—that was once elusive. It's upon us to figure out how to filter and digest it and how to *act* on what is true and *consequential*. When to focus and how to tune out.

Effective leaders know how to do this. For the president of the United States, information is condensed into what is known as the Presidential Daily Briefing, typically three pages of top-secret information about international developments and concerns, delivered, as the name implies, daily, with in-person explanations and summaries. The best presidents listen intently, ask questions, and then apply what they've learned to their day-to-day decisions.

Trump was never interested in access to the best intelligence on earth. "I don't have to be told the same thing in the same words every single day for the next eight years," he had said during his first campaign. This news junkie was in no rush to get the lay of the land after his victory in 2016 either. Other presidents-elect begin their daily briefings months before their inauguration, understanding that the hard jobs have steep learning curves. In the ten-week transition period, President-Elect Trump received just fourteen briefings.

It seemed that his lifelong frustration with school, and his bully's worldview in which calling someone "professor" is an epithet, came flooding back in resentment at demands that he pay attention. One of his first requests was that the briefing be shortened and that the oral briefing come in the form of a "narrative," to be more like the news he watched on TV. Even with these tweaks, Trump was hardly a willing student.

"He touched it," Trump's first CIA briefer said when asked if Trump had read his briefing. "He doesn't really read anything."

Instead, Trump tended to skim the document—itself a summary of insights that were often written with the sweat (or blood) of intelligence operators and informants, secured through great expenditure—his attention only occasionally piqued by graphics and pictures. He liked bullet points. He talked more than he listened, so that, according to one observer, "there might be eight or nine minutes of real intelligence in an hour's discussion." And even this expert opinion has to battle it out with whoever Trump talked to last—the president, as one adviser put it, will ask forty-nine people for their opinion and stop at the fiftieth . . . if he likes the answer.

A fool hears only what they want to hear.

This is perhaps why when Trump complained to the media that he hadn't been warned about the rising threat of the coronavirus, he was partly correct. It had in fact been mentioned *dozens* of times in the winter of 2020. Briefers had given him the facts. They had told him what the scientists thought. They led the horse to water, but the horse didn't like to drink.

All of us are manipulated by algorithms. All of us scroll past what we don't like and gravitate toward the simple over the complex. It's a human tendency to prefer entertainment over information. The filter bubble finds its way to surround us all.

We all fool ourselves. We all consume too much garbage.

It's just that for some of us, the consequences are more pronounced.

Elon Musk went from reading rocket manuals to obsessively refreshing his Twitter feed, from following the science to listening to podcasts and viral videos. As the quality of his information diet degraded, so too did his mental state—a brilliant, original thinker was suddenly impressed by "galaxy brain" nonsense. He went from first principles to settling issues with Twitter polls.

He has been critical of other people's media diets, saying that people "who get their news from legacy TV live in a fake alternate reality." Both he and Trump share similar versions of the same affliction, hooked on mediums almost antithetical to the transmission of wisdom. Musk could pay for a daily briefing rivaling even the most powerful heads of state, yet he prefers to mainline it from his feed of trolls and pundits.

Even an ordinary person today has access to the kind of information that emperors could have only dreamed of. This is real power, but as always, power corrupts and disorients and distracts. We have *more* information than emperors could have dreamed of. We are also subjected to more *mis*information than they could have conceived of in their worst nightmare.

Audio. Video. Text. It comes at us at incomprehensible speeds.

It takes discipline and wisdom to manage your information diet properly, to be a discerning and selective conduit for everything that's coming at you.

"The art of not reading is a very important one," Schopenhauer said of avoiding popular rubbish. It's not how much you know, but that you know the right things. It's not that you read, it's what and how you read. "Do not be eager to know everything," Democritus reminded himself in the fifth century BC, "lest you become ignorant of everything."

Go straight to the source when you can. *Check* sources always.

Choose quality over quantity.

Find experts you can trust. Verify them first.

Favor information that has staying power over what is "developing" or "just in." Try to get the big picture. Try to make connections between what's happening now and what has happened before.

Seek out things that challenge you. Hear what the other side has to say.

Don't be distracted by trifles . . . and don't ignore essential details.

Beware of information overload. Beware the tendency to doomscroll.

And never, ever mistake gathering information and opinions about an issue with *doing* something about a problem.

Think for Yourself

~

Richard Feynman was an iconoclast. A freethinker. A disruptor in his field. A *character*.

His memoirs were titled *Surely You're Joking, Mr. Feynman!*— a nod to the kind of reaction that mavericks provoke. *Are you serious? That's crazy!*

This title wasn't a reference to Feynman's groundbreaking work in quantum electrodynamics or his contributions to the atomic bomb, however. It wasn't even an expression of shock at his untraditional hobbies, including his love of drawing graceful human forms, which he often practiced at a local strip club.

No. It was Feynman's request for both lemon *and* cream in his tea that made his colleague's wife gasp in disbelief.

The horror!

It doesn't take much to shock people, because people have very narrow views of what is and isn't normal. Generally, they just do what other people are doing and want what other people want and are appalled when people want something different.

This was the insight of the philosopher René Girard, who coined the theory of mimetic desire. He believed that since we don't know what we want, we end up being drawn—subconsciously or overtly—to what others want. We don't think for ourselves, we follow tradition or the crowd. We imitate instead of innovate.

To achieve wisdom, to do anything important, one must swim upstream against this tendency. That's what first-principles thinking is at the most basic level. Instead of engaging with an issue from a headline or a tweet—something everyone else is engaging with—the wise person goes to the beginning. The wise person approaches the problem with a fresh set of eyes and an open mind.

Standard operating practices are rarely questioned by individuals or institutions. "Don't ever use the word *budget* with me," Musk has been known to tell employees, "because it means you've turned off your brain." "Their heads are so flattened between boards of Army discipline," Florence Nightingale once marveled as she battled layers of bureaucracy, "that they remain children all their lives." The same is true even for the words of the ancients. Just because someone said it a long time ago doesn't mean it's true now. It might not have even been true then!

When a grad student tried to argue with Feynman that some theory he disputed had been established for some time, he replied, "OK. So not only is it bullshit, it is *old* bullshit." "I'm just doing my job" and "This is how it was explained to me" have rationalized incredible stupidity for generations. We accept too much because it was passed down to us, because we have never bothered to test it or subject it to any scrutiny, to ask, "What if there is a better way?"

We need to question the status quo. We must think for ourselves . . . and yet there is a reason that we have precedents. If we rethought every single issue, every single time, we would never get anywhere. If we were contrarian on every issue, we'd often be wrong—because sometimes things are the way they should be.

In this way, having a contrarian opinion that turns out to be right—turning out to be smarter than everyone else—can be a real brain-destroying experience. Nothing is safe.

There is a story about Musk flipping down the visor on a prototype of the Model S. "What the fuck is this?" he said as he noticed, apparently for the first time, the mandated yellow-and-white warning label reminding parents to disable the airbag if a child is placed in the front seat. The employee tried to explain the government's reason for requiring these labels, but Musk decided it was unnecessary. "People aren't stupid," he said. "These stickers are stupid."

But obviously the stickers were there *because people are stupid.** Because it's usually better to be safe than sorry when it comes to children and car crashes. Instead of deferring to some harmless conventional wisdom here, Musk and his team spent countless hours trying for a technological solution that would turn the airbag off automatically as well as arguing with the National Highway Traffic Safety Administration. It would deal with at least two recalls over the issue as well.

"Factory settings are always idiotic," he once told employees as he sped up a machine on the production line, which is, of course, an idiotic thing to say. Sometimes they should be disregarded. *Sometimes* they'll save someone's life.

Blindly trusting convention is stupid . . . and so is blindly trusting your gut, assuming you simply know better than convention because you have proven it wrong before.

Precedent is often the result of hard-won wisdom. You can't just toss it out. A colleague of Churchill's once observed that Churchill "venerated tradition but ridiculed convention." This is perhaps the best way to split the difference: We both question and respect; indeed, we question tradition because we respect it.

Memetic desire is a shortcut. It's a curtain that cordons off scary or uncomfortable or complicated things. We are saving ourselves the trouble of having to ask those fundamental ques-

---

*It's also a strange take given that Musk is notorious for calling people idiots.

tions about ourselves and life: *What do I think? What do I want? What is actually true here?*

When everyone is thinking the same thing, no one is really thinking at all.

There's a famous psychology experiment that captured how people will change their mind about which of two lines is longer based on how other participants are answering—even though it directly contradicts their own observation.

We've all done it. Almost never does it work out well.

The bubble eventually pops. The fever passes. The truth comes out. We look back and think, we were so stupid, and worse, *we knew better.*

It's OK to stand alone. It's OK to come to your own conclusions. In fact, it's more than OK.

It's the job.

"If I wanted to be part of the mob," an early Stoic once said, "I would not have become a philosopher." *Thou shalt not follow a crowd to do evil.*

You are unlike anyone who has ever lived . . . why would you think and act like everyone else?

In these times of "the herd's rampancy," as Stefan Zweig would say of the rise of fascism in Europe as well as the religious fervor of Montaigne's time, courage and resolve and sincerity are required. We must resist the impulse to assume and defer. We must not join in with the mob. We must not default to the laziest, easiest, most comfortable of opinions.

We must think for ourselves.

We must go to first principles.

We must respect precedent, but question it. Challenge it without tossing out what matters.

Don't be lazy.

Do the work.

You have a brain.

Use it.

Don't Break Your Brain

Like Montaigne, John Stuart Mill had an unusual education. He was taught Greek at age three. As a toddler, he was reading Xenophon in the original, and shortly thereafter was given Herodotus, which he was expected not just to read, but to understand. By seven he was assigned the dialogues of Plato, which he was to figure out himself.

That was the rule: His father wouldn't explain anything until his son had exhausted every avenue on his own.

By eight, Mill was on to Latin and the great English writers. Cicero, Tacitus, Livy, Juvenal, Quintilian, Thucydides, Demosthenes, Aristotle, Shakespeare, Gibbon, Smith, Hume; logic, philosophy, literature, politics, history. Hour by hour, day by day, he was steeped in great thinkers, at first struggling but eventually mastering them, to the shock of everyone who encountered this prodigy.

"My father," Mill recounted, "demanded of me not only the utmost that I could do, but much that I could not possibility have done." For not only did he have to learn all this, it was also his responsibility to teach what he had learned to his eight younger brothers and sisters.

There's no question that these methods created a great mind, all before puberty. By seventeen, Mill was working as an administrator in the colonial office, dazzling the great minds of his time in debate societies, an incredible career laid out in front of him. He had big ideas. He was the product of relentless ambition, a young man poised to change the world, shaped by an education few receive.

All was well on the surface, but beneath lay dangerous, destructive currents. Anyone subjected to this much pressure was bound to crack.

A seemingly innocent question popped into his head: What if all his intellectual ideas succeeded? What if he achieved the enlightenment he had worked so hard to attain? "Would this be a great joy and happiness to you?" Mill asked himself.

And the devastating answer hit him like a train: "No!"

He would later write that the whole foundation of his life collapsed right then. It wasn't some passing depression but a full-blown intellectual and emotional crisis. The books that had been, in many ways, his friends now failed to capture his attention. He lost all motivation. Everything felt purposeless. There was no one he could talk to, no way he could explain what he felt. He was hopeless. He very nearly killed himself.

In time, such an experience would come to be called a nervous breakdown. Today, we'd call it burnout. It was depression brought about through strain and overwork and the crushing weight of expectations he never chose for himself.

One does not have to be a trained psychologist to properly point a finger at Mill's father, who had treated his boy more like a machine than a son (indeed, Mill would write that his father was the last person to whom he could possibly reveal the mental anguish he was under).

Wound tighter and tighter, his mind eventually broke. Sadly, this is not a rare experience. "Much learning doth make thee mad," Festus tells Paul in the Bible. Nietzsche went insane. Agassiz became a delusional racist. Hunter S. Thompson succumbed to the effects of the Dexedrine he took for energy and focus. It ran his mind hot and fast until his mind wore out, turning the last thirty years of his life into a creative desert.

"From the sublime to the ridiculous," Voltaire observed, "is only one small step."*

It is an especially short trip when so much of one's brilliance is based on *questioning*. You can end up kicking out all the legs of the stool, leaving nothing left to support you. If you question everything, what's left standing? You get so good at arguing that now you're arguing with yourself.

---

*It is said that Napoleon repeated this observation after his disastrous defeat in Russia.

Compulsive, obsessive focus was what drove you to brilliance, but this is a dangerous thing to play with. How do you know the difference between your secret weapon and unhealthy overthinking? When you push yourself so hard because discipline has been your strength, but you go without sleep and without balance, it becomes impossible to know the difference between a transgressive idea and an insane one.

People used to say of Musk, "He's so brilliant." Now they say, *"What happened?"*

There are many plausible explanations for Elon Musk's behavior, but the combination of drugs, fame, and overwork is the most plausible . . . and preventable. It's not normal or healthy to get attention from hundreds of millions of people throughout the day—and although attention can produce a kind of high, his admitted use of ketamine (a drug that can impair cognition, focus, and decision-making) and grueling hours is even more alarming. "And one lesson I've learned is, don't tweet on Ambien," Musk once said. "You may regret it." This is not a lesson one should have to learn the hard way when one runs multiple public companies of such importance.

Too much information. Too much *bad* information. Too much stress. Too much stimulation. Not enough time, not enough nourishment, not enough recovery, not enough care.

Not enough stillness. Not enough friendship. Not enough love.

You can't just sit around and think all the time. You can't live without sleep or hobbies or joy.

Only a fool abuses the only mind they'll ever get.

This is the main task: to protect this gift we've been given, to buck the trend and not go crazy as we become more successful.

But there is some good news. With care and nourishment and self-compassion, the mind can be put back together. It can be made stronger in the broken places, even.

Mill's breakdown at twenty may in fact have saved him. It was a wake-up call. It was a crossroads moment.

He realized that his father's methods were not sustainable. Mill turned to poetry and art. He fell in love with music.

Quitting the debating society where he had spent so many hours fighting over arcane topics, Mill began to approach philosophy differently. No longer was it an academic contest, but a real thing in the real world. He went to France to meet Lafayette. He became engaged with the political issues of his time. His wife opened up his world too—not just to women's rights but to a lightness and happiness and connectedness that he had not known in childhood.

His great contributions came after the breakdown. They came after he put himself back together. They came because he was brave enough to be vulnerable, brave enough to reimagine his life and his priorities.

Wisdom emerges when we slow down. When we have quiet. When we take care of ourselves.

Wisdom is realizing that even if what you do is important . . . it's not that important.

Wisdom is realizing you are not a prison experiment. You are not a machine. You are an ecosystem.

None of it works if some of it doesn't work.

Be careful. Take care.

Change Your Mind

~

Richard Wright introduced Ralph Ellison to communism. It makes sense that these two writers were both attracted to the ideas of the radical left. How could they not be? The world seemed like it was falling apart. The pointlessness and slaughter of the First World War had been followed by a great global depression.

Imperialism had been exposed as bankrupt. Capitalism seemed like it was failing—the lines at the soup kitchens in the thirties made that very clear. And certainly humanity had failed those two men specifically, subjecting them to terrible discrimination and Jim Crow racial violence.

Besides, the Communist Party had made very specific plans to recruit and cultivate Black artists and workers in Harlem, making it the epicenter of their operations in the United States.

So of course, they both joined the movement in the 1930s—it was perhaps the *only* one in the country, perhaps in the world at that time, that purported to recognize an equality between the races. Joining was not a big deal; you just signed up and suddenly were part of a scene where people treated you with respect, offered you opportunities, and claimed to care about making the world better. Ellison and Wright flourished in Communist circles, developing as writers for Communist publications like the *Daily Worker* and the literary magazine *New Challenge*. Ellison often slept at the offices. Both men were able to survive as artists because of the money they earned and the support of party donors.

Here, they had a place of their own. There was energy! Light! Every question had an answer. Everything *made sense*.

But like all radical political movements, all was not what it seemed. There was something stifling about communism. In one of his books, Wright brought up listening to party officials and being struck by their "fanatical intolerance . . . minds sealed against new ideas, new facts, new feelings, new attitudes, new hints at ways to live." He and Ellison believed deeply in the class struggle, but they didn't like being told what to think. They found plenty of disagreement with the party on issues of race and the role of literature.

As novelists, they understood that people and life are complicated—that human beings contain multitudes that can never be captured in simple theories. They sensed, for all the talk about the arts, a profound anti-intellectualism in the movement (in fact, Wright recalled a heavy-handed reminder from one party leader about how many "intellectuals" had had to be executed in Russia). They had come to the ideology as seekers of ideas. Instead, it was starting to feel like an intellectual dead end. "They denounced books they had never read, people they had never known, ideas they could never understand, and doctrines whose names they could not pronounce," Wright complained. "Communism, instead of making them leap forward with fire in their hearts to become masters of ideas and life, had frozen them at an even lower level of ignorance than had been theirs before they met Communism."

And then there were the Soviet show trials, the rise of the secret police, Stalin's pact with Germany, and the outbreak of World War II, all of which chipped away at the revolutionary façade.

For a time, the two men were able to rationalize all these contradictions, as most of us are. It's very difficult, it's been said, to reason your way out of a position you didn't reason yourself into. Ellison and Wright were attracted to communism in part because of its emotional appeal, its promise to solve the unsolvable problems of the human condition. They bought a dream, not a reality.

Nor were they the only ones—a generation of earnest young people was swept up in this appeal in the years between the Russian Revolution and the rise of the totalitarian Soviet state. The alternatives weren't much more appealing! What case were democracy and capitalism making for themselves in 1935, when Americans were living in Hoovervilles and waiting in breadlines? At least the party claimed to care about people.

Hope deceives. Wishes distort.

But with time, both Wright and Ellison would break with the party, Wright in 1942, Ellison a bit earlier. "So you and Wright are together?" one professor asked Ellison about their leaving the party. "No, Wright is by himself and I am by myself. We are individuals."

Changing their minds and their beliefs was not easy. Wright ended up exiled in Europe, telling Ellison that it was because "after I broke with the Communist party I had nowhere else to go." Both dealt with guilt and shame about how long they were under the sway (and control) of the party. Both would take heat from the authorities for their past association with the party. All the same, this was a critical step in their evolution—as artists and as activists. "The break with the [Communist Party]," Ellison would tell Wright, "has allowed me to come alive."

The philosopher Diogenes the Cynic was once confronted about something he used to believe. "And there was once a day when I would piss in my bed," he said as a way of reply, "but no longer." John Maynard Keynes had a good reply to the same proposition: "When the facts change, I change my mind. What do you do, sir?" That's what the lyrics to "Amazing Grace" are about, after all, written as they were by an ex-slaver who had seen the evil of his ways: "I once was lost, but now am found / Was blind, but now I see."

Sure, it would have been better to have been found earlier, to change earlier.

Most people stay blind. Let's give some credit to those who don't.

Changing is hard because it means that you probably should have changed earlier. It means you did and said things that, as it turns out, were based on incorrect beliefs. Awful things, in some cases. Deeply embarrassing in others.

Some people can't bear losing face. So they double down.

Not only do we have trouble changing our minds, but sometimes we are so fragile that we resent people who do. We accuse politicians of being "flip-floppers." We call it a betrayal. Or we mock someone for what they used to believe—how could they have ever been so stupid as to think *that*?

The real failure, however, is to have never changed. Imagine still believing all the things you believed as a kid! Imagine still believing in and acting the same way you did before *something* happened. When someone calls you stubborn, it's not a compliment!

Only a fool stays the same.

"To doubt one's own first principles is the mark of a civilized man," Admiral Hyman Rickover told future naval officers. "A foolish consistency," Emerson said, expressing the idea in the negative some one hundred years earlier, "is the hobgoblin of little minds." "If I am true to myself from moment to moment," Gandhi said, just after using that word *hobgoblin* to dismiss the virtue of consistency, "I do not mind all the inconsistencies that may be flung in my face."

Wisdom is the ability to go through life *ready* to change your mind. This doesn't mean we abandon our values because they're inconvenient, but our thinking is *supposed* to evolve. We are supposed to grow. New things are going to come to light. Feedback follows belief and action, which should create new beliefs and actions.

Certainly, this explains much of the shift in Ellison. He was a young musician from Oklahoma when he first came to communism. In the intervening years, he read, met many people, wrote and experienced much. The world convulsed itself through a world war. Stalin revealed what no amount of propaganda or wishful thinking could cover up. The civil rights movement began in fits and starts. How much did he see of human nature in that time? How much more did he know?

"I said a lot of stupid things when I worked with the Conservative Party," Winston Churchill said when he changed political parties at age twenty-nine, "and I left it because I did not want to go on saying stupid things." It would be better if we'd never been wrong in the first place, sure, but the second-best thing is to change our minds now.

It's an interesting question to ask people you want to learn from: What was the last thing you changed your mind about? What's something you think very differently about now than you used to? What have you been proven wrong about?

Honest answers are indications of mental strength and moral character.

No one thinks Lyndon Johnson was weak for changing his mind on segregation. On the contrary, we think *about damn time*.

We consider new facts. We listen to advice. We ask questions. When we find something that doesn't add up, we don't ignore it—we keep exploring until we accept either that it was wrong or that we were.

This is how science works, by the way. People think breakthroughs happen in moments of grand discovery or divine inspiration. Epiphanies do happen, but they are the exception and not the rule. No, science is a gradual process, and change in science is usually the result of an old paradigm slowly breaking down, the conventional wisdom becoming less and less sufficient to explain what's happening, until eventually a new paradigm emerges and is then adopted.

The world is complicated. Things are always changing. We are constantly learning, being exposed to things we didn't know or consider.

Our minds must be flexible and open enough to accommodate this.

Grow Up

~

It must have been a horrendous childhood.

Even if his family was wealthy and privileged, the evil of apartheid hung over South Africa. A society built around oppression oppresses *everyone*, finds a way to infect *everything* with oppression, and so Elon Musk was relentlessly and violently bullied for being different and weird.

One of those bullies put him in the hospital, something his father promptly blamed on his son.

Home is supposed to be a place of safety for a child. For Musk, it was the opposite. "He was such a terrible human being," Musk has said about his father, Errol Musk. He has been known to cry when attempting to speak of his childhood. "You have no idea about how bad," he said. "Almost every crime you can possibly think of, he has done. Almost every evil thing you could possibly think of, he has done."

No kid should have to say that. No one could emerge from that "normal."

"[Our father] definitely has serious chemical stuff," Elon's brother said. "Which I am sure Elon and I have inherited." Their father would regularly refer to them as idiots and morons. He regularly tells reporters deranged and racist things. "He changes reality around him," Kimbal said of their father. "He will literally make things up, but he actually believes his own false reality."

Sound a little familiar?

"Inside the man," Elon's first ex-wife once said of her ex-husband, "he's still there as a child, a child standing in front of his dad."

In a way, we're all that child standing in front of our parents. Especially if that childhood was rough—emotionally, physically, or otherwise. Psychologists call the mechanisms that "wounded children" create to protect their scared, neglected, or overwhelmed selves the "adapted child." We are supposed to become "functional adults," but some adapted children, defined by what they didn't get, can't.

When I was a child, I spake as a child, I understood as a child, I thought as a child. And so they remain.

The problem is that we're not children anymore. We can't afford to be. If we do, we risk making child-*ish* decisions. Having very child-*ish* reactions. Reverting to child-*like* opinions.

You need to grow up. Or it'll cost you.

Alexander the Great went to the ends of the earth to surpass his father and impress his mother. Leonardo da Vinci, never fully accepted by his father, wasted years of his life trying to find the perfect patron who would support and celebrate him. Richard Nixon, the most powerful man in the world, unable to see himself as anything other than the underdog, became terrified of being perceived as weak or vulnerable. "Can you imagine what this man would have been like if somebody had loved him?" Henry Kissinger once said about Nixon.

Imagine letting an unloved nine-year-old make decisions of global importance. Imagine handing the future of your personal life over to an insecure teenager. Imagine expecting a bewildered four-year-old to understand the complexity of human motivations or navigate the trade-offs between short- and long-term interests.

Yet this is precisely what many successful and otherwise brilliant people do!

"No one is willing to believe that adults too," Goethe wrote in one of his novels, "like children, wander about this earth in a daze, and like children do not know where they come from or where they are going, act as rarely as they do according to genuine motives, and are as thoroughly governed as they are by biscuits and cake and the rod."

But this is what enlightenment must be, as one philosopher said: the exit from our "self-incurred immaturity."

You can't be wise if you're still operating on the assumptions you made about the world as a girl. You can't be rational if you're still ruled by the same emotions you felt as a boy. You will not make good decisions if you are still motivated by the same things you were motivated by as a kid. You are not enlightened if you have not put away your childish ways.

Fools try to maintain their childlike view of the world. Our ego, our conceit, our insecurities are compensating for something. Our need for validation, our hunger for control, our fear of failure, our aversion to discomfort and inability to deal with hard truths—all these impulses mask deeper vulnerabilities.

We might be brilliant. We might be experts in a topic. But unless we are vigilant, we can still be subconsciously directed by assumptions we made about the world as children.

The decisions Musk makes affect not just the livelihoods of tens of thousands of people but the *lives* of millions who drive his cars and use his autopilot, whose internet and satellites depend on his rockets, whose culture is shaped by the social network he controls, who are ruled by the government he has taken a wrecking ball to. He, like every leader, is obligated to not be ruled by the whims of his impulses or the shadows of his demons. It's unacceptable that such a powerful man would be ruled by such a stunted child.

Musk didn't get the love he needed as a kid, so he gets it from the rabid mob. Deprived of stability, he seeks chaos and attention. Should it surprise us, then, that he has had fourteen children of his own? Or that he reportedly offers strangers his sperm for IVF pregnancies? Or that he has referred to one of his younger children as his "emotional support human"? Musk, perhaps channeling his own father, shows no empathy for his transgender child, claiming that "the woke mind virus killed my son." Musk, like so many broken people, seems to see not dealing with his trauma as a badge of honor. Asked by his biographer how he deals with his mental health issues, Musk sighed and said, "Just take the pain and make sure you really care about what you're doing."

Only a fool leaves their wounds untreated. In fact, it makes them a traumatizer, inflicting a self-perpetuating cycle on future generations. They make it impossible to grow and change and move forward.

It's our responsibility to treat and deal with our demons, not embrace and excuse them.

We can't be too great for introspection. Too egotistical to get vulnerable. We can't be too old to grow up.

Don't Be a Snowflake

~

Early American slave owners knew what they were doing was wrong.

They admitted it in private. They felt the guilt and shame. Jefferson's writings clearly reveal this (as do his hopes for a future where slavery was gone). There were, at least for a while, debates and discussion about the legitimacy of the institution along with earnest attempts to reform it. These concerns were what Thomas Clarkson was able to mobilize into the abolitionist movement, which eliminated slavery in the British Empire.

But in America, at the turn of the nineteenth century, wave after wave of preposterous pseudoscience was published to help slave owners rationalize what was obviously wrong but incredibly profitable. Speech criticizing slavery was policed. Books were banned; possession of some, like *Uncle Tom's Cabin*, were *criminalized*. Abolitionists were lynched and driven from the South. Slave owners' sublimated guilt was so fragile that they needed soft and hard power—indeed, the entire force of culture and government—to maintain the specious lie that slavery was not only not bad, but that it was a *positive good*.

It wasn't enough to hide it away and reap the profits, it needed to be justified.

The Civil War was driven by greed and cruelty, but another way to see it is that it was started rashly and stupidly by men and women who lived in a delusional, paranoid bubble in which *they* were the victims, that *they* were the ones being persecuted (by the North) instead of being the villains who enslaved and raped and killed. Slave owners were monsters, but they were also incredibly sensitive and fragile, unable to face what they'd done and terrified of living in a world where they couldn't keep doing it.

As Tocqueville noted in 1835, men and women of the South had been raised for generations as "domestic dictators," their every wish a command and every belief confirmed with a "Yes, master." The education system—and the culture—had given the slave owner the character of a "supercilious and a hasty man; irascible, violent, and ardent in his desires, impatient of obstacles, but easily discouraged if he cannot succeed upon his first attempt."

In short, slave owners were little snowflakes to whom even the notion of equality seemed like oppression, and for whom disagreement was literally a dueling offense.*

---

*In 1856, Senator Preston Brooks beat fellow senator Charles Sumner nearly to *death* on the floor of the Senate for criticizing his first cousin once

Sound familiar? It should, because this type has always been with us. And even the smartest people can develop reinforcing, preposterous systems for protecting their egos, their assumptions, their intellectual comfort.

Fundamentalists have been banning and burning books and people they didn't like for centuries, as Montaigne could tell you. People have always combatted what they didn't want to hear. People have always been afraid of ideas. What are honor cultures but ritualized snowflakery? Oh no, someone insulted you? Guess you'll need to fight to the death about it!

How did Elon Musk respond to Mark Zuckerberg's criticism and competition in 2023? By challenging him to a cage match. The guy who once said that "a well-thought-out critique of whatever you're doing is as valuable as gold" has taken to banning media outlets and siccing mobs on reporters he doesn't like. Musk is apparently all about free speech, but one word he'll censor is "cisgender"—because it singles him out.

Look, people are allowed to be stupid. You're just not allowed to insist that other people indulge in your nonsense because the truth makes you feel fragile.

It's a cliché to complain about how sensitive and weak young people are these days. Maybe they are. But if they are, whose fault is it? They learned it from somewhere . . .

---

removed in a speech about slavery. That's how dangerous intellectual babies with a guilty conscience are.

They say that the truth will set you free, but that's not really true. Truth is heavy. It's uncomfortable. It challenges you, or worse, it *obligates* you. Once you know how the other half lives, your sense of right and wrong means you may have to do something about it. Once you hear about something you've been screwing up, you have to fix it.

We are offered, Emerson once said, a choice between truth and repose. "Take which you please," he said, "but you can never have both." Once you have been disabused of your notions about something, or the paucity of your knowledge about something, you're not free at all. Now you have to go learn. Now you have to change your mind. Now you have to admit you're wrong. Now you have to go do some real work.

This is painful. This is scary. It is no fun.

But courage and wisdom are related—the former allows for the latter. If you can't bear to engage with new information, you can't learn. Cowards are fools, and fools are usually cowardly.

As you become successful, it becomes easier and easier to become cocooned in your own comfortable certainty. This is also one of the downsides of finding your people—you may well surround yourself with people who think like you do, who act like you do. All the while, your intellectual immune system is growing weaker and weaker because it's no longer being exposed to new and interesting ideas.

Exposure to conflicting and challenging ideas makes us

stronger. Why do people fall for scams and silly ideas? Because they don't know what a good argument looks like. They don't know their own arguments well! Why do smart people overreach? Because they've stopped subjecting their work to the rigor of challenges and dissent—they've become convinced of their own infallibility, their own genius.

We must seek out disagreement. We must seek out discomfort. We can't rig the game in our favor.

History should make you feel angry. Art should break you open, touch you in places that are raw and sensitive. Trigger warnings? The point of art is to trigger. *You've been warned.*

There is a world of different opinions, views, experiences. People have different beliefs and philosophies. Pretending otherwise doesn't help you, and it won't help you change other minds (if, in fact, they're wrong).

Oh, this teacher, this topic makes you feel stupid? Good. It's hard to improve unless you feel that way. And if what you believe makes you feel comfortable and superior . . . question it.

You're not special.

You are also not a delicate little flower that needs to be protected.

Political correctness. Censorship. Shouting people down. This doesn't make anyone smarter or better or safer. In fact, it makes us weaker, more susceptible to groupthink, more delusional, more likely to overreach or misread.

The leaders of the South were convinced they would win the Civil War. They were convinced that England—which was adamantly opposed to slavery—would recognize this new nation and support its cause. This insanity was belied by facts clear to nearly everyone else, as obvious as the monstrous evil of their enterprise.

"If slaves will make good soldiers," one general wrote to the Confederate secretary of war, "our whole theory of slavery is wrong but they won't make soldiers." So it was the North who armed formerly enslaved men—some one hundred thousand ultimately served in the Union ranks—driving the final nail in the Southern coffin.

Snowflakes make bad decisions because every decision is decided by the least consequential variable: *Does this align with what I want to be true?*

No wisdom is possible for the fragile. No growth.

No truth.

Seek Criticism

~

Sometime around the year AD 138, a young Marcus Aurelius received two letters on the same day from his rhetoric teacher and adviser, Fronto. The first was a line-by-line criticism of a recent essay that Marcus had written. The second praised his efforts elsewhere.

"I swear to you," he told his beloved mentor in reply, "that the first letter gave me the greater pleasure and that as I read it I exclaimed several times, 'How lucky I am!'"

This may seem strange, but we are lucky to be criticized. Not least because criticism means you are alive and doing something people notice, but also because criticism makes us better.

As the heir apparent to the Roman Empire, Marcus Aurelius knew that honest feedback was a rare commodity, one that would only get rarer the more powerful he became. Which is why he so appreciated Fronto's "fault-findings" and "guiding reins." He understood that they came from a place of love, as piercing observations often do.

"The hostile critics are doing me a service," Gandhi once told a friend. "They teach me to examine myself. They afford me an opportunity to see if I am free from the reaction of anger. And when I go to the root of their anger I find nothing but love."

But it takes work to see it this way . . . especially when you have a lot of critics. Especially when the criticism doesn't seem loving on the surface.

Martin Luther King Jr. was attacked physically and verbally by people who disliked him. He was libeled in the press and from governors' mansions. As late as 1966, just one-third of Americans thought favorably of him, and nearly half viewed him very *unfavorably*. He was not universally beloved by his own supporters or among Black Americans either. Some accused him of being too radical, others for not being radical enough.

It's hard to be a public figure. You need tough skin. At the same time, if your skin is too thick, you'll never be able to receive the information you need to improve and connect.

This is one of the most impressive parts of King's rise, his ability to listen and learn, even from those he disagreed with— to keep his heart and mind open despite all those who were trying to get inside it, his ability to separate attacks from feedback, to correct course and steadily convert people to his cause.

He was able to hear the students in the Student Nonviolent Coordinating Committee who believed that King was sheltered, that he wasn't fully out on the front lines, willing to get arrested with them. And then, when the Black Power movement began to emerge and King disagreed with many of their tactics (and they his), King had to figure out how to navigate divergent opinions inside the movement and prevent it from splintering. "If Stokely [Carmichael] is saying the same things I am saying," King would say as the Black Power movement criticized him, "he becomes like my assistant."

In fact, King expected his assistants to be critical too, and to speak up when they disagreed. This was especially important when so many of the activists believed in their cause with near-religious fervor.

At one meeting, Andrew Young, a staffer whom King often leaned on to be the voice of reason in group discussions, was quieter than normal. King immediately noticed. "Look," he said as he took the young man aside, "you know that most of us are certifiably insane." He couldn't afford *yes-men*, King explained, the stakes were too high. He wanted people to speak up, to point out the problems with various ideas and to prevent their plans from going too far. "I don't mind risking my life," King told Young, "but I don't want to throw it away over some foolishness."

How to stay rooted in reality is a key challenge of activism. But it's also essential in the pursuit of wisdom. Can you listen? Can you learn? Imagine Martin Luther King being strong enough to endure beatings but not strong enough to endure dissent! Too sensitive to be corrected, wilting under the slightest questioning, too much of a snowflake to have his assumptions challenged.

"Criticism may not be agreeable," Churchill once said, "but it is necessary; it fulfills the same function as pain in the human body, it calls attention to the development of an unhealthy state of things."

The first step in being able to endure is to put up with the pain. The second step is moving beyond simply *weathering it*, instead actively seeking it out, coming to enjoy and appreciate it.

We have a remarkable ability to convince ourselves we are right. We have blind spots. We have biases. This is why we need help. This is what critics are for!

And Gandhi was right—this service is often done out of love.

If your enemy were in error, would you speak up? No. That's one of the dictums of business and war—never interrupt an opponent in the middle of making a mistake. It's when we don't want someone to fail that we take the risk of saying something.

For Admiral Rickover, yes-men were a scourge. "If a subordinate agrees with his superior," he would say, "[they are] a useless part of the organization." He would speak admiringly about one admiral who called an otherwise stellar officer in for a performance review. The man was failing, he said, and he was disappointed in him. Why? Because, the admiral said, in all the time they'd worked together, the officer had never once disagreed with him.

Fools nod their head to everything. The fools above them often take this nodding for more than what it is.

"Very often an idea of yours is possessed of no innate magnificence," Mark Twain warned Cornelius Vanderbilt, then the richest man in the world, "but is simply shining with the reflected splendor of your seventy millions."

One of the foolish things that success can engender is a sensitivity to disagreement and criticism. Elon Musk's relationship with the press soured as the media began to cover his companies less as scrappy upstarts and more as the industrial behemoths they are. "FUCK YOU!" Musk reportedly screamed at the employee who called him out for his disgusting Paul Pelosi tweet. In another famous exchange, he fired a Twitter engineer when the man tried to argue against rigging the site's algorithm to make Musk's tweets more popular (and to tell his boss that he was, in fact, increasingly unpopular). But what was most remarkable was the question Musk asked to the silent room immediately after. "Why is nobody else speaking?" he said in surprise.

We think that eliminating dissent and attacks will make our lives easier. In fact, it makes things tougher for us in the long run—requiring us to learn very expensive lessons that feedback and disagreement might have saved us from.

Does that mean all criticism and dissent is valuable? Hardly.

Wisdom is the ability to separate good advice from bad, knowing which notes to take and which to ignore, how to separate the raising of a problem from the proposal of a solution—how to take what we can use and discard the rest. Wisdom is, in all things, a matter of *discernment*.

Without criticism, without competition, without dissent, the probability that we will get better is zero.

Don't be a snowflake. Seek out criticism. Sift through it. Apply what you can use and discard the rest.

Make Mistakes

~

L ou Gehrig was not a natural athlete. He made himself one in the gym.

He was not a natural baseball player either. He made himself one . . . one mistake at a time.

In 1921, Gehrig let a ball go through his feet at first base during a tryout with the New York Giants, and it cost him a spot on the team. In 1931, Gehrig passed a runner while rounding the bases and was called out. Worse, it cost him a home run title. In between these career-defining errors, before and after, he made hundreds of mistakes—he's credited with 196 of them in career stats—some more painful than others.

Do you think it was fun for him to get sent down to the minors, as he was in 1923? "It takes the heart of a fellow," he said after he got the news. Except it didn't. He understood that playing time was the best teacher, and that in Hartford, Connecticut, he would actually have room to make *more* mistakes and to get better faster.

"When he came here," his Yankees manager Miller Huggins once said, "he was one of the dumbest players I've ever seen. But he's got one great virtue that will make him: He never makes the same mistake twice. He makes all the mistakes, all right, but not twice."

This is what experience is about: learning in real time with real stakes.

Not that Gehrig was stumbling and fumbling about like a dunce. He was a student of the game and actively sought his coaches' feedback and criticism. "In the beginning," he explained, "I used to make one terrible play a game. Then it was one bad play a week, then finally I'd pull a bad one once a month."

Making a mistake doesn't make you a fool. As the Roman expression, sometimes attributed to Cato, explains, a fool is someone who stubs their toe *on the same rock twice.* It's the ability to get better, to learn painful lessons, that is the hallmark of wisdom. Or at least, the sign of progress along the path to wisdom.

Within each mistake is a reminder. An insight. A truth. The world is telling us, Hey, this is how things work. Hey, there's a reason for that. Hey, you forgot something important.

Yet it is our shame, our ego, our stubbornness that impede this process. We deny the error. We excuse the error. We continue in error.

Everyone makes mistakes. Not everyone learns from them.

Because it's easier not to learn. Because it's less expensive. Because we're smart enough to get away with it. Because we're cowards.

One of Churchill's most withering appraisals of a political rival (one of many) was that while the man occasionally "stumbled over the truth . . . he always picked himself up and hurried on as if nothing had happened."

We've all done it. Yet we reject wisdom when we say, "Nope, I'd like to continue as I was."

And then we pay for it again later, with interest accrued.

No one can make us learn from our mistakes, especially as we make our way upward in life. Imagine you're Marcus Aurelius. You head an enormous army. You're the most powerful person on earth. You're worshipped as a god. People are going to be constantly covering up your errors, trying to tell you why things are not your fault, how great you are.

This is why *Meditations*, his private notebook, was so important. It was his place to reflect on his mistakes and errors. It was where he held himself accountable—or at least tried to. "Remember that to change your mind and accept correction are free acts too," he reminded himself. "The action is yours, based on your own will, your own decision—and your own mind." He wanted people to speak truth to him (as he had to Hadrian as a young boy, thus paving his path to become emperor). He wanted to be regarded as a man and not a living myth. "If any-one can refute me," he would say, "show me I'm making a mistake or looking at things from the wrong perspective—I'll gladly change. It's the truth I'm after, and the truth never harmed anyone. What harms us is to persist in self-deceit and ignorance."

We have all said stupid things. We all have faulty assumptions. We all make blunders.

Will we mend them, or will we make them again and again?

This is the difference between the wise man and the fool.

You don't have to be perfect. Indeed, you are not and will not be. But if you are someone who gets better as you go, who faces errors fearlessly and corrects them, then you will eventually, inevitably, do more than those who are precious and fragile.

Speaking of Churchill, he made *plenty* of mistakes of his own in his nearly seventy-year career. But as he said in a famous letter to his wife, referring to the catastrophic failure of his Dardanelles campaign, from which he was still reeling, "I should have made nothing if I had not made mistakes."

Indeed, years later, as the Allies contemplated invasions of Italy and then of France, the once impulsive Churchill was the voice of reason and caution.

Wisdom is not only making mistakes and learning from them, it's also not being *ashamed* of having made them. In fact, we talk about our mistakes openly so we can codify the lessons not just for ourselves, but for others.

Listen to advice. Debrief. Find the lesson. Get better. Don't get yourself in the same mess again if you can help it.

Err and err, goes the famous poem, but less and less.

Go Deep

~

D a Vinci had a pretty good eye. He could capture what he saw with relative ease.

But for him that wasn't remotely enough.

We can tell this from his notebooks. Across the thirteen thousand pages that survive, we see a man intent on *figuring stuff out*. He wasn't content to simply paint a person. Never content with a first look.

"Blink your eye and look at it again," da Vinci admonished. "That which you see was not there at first, and that which was there is no more."

Fools stay at the surface. The wise want to know what lies beneath.

This was why da Vinci dissected something like thirty corpses. It took a minimum of three dissections just to *begin* to understand an area of the human body, he said. He made casts of organs. He measured proportions. He studied how the heart pumped blood through the body. He compared female and male bodies, noting the subtle differences. He did so many dissections that people accused him of being into the occult, and eventually the pope had to forbid him from doing more. But the work was already done. Da Vinci's observations on anatomy were documented in tens of thousands of words and hundreds of pictures, dwarfing both in volume and in understanding the medical minds not just of his time but for the next several centuries.

He was like this about everything that interested him.

He refused to defer to ancient authors. He needed to see for himself. He couldn't possibly paint water without understanding nearly every facet of how oceans and rivers work. He studied how the moon affected the tides, explored the fossil records of ancient seabeds, and tracked the winding courses of rivers. He could not design a statue of a horse without watching them run, without measuring their proportions and examining other famous statues. He couldn't depict an awful monster on a military shield without first collecting lizards and crickets and bats and snakes and studying them, combining their features to create something new and terrifying.

"You must go about, and constantly, as you go, observe, note and consider the circumstances and behaviors of men in talking, quarreling or laughing or fighting together—the action of the men themselves and the actions of the bystanders, who separate them or who look on," he advised. "And take a note of them with slight strokes, in a little book which you should always carry with you . . . for the forms and positions of objects are so infinite that the memory is incapable of retaining them, wherefore keep these sketches as your guides and masters."

Lurking beneath da Vinci's paintings or inventions or insights was, like the proverbial iceberg, much that was unseen. Although experts would lament da Vinci's awful handwriting, we remain—more than five hundred years later—amazed at the sheer depths of the exploration he did on even the simplest of subjects. And we have only a *fraction* of what he created; a full two-thirds of his notebooks did not even survive.

As an old man Marcus Aurelius would reflect on the most important lesson he had learned from his philosophy teacher Rusticus: "to read attentively—not to be satisfied with 'just getting the gist' of things."* Da Vinci appears not even to have known what that phrase meant.

He did not learn in half measures. His curiosity demanded he go *as far as he possibly could* to understand something. A superficial grasp was not acceptable.

Nor should it be.

If we want to understand something we don't just read *a* book on a topic. We have to read everything we can find on it. We don't just ask *a* question or find *an* expert, but we want to find every expert we can and ask them every question they're

---

* It was Rusticus who loaned Marcus his own copy of Epictetus's lectures, a book that Marcus read dozens and dozens of times, quoting it from memory throughout his life and in his own writing.

willing to answer. We don't just look at what's there; we must explore the remotest corners, every facet, from every angle.

We want to hear from people we agree with. We want to hear from people we disagree with. We have to go out and get real experience.

Was this not what the abolitionist Thomas Clarkson did? He thought that slavery was wrong. He wrote a convincing essay on the topic. But then he realized that if he was going to be the person who did something about this, he would *really* have to understand slavery as a business, as a logistical enterprise, as a series of cultural assumptions that humans had passed down to justify it for thousands of years. His first mentor was the publisher James Phillips. He was not just interested in publishing Clarkson's antislavery essay but immersed him in the abolitionist scene. He introduced Clarkson to Quakers, who had been the earliest activists in the field. He introduced him to Granville Sharp, whose legal work had helped ban slavery in Britain, and to Olaudah Equiano, a brilliant writer and thinker who was also likely the first freed slave Clarkson had ever met. He introduced him to James Ramsay, a doctor and a minister who had treated slaves on slave ships as well as hosting them in his own home and church in St. Kitts, then the site of numerous sugar plantations.

It was after this that Clarkson visited his first slave ship, then in England by way of Massachusetts and Ghana. What he witnessed, the almost uninhabitable quarters, the chains and the grates, filled him "with melancholy and horror," kindling, he said, "a fire of indignation." But this anger was now fueled by real facts, and he wanted more. Clarkson made an effort to speak to every person he could find who had been to Africa. He interviewed them, recording what they told him in his notebooks. He sorted through records at the Custom House, poring over muster rolls and ship logs. He reviewed trial transcripts and insurance records.

Clarkson often fell asleep over paperwork, surrounded by his research. But by the end of this period, which lasted for years, nobody knew more about the slave trade than Clarkson— he was more informed than many of the slave traders and their investors, since so much of the horror of what they did required deliberate ignorance.

You can't solve a problem you don't understand. You can't lead a field you haven't immersed yourself in. You must go down the rabbit hole. You must swarm the topic. You must go deep.

"I have the advantage of having found out how hard it is to really get to know something," Feynman explained. "How careful you have to be about checking your experiments. How easy it is to make mistakes and fool yourself. I know what it means to know something, and therefore I see how they get their information, and I can't believe they claim to know something. They haven't done the work necessary. They haven't done the checks necessary. They haven't done the care necessary."

A fool doesn't care enough to do the work.

The jazz legend Miles Davis didn't just go down to the club and listen to music. "I would go to the library and borrow scores by all those great composers, like Stravinsky, Alban Berg, Prokofiev. I wanted to see what was going on in all of music," he explained. *All of music.* Old stuff. New stuff. The greats. The weirdos. "Knowledge is freedom and ignorance is slavery," he said, "and I just couldn't believe someone could be that close to freedom and not take advantage of it."

It's all there. Will we take it?

The Wright brothers did not discover the secret to flight in some single epiphany; it was the result of countless hours of watching birds in the air. "We couldn't help but thinking they were just a pair of poor nuts," one resident of Kitty Hawk remembered. "They'd stand on the beach for hours at a time just looking at the gulls flying, soaring, dipping." They had even watched how paper fell and floated to the ground, over and over again.

Wilbur's notebooks are filled with drawings he made of birds, observations about differences in flight techniques between various species, how weather conditions seemed to affect their ability to fly. It's filled with drawings and notations about how different designs worked in the wind tunnel they built. Other people had noticed details about bird flight, of course, but no one had gone quite that deep, no one had ever spent more time intently looking at the mechanics of flight and wings.

That is the difference.

We all see through a glass darkly, but then face-to-face. That extra look, that extra hour watching birds, one more dissection, one more book, one more angle, one more ponder—it's this "extra" that becomes essential.

You have to take the time.

There is always more to learn.

Always something new.

Look for it.

Don't Fall for It

~

There was a time when Kyrie Irving was sure the earth was flat. He saw some stuff on the internet and was convinced. "I'm telling you, it's right in front of our faces," he said, referring to the scientists who claim that the earth is round. "They lie to us." Taking it further, Irving started to doubt whether the earth even revolves around the sun.

It is not surprising, then, that Irving was convinced by online chatter about vaccines and refused to get a COVID-19 shot during a global pandemic, a decision that cost him nearly an entire NBA season. After that, he fell for perhaps one of the oldest and darkest conspiracy theories there is—the idea that Jews control the world—when he recommended a preposterously awful documentary alongside a clip from Alex Jones. When asked to disavow his anti-Semitism, Kyrie replied, "Any label you put on me I'm able to dismiss because I study. I know the Oxford dictionary."

Well, that settles it then.

The problem isn't that Kyrie Irving is dumb. Many people

are dumb and go through life just fine. The problem is that Kyrie Irving is so convinced that he's smart—smarter than everyone, in fact—that it makes him a very easy mark. A mark for bullshit. A mark for extremists. A mark for conspiracy theories. A mark for con artists.

"If you're vain," Angela Merkel said, "you can be seduced."

In other words, you can be fooled and turned into a fool.

Kyrie Irving paid dearly for his words—destroying one of the most talented teams in basketball history and losing his Nike deal over these controversies. But the public also paid. Stupidity, like the pandemics and other diseases it so flippantly denies, is contagious. Foolish people infect and create other foolish people who do foolish things with what they "learn."

One of the things Marcus Aurelius said he learned from Rusticus was the discernment to "not fall for every smooth talker." From him Marcus must have also learned to "avoid rashness and credulity."

Somebody failed Kyrie Irving in that regard.

Many of us have been similarly failed.

We fall for conspiracy theories. We get conned out of money. We support obvious grifters. We excitedly participate in bubbles and fads. We try snake oil remedies. We rush to conclusions. We assume we understand a complex topic that we have thought about for literally two minutes.

It has always been thus.

The Sirens in the *Odyssey* didn't just sing beautiful songs that led the sailors astray. They spoke seductively to them, telling each what they wished to hear, promising them secret knowledge, bringing them closer and closer to the rocks that would destroy them.

History shows us how this happens over and over again. "Mankind are, in all ages, caught by the same baits," David Hume observed in 1752. "The same tricks, played over and over again, still trepan them."

Not just on fools but on very smart people.

Steve Jobs and Gandhi both fell for quack scientists and medical advice. Sir Arthur Conan Doyle, the creator of Sherlock Holmes, famously fell for the Cottingley Fairies hoax (believing there was photographic evidence of *fairies*). Mary Todd Lincoln wanted desperately to believe that mediums could help her communicate with the children she had lost, even holding séances at the White House. Two-time Nobel laureate Linus Pauling was swayed into promoting high-dose vitamin C as a cancer treatment. Elon Musk, who was once so good at sussing out bullshit when he heard it from bureaucrats and lawyers and even his own employees, now falls for propaganda tweeted by Russian agents and links from garbage websites.

We drink the Kool-Aid. We accept the theory, the single trick, the big explosive idea that *explains it all*!

Why? Because we want it to be true.

That's where we are so vulnerable—not just to silly new beliefs, but to what the foolish part of us already thinks. And bad actors are all too ready to help us with this self-deception.

In the ancient world, the *sophists* were the kind of smooth talkers whom Marcus Aurelius was taught to be skeptical of. They argued for a living, told a crowd one thing one day and a different crowd the opposite the next. They were dumb people's idea of smart people, and they were experts at parting fools from their money and time. They're still in business today, purveying their wares on cable news and social media, surfing the algorithm, profiting from rage and confusion and misinformation as in the old days.

There have always been charlatans and snake oil salesmen. There have always been cult leaders and gurus. They sell what we wish could be true. They promise that we can manifest our reality. That for a fee we can be absolved of our sins, that they can get us into heaven or deliver us riches if we just follow their simple framework . . . if we just overlook their previous conviction . . . if we just purchase the secret formula . . . if we just ignore the glaring inconsistencies, the questionable motives, and common sense.

One of the secrets to accumulating wealth is just *not* falling for scams or shortcuts. Most research shows that the average investor does better when they stop thinking they can beat the market and just passively invest in various index funds. But the glittering promises of riches, of enormous or immediate returns, is difficult to resist. Wise is the person who knows what's too good to be true, what's reasonable and realistic. A fool gets excited when a Nigerian prince sends them an email, a friend invites them to join a multilevel marketing scheme, or they see a pitch deck for *the next big thing*. They can't tell a crooked game from a real one, separate an exciting opportunity from something too good to be true.

This is why, as the saying goes, a fool and his money are soon parted. They don't manage to hang on to their dignity or sanity very long either.

The sophists had peers who are also unfortunately still with us today. These were the *demagogues*, the rabble-rousers who were particularly good at convincing the common people that the system was rigged and that they alone had the solutions. "The demagogue," James Fenimore Cooper explained in 1838, "is usually sly, a detractor of others, a professor of humility and disinterestedness . . . a man who acts in corners, and avoids open and manly expositions of his course, calls blackguards gentlemen, and gentlemen folks, appeals to passions and prejudices rather than to reason, and is in all respects, a man of intrigue and deception, of sly cunning and management."

Sound familiar?

The Athenians had Cleon, and Rome had Cataline. Montaigne's time knew the Savonarolas who burned books and persecuted heretics. Germany had its Hitler and Italy its Mussolini. In the same period America produced Father Coughlin and Huey Long. Today, we've got Orbán in Hungary and Netanyahu in Israel. We've got a thrice-married, six-time-bankrupt reality television star convincing evangelical Christians that he's their savior, convincing the poor and the downtrodden and the uneducated that he—the guy whose dad gave him hundreds of millions of dollars and pulled strings for his Ivy League admission—is their weapon against "the elites."

In between and for all time, there have been preachers and mystics, politicians and entertainers, entrepreneurs and marketers who have figured out how to play people, to convince them that complicated issues are simple and simple issues are complicated and that they, the maligned or misunderstood, are the only ones who know the truth.

Sometimes the opportunities these people sell are not without value. Maybe the real estate market *is* booming, maybe some new kind of technology really *is* a big deal. Charisma is a powerful weapon . . . and it feels good to believe. Sometimes the grievances being hammered are legitimate. The ravages of the Great War and the Great Depression created the conditions that made so many of those mid-twentieth-century demagogues possible. The system *is* rigged in many ways.

But this is never the whole story.

Even if we're smart, even if we're successful, we can still be marks. Plato was repeatedly suckered by Dionysius, a savvy tyrant who convinced Plato that he was interested in democracy, when really he just wanted to glom onto Plato's reputation. Seneca fell for Nero's charms, for the oldest lie in the world—that people can change. He also fell for a hope we all fool ourselves with—that we're the one who can change them.

Malcolm X converted to the Nation of Islam while in prison, and the repeated injustices and the hypocrisies of America at that time made him susceptible to the group's arguments. The problem was that the group was a cult and had its own hypocrisy. He became a demagogue, preaching separatism and violence, as if these could possibly solve the timeless problems of race and religion. In 1961, George Lincoln Rockwell, the head of the American Nazi Party, would be invited by the Black Muslims to come see Malcolm speak. Malcolm X would himself secretly meet with the leaders of the Ku Klux Klan in Atlanta that same year. These extremists were on very different ends of the spectrum, but their tactics and temptations—and, in some ways, what they sold—were the same.

"The thing you have to understand about those of us in the Black Muslims was that all of us believed 100 percent in the divinity of Elijah Muhammad," Malcolm later explained. "We actually believed that God, in Detroit by the way, had taught him."

What's so striking is that years later the beliefs underpinning the worst actions humans have taken against one another, from slavery to the Holocaust, are almost incomprehensibly stupid. It's not just that they're offensive and dangerous, it's that they are almost childlike in how nonsensical they are. Yet people were marched off in chains and into ovens over them all the same.

Voltaire said that if they can make you believe absurdities, they can make you commit atrocities. It's why we must be skeptical. Why we must constantly reexamine our beliefs.

It's to Malcolm X's credit that he eventually woke up to the con that had been perpetrated against him, first turning against Elijah Muhammad, who had exploited the faith of his followers for personal gain while engaging in numerous extramarital affairs, and eventually, during a visit to Mecca in the final months of his life, Malcolm turned away from the hatred and the conspiracy theories that had deformed his understanding of the world.

This is an *incredibly* hard thing to do.

Who wants to admit they have been fooled?

We should absolutely "do our research"—to borrow the term popular with conspiracy theorists—but by that, we mean *actually* do the research. Like, read real and credible authors on a topic, lots of them. Do *actual* thinking, not what *feels* like thinking. Ask real questions, instead of "just asking questions." Listen to the answers. Allow ourselves to be proven wrong. Allow ourselves to learn new things. A podcast is not a sufficient briefing on a topic!

We must be ever vigilant against bullshit, which can be spread today in ways that the ancients could not have imagined. We are besieged by falsehoods designed to prey on our biases, to exhaust us, to wear down our ability to see what is obviously in front of us.*

---

*Artificial intelligence is very intelligent, but it also "hallucinates" complete nonsense.

For intelligence is not just useful for solving the mysteries of the universe or creating groundbreaking insights. It serves more practical purposes too. To keep you out of cults and away from scams. To help you see through what's being sold, to see past those attractive, reassuring, exciting beliefs being offered.

It's patience and skepticism instead of rashness and credulity.

This is wisdom.

Don't fall for the smooth talkers and slick salesmen.

Ignore the sirens and the tempting fictions.

Don't fool yourself.

Understand People

～

ocrates was brave, fighting with honor in the Pelopon-nesian War.

He was brilliant, bringing philosophy down from the heavens.

He was also pretty obnoxious.

Although many of his probing questions live on through his philosophical dialogues, they could not have been all that fun for the real people on the other side of them.

No topic was off limits to Socrates. No person was either. He would question and question, sometimes until his interlocutors—*victims*—were thoroughly humiliated. And what exactly had been proven? What had Socrates himself affirmatively stated in these exchanges? What positions had he committed to?

Ah, that was the trick of his method!

It's ironic that Socrates would come off as a know-it-all, but that's sort of what he was.

He was also kind of weird. He didn't have a real job. He hung out in the market and the gymnasium. He lounged about the city, blissfully unaware of the resentment this almost certainly provoked. More gratingly, he seemed to think his lifestyle was superior to those of the hardworking, "normal" Athenians just going about their lives. What's more, he was trying to persuade their children to be more like him.

Socrates said he was the "gadfly" of his country . . . but people don't like flies.

In 399 BC, they swatted back hard, bringing Socrates up on charges of impiety and for corrupting the youth. In fact, the only surprising thing about his arrest is that it seemed to surprise Socrates. The guy who questioned the gods, who got between parents and their children, didn't see a backlash coming.

And yet, even after his conviction, all was not lost for Socrates. Given a chance to speak at his sentencing, he could have brought in his family and asked for mercy. He could have suggested exile or a large fine. He could have shown that he had at least learned something from the experience, that he might be willing to reconsider some of his methods and choices.

Instead, Socrates proposed that this angry court *award him a pension*, the same honor that was given to champion athletes or war heroes. "I had not the boldness or impudence or inclination to address you as you would have liked me to address you," he told the people who held his fate in their hands, "weeping and wailing and lamenting, and saying and doing many things which you have been accustomed to hear from others, and which, as I say, are unworthy of me. . . . I would rather die having spoken after my manner, than speak in your manner and live."

Was it brave? Sure. Was it also stupid? Yes.

Athens was not inclined to pay him off, but it was happy to let him die.

A thin majority of the five hundred jurors had voted to convict Socrates. After the wisest man in Athens addressed the jury, however, a larger majority voted for the hemlock.

How poorly do you have to read a room to make a juror who just voted to acquit you—who had sworn an oath to put aside "favor or enmity"—think you should be *sentenced to death*?

"The more I read about Socrates," Macaulay said, "the less I wonder that they poisoned him." Socrates was brilliant, but he lacked social grace and social intelligence. In the end, it was this, not his supposed "crimes," that sealed his fate.

Someone once said of the writer Gertrude Stein that "she knew persons, but not people." Perhaps this was Socrates's problem. He understood the human condition but was oblivious to his effect on human beings. The wise man was, in this regard, a bit of a fool.

If someone is arrogant and obnoxious, totally unaware of the problems they stumble into and the controversies and offenses they cause, we would not consider them to be very smart.

Yet for some reason we often excuse obviously brilliant people when they do the same thing. The absent-minded professor.

The imperious writer. The clueless scientist. The superstar engineer without any friends. The successful businessperson who falls for a scam.

Without people skills, how smart is a person? How effective can they be?

Social intelligence is an attribute like any other. It's something you accumulate with hard work and experience. Some have mastered it. History is filled with examples of people exerting it. It's also full of cautionary tales of people who blew it.

There's General George McClellan, whose strategic genius could not overcome his haughtiness and his crippling anxiety. Plutarch tells us about how Cicero turned his greatest accomplishment (saving the republic) into a liability, that "one couldn't attend a Senate or public meeting . . . without having to listen to the endless repetitions." Did Elon really think this bargain with Trump was going to end up differently than it has for anyone ever?

We can contrast these fumbling self-owns with the actions of someone like Benjamin Franklin.

Franklin was brilliant. He too brought things down from the heavens (electricity, no less!). Widely believed to be the smartest man of his time, he was also one of the most famous men of the age, feted by kings across the globe. Yet he was equally beloved by the common man. Despite his intelligence and wealth, he did not make people jealous. He managed to spend years in the business world without many feuds or expensive rivalries. Unlike Socrates, he did not enjoy arguments—he put his intelligence to work on inventions that benefited regular people, from the potbellied stove to lending libraries and fire departments. He liked people, so he was able to deliver important—sometimes wildly groundbreaking—ideas in a way they welcomed and celebrated.

Our curiosity, our desire for understanding, should extend not just to the person in front of us but to how people function within groups. Both because it is an endlessly fascinating topic and because it's essential to getting things done.

If nobody likes you, if you constantly find yourself embroiled in disagreements and bumping up against resistance, what does that say about you? If you can't understand people, you will not only be unpopular, you will be ineffective!

It may well be that some of us are not as well-disposed or naturally astute at reading social cues as others, but that only means we have to work extra hard at it.

Acquiring social skills is a contact sport. Spending countless hours on social media, as Elon Musk does, does not actually help one develop their social skills. It does the opposite, deforming and warping our humanity and making it harder to connect with others. Wealth and success can exempt us, to some degree, from some social obligations, but one stops caring about others at their peril.

Being an asshole is a bad strategy, but social acuity is about more than how you treat others. It's also your ability to read and understand how others act in relation to you—which is key to motivation and to discerning motives. No one is more easily deceived than a narcissist, because no one is clearer about what they want to hear.

Socrates lived bravely and according to his principles. His sentence wasn't fair. Being annoying shouldn't be a crime, and the leading citizens of Athens behaved like little snowflakes, unable to handle the questions from a man who just wanted to help people discover the truth.

But still, so much suffering could have been avoided! With a little more savvy and a little more restraint, Socrates could have kept going.

A quote often attributed to Andy Warhol says that art—especially transgressive art—is about *getting away with it.*

Socrates didn't get away with it.

The world lost him early. His family lost him early.

We are all dumber for that.

We ignore social dynamics at our peril.

From Humility to Wisdom . . .

~

To know that one does know is best;
Not to know but to believe that one knows is a disease.
Only by seeing this disease as a disease can one be free of it.
Sages are free of this disease.
Because they see this disease as a disease, they are free
of it.

—*DAODEJING*

We should not be too harsh on fools—they are not usually having a good time. Nor are they aware of the wisdom they are missing. Someone has failed them. Someone has taken advantage of them.

Although the Bible can be harsh on the foolish, Jesus had much sympathy for them. Especially those who, as Plato described, were cut off from truth against their will.

"Like all poetical natures [Jesus] loved ignorant people,"

Oscar Wilde would write from his prison cell. "He knew that in the soul of one who is ignorant there is always room for a great idea. But he could not stand stupid people, especially those who are made stupid by education: people who are full of opinions not one of which they even understand, a peculiarly modern type, summed up by Christ when he describes it as the type of one who has the key of knowledge, cannot use it himself, and does not allow other people to use it, though it may be made to open the gate of God's Kingdom."

Being wrong is not the sin. Being confidently wrong? That's the problem. That's the difference between ignorance and stupidity.

The ignorant are not nearly as dangerous as the smug and arrogant morons who feel entitled to tell others what to do. It's fanaticism that is responsible for most of the evil in the world. It's the fundamentalists who do the most damage.

We have all had foolish beliefs. Some of our current opinions will not hold up well.

This is nothing to be ashamed of. This *is the point.*

We want to outgrow our childishness and evolve beyond our biases and ego. We want to achieve not just knowledge but *self*-knowledge. We want not just facts but *understanding.*

Ignorance is a solvable problem . . . but it requires admitting the problem first.

You can't learn what you think you know.

You can't learn if you think you know everything.

You can't get better if you think you're perfect.

We must be humble. We must be open.

We must want to grow, to be challenged, to be questioned.

This is the key to wisdom.

PART III
THE APOTHEOSIS
(TOUCHING THE DIVINE)

Knowledge comes, but wisdom lingers,
and I linger on the shore,

And the individual withers, and the world
is more and more.

—TENNYSON

We are all born equal . . . and then some of us discover philosophy. Some people try to pile up money, others experience. Some sculpt their body, others cultivate wisdom. They talk to the dead. They do the work. They achieve insight, peace, and understanding. They stand apart from the rabble. They beat back against the current, they go their own way. This takes courage. This takes discipline. That's what makes them great. This is how we bring justice into the world. Will we avail ourselves of the greatest minds that ever lived? Will we seek truth? Will we challenge ourselves and our assumptions? Will we begin this journey that never ends? We must fight for enlightenment, against cynicism and despair. We must be patient. We must see what is really there. We must fulfill our potential. We must share what we have learned, use it, move *forward* through it.

Shrewd, Sensible, Sound, *Strong* . . .

⁓

Late in his life, Leo Tolstoy visited a remote tribe in the North Caucasus mountains, where Eastern Europe transitions into Asia. As Tolstoy told stories of old heroes, their chief stopped him and asked why he had not spoken of the "greatest general and ruler of the world."

The man could have been talking of number of conquerors, those towering figures who had over the centuries remade entire continents in their image. But the hero the people in the distant camp far from the center of civilization wanted to hear about was a long-dead American president . . . a man Tolstoy had never met, whose picture they had never even seen, whom they could have only known through snippets of legend and myths.

Tell us of the man who clawed his way up from nothing, they said, the man with "the voice of thunder" and "deeds as strong as the rock."

They wanted to know about Abraham Lincoln.

Why?

Because at some intuitive level, even these remote people seemed to understand, Tolstoy felt, that "of all the great national heroes and statesmen of history Lincoln is the only real giant." That Lincoln transcended Alexander and Caesar and Napoleon in wisdom and character and moral power. "Lincoln was a man of whom a nation has a right to be proud," Tolstoy later wrote; "he was a Christ in miniature, a saint of humanity, whose name will live thousands of years in the legends of future generations. His genius is still too strong and too powerful for the common understanding, just as the sun is too hot when its light beams directly on us."

And yet that man grew up in a primitive backwoods cabin, barely fit to be called a house, not too different from those the tribesmen would have known.

There would be no special schools or private tutors for young Abraham Lincoln. His formal education would amount to less than a year. There was simply no opportunity. Instead of sending him to college, his father rented him out to neighboring farms. It was backbreaking labor, pulling stumps, planting seeds, working animals, splitting rails, chopping firewood, eking out a subsistence-level existence in a violent, unforgiving place.

He was not born to wealth. His family did not own an emerald mine or vast estates that bore his name. His grandfather had been killed by Indians in front of his family. "The panther's scream filled night with fear," Lincoln wrote. "And bears preyed on the swine." Man was pitted not just against the wilderness but against society—the Lincoln family was repeatedly swindled by land speculators and moneyed interests.

Years later, when asked for a description of his early life, Abraham Lincoln said the whole of his family history could be captured in a single line from the poet Thomas Gray: "The short and simple annals of the poor."

Montaigne had been taught Latin as his mother tongue. Growing up, Lincoln did not even know anyone who could read a word of it—recalling with a laugh that a man who spoke Latin in their provincial world was "looked upon as a wizard." Montaigne had an arrangement with a teacher who allowed him to read outside their curriculum. Lincoln's father, who could not even sign his own name, resented his son's reading, thought it a distraction and an indulgence, and sometimes destroyed his priceless books out of spite.

Reading was the boy's escape from an oppressive existence, his first exposure to a world bigger than his own. "I don't always intend to delve, grub, shuck corn, split rails and the like," he told a family friend. He read and read and read . . . no matter how many lashes it earned him from his father.

"I never seen Abe after he was twelve 'at he didn't have a book som'ers 'round," a cousin said. "He read all the books he could lay his hands on," his stepmother recounted. "He read diligently—went to bed early—got up early to read." After work, he'd grab a hunk of corn bread from the cupboard, splay out in a chair, and read for hours. She watched as this strange, lanky boy, exhausted from farm work, not only read, but when he came across a particularly striking passage would write it down and rewrite it just to feel the words run through his fingers. It broke her heart when they couldn't afford paper, but Lincoln didn't mind, inscribing the passages on old wooden boards instead. It wasn't the most glamorous process, but it worked, and the things he read and heard became "fixed in his mind . . . he never lost the fact or his understanding of it."

"I can remember going to my little bedroom," Lincoln once recounted, "after hearing the neighbors talk of an evening with my father, and spending no small part of the night walking up and down, and trying to make out what was the exact meaning of some of their, to me, dark sayings. I could not sleep, though I often tried to, when I got on such a hunt after an idea, until I caught it; and when I thought I had got it, I was not satisfied until I had repeated it over and over,—until I had put it in language plain enough, as I thought, for any boy I knew to comprehend."

Perhaps it was this laborious process that first impressed upon Lincoln a metaphor for how his brain worked. "My mind is like a piece of steel," he would later tell a friend, "very hard to scratch anything on it, and almost impossible thereafter to rub it out." Like Cleanthes, Lincoln was a slow learner but he didn't forget what he learned—and that is a powerful combination.

Not that the man himself was made of steel. "All that I am or hope ever to be I get from my mother," he said of the sweet and loving woman who died when he was nine. Her last words, as she called her children to her deathbed, were to remind them to "be good and kind . . . to one another, and to the world." He was the product of his loving stepmother too, who moved in with the Lincolns and found the children all but feral in a shanty. It was she who washed them, who provided the tenderness and affection that would help form a man very much apart from the widespread cruelty of his time.

One book that Lincoln read over and over was *Lessons in Elocution* by William Scott, which his stepmother had brought with her. It was filled with lines he inscribed not just on boards but into his soul. There was Gray's bit about the annals of the poor. "You must love learning, if you would possess it," said another passage in Scott's book. "A man acquainted with history may, in some respect, be said to have lived from the beginning of the world. . . ." "Never sport with pain and distress in any of your amusements, nor treat even the meanest insect with wanton cruelty."

His education, then, was not something he got, but something he fought for and gave himself. A friend described him as a *stubborn* reader. He didn't quit a topic or an author just because it was hard. "Get the books," Lincoln once said, "and read and study them till you understand them in their principal features; and that is the main thing." He would never be as well-read as his peers who were able to go to Harvard or West Point. There were some Shakespeare plays he'd never even gotten to read, he would explain, but the ones he had read, he'd read as much as anyone alive.

His love of learning sat on top of a toughness—a mental discipline to absorb the judgments of people around him and a physical discipline to endure the hardscrabble life he had been born into. He came to an understanding with his neighbors: If there was a book within a few days' walk, he was going to come read it. Reading, then, meant miles and miles of walking, even after those hours in the field.

"I can outlift any man," he was still saying as president. "When I was young, I was never thrown," he said of his wrestling prowess. Just a few days before his death and after a long day of shaking hands, a fifty-six-year-old Lincoln stunned a group of soldiers when he picked up a seven-pound ax around the handle and held it outstretched, parallel to the ground, perfectly still, at length. Not a single one of the younger men could match the feat of the former rail-splitter. "A man of less iron frame," a friend observed, "would have sunk under the enormous burdens laid upon him during four years, marked by Executive cares that have no parallel in history."

Although he had traveled through many distant lands and all the eras of the past through his childhood reading, Lincoln was nineteen years old when he made his first trip across the burgeoning country. Twenty-three centuries earlier, Herodotus had been amazed at the way the Babylonians had built boats for the Euphrates River trade, only to break them up and sell them for parts on arrival. Twice, Lincoln would do the same on a journey down the Mississippi, traveling from Illinois to New Orleans—through Memphis, Vicksburg, Natchez, St. Louis, Baton Rouge—his fifteen-by-forty-foot wooden boats repurposed into housing stock, while he walked a good chunk of the journey home. Along the way, he fought off bandits and heard new languages (Creole, French, Spanish). He saw great wealth and great poverty, huge buildings and new technology.

Little did he know that it was this intimate relationship with the "Father of Waters" that would inform his strategic plan for winning the Civil War. Or that a scramble to get his boat unstuck in New Salem would inspire him to file a patent for lifting boats on the river—the only American president to patent something.

But that's what an education is: sowing of seeds we will reap later.

There is perhaps no world leader to ever have tried their hand at more professions than Lincoln. In addition to his early farm labor, Lincoln would work as a surveyor, an elections clerk, a shopkeeper, a flatboatman, a captain in the militia, a postmaster, a small-town prairie lawyer, a local legislator, and a millworker, among others.

At just twenty-three, Lincoln, resolving not to be an "idiot," first entered public affairs by running for the Illinois State legislature. Although he lost, he did meet his first of many mentors, including John T. Stuart, who allowed him to borrow some of his law books. As always, he was a diligent student.

"If you wish to be a lawyer," Lincoln would later tell a young man, "attach no consequence to the *place* you are in, or the *person* you are with; but get books, sit down anywhere, and go to reading for yourself. That will make a lawyer of you quicker than any other way."

He'd practice law for the next twenty-five years. As much as he got from books, it was Lincoln's experience in the courtroom and the legal system that shaped him as a lawyer and as a student of human experience. Between 1837 and 1860, he would work on over five thousand cases. He handled wills and deeds, libel cases and property disputes. He processed bankruptcies. He represented slaves and slave owners, criminals and the wrongly convicted, railroads and day laborers. He handled not one but *several* cases for clients accused of bestiality and tried seventeen homicides (two as a prosecutor). He argued in front of the Supreme Court. He mediated between squabbling spouses.

After a single term in Congress from 1847 to 1849, Lincoln returned to the law, "riding the circuit," as lawyers did in those days, traveling tens of thousands of miles over muddy, broken roads across the Midwest. He tried cases in Tremont and Metamora, Bloomington and Mount Pulaski, Urbana and Danville, Shelbyville and Decatur. He shared rooms in dingy inns in rural towns. He spent hours on horseback. He waded across swollen rivers. He met strangers and ruffians. He slept on trains. He dealt with corrupt judges. He entertained in taverns and charmed waitresses in greasy restaurants. He encountered human decency. He missed his family. All the while, he carried the volumes of Euclid in his saddlebags, so that he might teach himself something new during the downtime.

"Mr. Lincoln possessed a quick intuition of human nature and of the strength and weakness of individual character," his two most trusted aides would later write. "His whole life had been a practical study of the details and rivalries of local partisanship." Lincoln knew people. He knew the world. He knew it *firsthand*.

Practicing law—on the frontier or in the big city—can warp a person's character. It is, after all, an adversarial profession, one built around the search for and exploitation of loopholes, where a strong sense of right and wrong can be impediments to a lucrative career. But it was *as a lawyer* that Abraham Lincoln earned his reputation as "Honest Abe." His fees were modest. He didn't cheat clients. He didn't deceive the court. He took his oath seriously. He discouraged litigation, urging both sides to compromise, often at the expense of his billable hours. He came to hate the idea, he said, that lawyers are, as a rule, dishonest. "If you cannot be an honest lawyer," he said, "resolve to be honest without being a lawyer. Choose some other occupation."

Still, he was not a rube. He knew how to play to the jury. He was a wicked cross-examiner, who lulled opponents into complacency, deceived them with his aw-shucks style and liberal uses of "Well, I reckon." Smart as a serpent, he was notorious for using the egos of witnesses against themselves. "Any man who took Lincoln for a simpleminded man," said a lawyer who tried many cases against him, "would very soon wake up with his back in a ditch."

What was all the learning for? "Every man is said to have his peculiar ambition," Lincoln explained. "I have no other so great as that of being truly esteemed of my fellow men, by rendering myself worthy of their esteem." He wanted to be important. He wanted to make his mark.

It was this drive—this little engine that knows no rest, as one of Lincoln's friends described it—that had pulled him up from poverty, that allowed him to cobble together a nice life for himself. But there was, as there is in so much of our striving, a hollowness to this ambition—a fragility to the thirst. In Lincoln's case, it would not survive the blows of fate that fell sporadically at first, and then so rapidly that they nearly killed him.

Although Lincoln had lost his mother at age nine from milk sickness, it was the middle of his life that was defined by tragedy and setbacks. He was defeated in his first run for office. He was laid off from his job running a store in 1831. When he started his own, it failed. His possessions were sold in a bankruptcy auction. He lost his first love to typhoid. His second fiancée dumped him. He broke it off with his future wife, Mary Todd, a few years later. His first law partnership dissolved. He was not reelected to Congress. He lost two Senate elections. He buried his three-year-old son Eddie.

He had always been dogged by what he would call his "melancholy," but for a good chunk of his twenties and thirties, in response to nearly uninterrupted failure and loss, it spiraled into suicidal depression. His friends took sharp objects from his room. He was "delirious," one of them said; "the most miserable man living," according to Lincoln himself. In a poem Lincoln would write and publish around that time, he's clearly a man tortured by his own mind.

> To ease me of *this* power to *think*,
> That through my bosom raves,
> I'll headlong leap from hell's high brink,
> And wallow in its waves.

Around the time of his second nervous breakdown, Lincoln was traveling through Kentucky when he encountered a group of slaves chained six and six together, for the purposes of being shipped farther south. He was struck by two things in this horrible scene. The first was the way these human beings "were strung together precisely like so many fish upon a trot-line." It was a vivid illustration to him of the brutal reality of the institution that so many of his fellow citizens sought to downplay and rationalize. The second was that these men and women, for all the injustice of their situation, still seemed to have within them a joy and happiness that he himself had not known in so long.

"How true it is that 'God tempers the wind to the shorn lamb,'" he wrote to a friend, "or in other words, that He renders the worst of human conditions tolerable, while He permits the best, to be nothing better than tolerable."

Lincoln, staggering under his own hurt, could have taken to drink. Many people would have been dehumanized by his kind of upbringing, would have been desensitized by the violence around them, become indifferent to the problems of others because of the overwhelming nature of their own. He could have given up. He could have numbed himself with accomplishments and power and fame. He could have done any of the things that people do to take away the pain of being alive. "To remain as I am is impossible," Lincoln said at his lowest ebb. "I must die or be better, it appears to me."

So that's what he did. He decided not just to become better, but to *do* better. He had done nothing, he told his friend Joshua Speed, to "make any human being remember that he had lived," done nothing to address the events and issues of his time, given nothing to future generations.

There were plenty of Americans who, by the middle of the nineteenth century, knew that slavery was obviously wrong. Lincoln's parents had known this—that's why they had moved from Kentucky (a slave state) to Illinois (a free state) during his childhood. But like most Americans who opposed slavery, he was not sure what he personally could do about it, mostly hoping the institution would just fade away. He hoped against hope that if left to its own devices, the South would come to its senses—fearing that attacks and criticism, as with many snowflakes, would only make the slave states double down.

The surprise passage of the Kansas-Nebraska Act in 1854, which opened up enormous swaths of territory to slavery, forced Lincoln out of this passivity. It "took us by surprise—astounded us," Lincoln said. "We were thunderstruck and stunned." The act had been the brainchild of Stephen Douglas, a venal politician, very much Lincoln's opposite. Short, rich, egoistical, Douglas was an ambitious race-baiter—guilty of "low . . . demagougeism [*sic*]," as Lincoln called it—who saw that pandering to the slave interests was his path to power, even if it meant jeopardizing decades of compromises and accommodations that had kept the Union together.

Douglas was proposing that people simply vote on the introduction of slavery into wide swaths of new territory as if it was no different than a bond to pay for road improvements. In some ways that was actually how Douglas saw it, he was playing politics so that he could direct the transcontinental railroad through Chicago! Douglas didn't care which way people voted, Lincoln was horrified to discover, slavery was to him "merely a matter of dollars and cents."

Lincoln, who towered over the five-foot-four-inch Douglas, could see much further—he knew there were always unintended consequences. With millions and eventually billions of dollars on the line, Lincoln understood that Southern interests could not be content with just preserving the institution; they would be driven to expand it, transforming America into a slave empire that stretched from coast to coast (with designs on neighboring Mexico, Canada, and Haiti). Bloody conflict with someone, somewhere, was inevitable.

"I look upon that enactment [of popular sovereignty] not as *law*," Lincoln said later, "but as *violence* from the beginning. It was conceived in violence, passed in violence, is maintained in violence, and is being executed in violence." And Lincoln's prediction would be vindicated, tragically, not just by the settler violence that raged across the prairies as territories fought over whether to allow slavery but in the war that followed.

When he had first seen that coffle of slaves at the market, he was deep in his own pain, but the scar of what he saw never left him. "That sight was a continual torment," he wrote to Speed again about the encounter in 1855, still ruminating fourteen years later. "And I see something like it every time I touch the Ohio, or any other slave-border."

As obviously immoral as slavery was to him personally, how to rid the nation of it was a problem he faced with much more humility. "If all earthly power were given to me," he had said in his first speech about the Kansas-Nebraska Act, "I should not know what to do, as to the existing institution." The lawyer in him came out here too. Not just that he respected the law—slavery was protected at the state and federal level—but having seen so many pointless, expensive conflicts in court, he tried to balance his sense of right and wrong with an amenability to compromise.

Some historians have tried to say that Lincoln was not really opposed to slavery, claiming that his sole concern was preserving the Union and citing remarks where he promised not to interfere with slavery.

This is wrong.

What Lincoln possessed, as a product of his painful, plodding rise from the dregs, was *prudence*, that essential element of wisdom—an understanding that progress comes slowly and that dangerous things must be done carefully.

"For I am never easy now," Lincoln said, "when I am handling a thought, till I have bounded it North, and bounded it South, and bounded it East, and bounded it West." The lawyer in him needed to understand the issue, needed to understand everything that had led up to it, just as the curious kid in him, his stepmother had said, needed to "understand Every thing—even the smallest thing—Minutely & Exactly." Thomas Clarkson began his campaign against slavery with a deep dive, and Lincoln's campaign began the same way. "He searched through the dusty volumes of congressional proceedings in the State library," William Herndon, Lincoln's law partner, recalled, "and dug deeply into political history." His way, Herndon observed, was to dig up a question by the roots and dry it out by the fires of the mind, until he could see it for what it was.

In his research, Lincoln found that most of the founders believed that Congress had the right to control and limit slavery, and that many others had clear antislavery views, whether they'd been called to vote on the question or not. It was notable that they had not used the word *slave* in the Constitution, as Lincoln noted, instead, out of shame and frustration, "the thing is hidden away . . . , just as a man hides away a . . . cancer." They knew it was indefensible, and thus employed the euphemism "Person held to Service or Labor." He noted that the founders had repeatedly regulated slavery: In 1794 they had banned the exportation of slaves; in 1798 they'd banned bringing them into the newly acquired Mississippi Territory; in 1800 they'd banned Americans from participating in global slave trading; and in 1808—the day the Constitution allowed it—they banned the African slave trade, which they knew to be barbarous and evil, entirely. And in 1820, what had they decided was the punishment for illegal slave trading? *Death*, Lincoln pointed out. "You never thought of hanging men for catching and selling wild horses, wild buffalos or wild bears."

Lincoln's argument was not what he was taught in school— because he hadn't gone to school, and besides, *no one* was taught about slavery at school at the time. This "maniacally detailed inspection," as one contemporary called it, was new research, a new understanding, a new reading of the American story. By the middle of the nineteenth century, there was no better student of the Constitution and the Declaration than Lincoln, no one who better grasped what America was and *could* be.

Properly armed, Lincoln began a series of barnstorming speeches that would put to words the feelings of millions of Americans across the country. Southern politicians, the judiciary, and powerful slave interests had conspired to redefine the fundamental premise of America, he said, all while cloaking themselves in language about elections and freedom. It was a "naked humbug," Lincoln said, one he could not abide.

What did the snowflakes in the South want? It was obvious, Lincoln said. "This, and this only: cease to call slavery wrong and join them in calling it right." The North, which had continually compromised and been bullied for decades by powerful Southern oligarchs, rejoiced, because finally someone was telling the truth, and doing it in plain language.

In his debates with Douglas, in his famous speech at Cooper Union, and across the country, Lincoln made the case against slavery and the case *for* a sustained political effort to retake proper, democratic control of the country. He did this all in a folksy, accessible way. "They say I tell a great many stories. I reckon I do," he admitted, "but I have learned from long experience that *plain* people . . . are more easily *influenced* through the medium of a proud and humorous illustration than any other way."

He would lose his 1858 Senate race against Douglas—

another defeat in a long line of election failures—but he won the war. "The fight must go on," he said after the election returns came in. "The cause of civil liberty must not be surrendered at the end of ONE, or even one HUNDRED, defeats." The loss, as it happened, propelled him in two years to the presidency.

It was good that Lincoln had not given up, because when the South foolishly split the ticket in 1860, they handed victory to the North. But, having grown so used to minority rule, for Southern leaders, even the thought of President-*Elect* Lincoln was too much to bear. Secession followed.

Perhaps they thought that bullying would work. For a generation it had. At every threat, in every fight, the North had given more ground to the slave interests to preserve the country. As a result, Southerners had come to believe their own lies—had broken their own brains—and now they careened toward self-destruction.

James Buchanan, Lincoln's predecessor, did nothing as the South seized arms depots and menaced federal forts. He did nothing as sedition and conspiracy ran wild in the capital, even in his own cabinet. Lincoln, though, knew what was what. He was not going to be pushed around. He was going to defend the country. He was going to keep it together. Asked what message he might have for wavering Kentucky at the outbreak of the war, Lincoln stood up from his chair, pointed at himself, and said, "Tell my friends: There is a man in here!'"

"If there were nothing else of Abraham Lincoln for history to stamp him with," Walt Whitman later said, "it is enough . . . that he endured that hour, that day, bitterer than gall—indeed a crucifixion day—that it did not conquer him—unflinchingly stemm'd it and resolv'd to lift himself and the Union out of it."

How did Lincoln know the North could win? How did a person who had never held an executive leadership position in his life manage to lead an enormous war effort? His administration faced not only secession but international conflict, frontier skirmishes, and an unfinished Capitol—on top of the ordinary responsibility of running an enormous country.

At the outbreak of the war, the standing US Army numbered fewer than twenty thousand men. By August of the first year of the war, there were nearly five hundred thousand men in uniform. At Antietam in 1862, the Union would lose more men in twelve hours than had been under arms in 1860. The speed and scale of this development would dwarf the build-ups for both world wars, and was done with considerably less technology. It was a political, cultural, and logistical operation unprecedented in human history, not just the first modern war, but in a way the first demonstration of modern centralized government.

Lincoln had to pass the country's first income tax to pay for it. He had to sell billions in war bonds. He had to build an army and hold together a shaky coalition of states. "His mind mastered the problem of the day," Emerson said of him, "rarely was man so fitted to the event."

The truth is that Lincoln had not known how to do any of this. What he did was *figure it out.*

No one made more mistakes than Lincoln—especially in the early days of the war. He made some of these mistakes more than once (hiring, firing, rehiring, and then refiring General McClellan in 1861 and 1862). But this is leadership. Leadership is not *knowing.* Leadership is *problem-solving.* "The pilots on our Western rivers steer from *point to point* as they call it—setting the course of the boat no farther than they can steer," Lincoln explained, "and that is all I propose to myself in this great problem." It was this that had most impressed Emerson about Lincoln, that "as the problem grew, so did his comprehension of it."

As it happens, his crucial first victory was not on the battlefield. Lincoln understood, as few presidents had before or since, the power of building a team that reflected opposing political, ideological, and regional perspectives. That to be successful, his aides explained, the president knew he "needed advisors, helpers, executive eyes and hands, not alone in department routine, but in the higher qualities of leadership and influence; above all, his principal motive seems to have been representative character, varied talent—in a word, combination." For his cabinet, Lincoln chose politicians of all stripes, even some who openly disliked him and had designs to succeed him in the presidency.

He eagerly chose Edwin Stanton, the Democrat who had once called him the "original gorilla" and tried to get him fired from an important legal case in 1855. But Stanton was the perfect secretary of war, and that's all that Lincoln cared about.* He had no right, Lincoln believed, to deprive the country of the best and most able operators, just because they had hurt his feelings or disagreed with him on many issues. "I will hold McClellan's horse if he will only bring us success," Lincoln said of the general who had repeatedly snubbed and insulted him.

Told by a friend that one of his cabinet members thought he was better than Lincoln, Lincoln replied by asking if the friend knew any others who thought so too. "Why do you ask me that?" came the puzzled reply. "Because I want to put them all in my Cabinet." The first question of this team of rivals that Lincoln had assembled, his secretary wrote, was who was best and brightest. "It is pretty safe to assert that no one," he said, "not even himself—believed it was Abraham Lincoln." Yet it was precisely this humility that ordained he would eventually outshine them all.

In fact, Lincoln's board of advisers extended beyond his

---

* "No men were ever so deceived," Stanton would say of his initial impression of Lincoln, "as we at Cincinnati."

cabinet. His wife, Mary Todd Lincoln, in time became an even more ardent abolitionist than Lincoln, and despite their occasionally tumultuous relationship, he looked to her for advice. Lincoln took frequent counsel from Anna Carroll, a fascinating and daring woman, who shaped his thoughts on military strategy and public relations. There was no one, Lincoln said, whose opinion he cared more about than that of Frederick Douglass, whom he met with multiple times during his presidency, almost to the shock of Douglass. "In no single instance," Douglass noted, did Lincoln do anything to remind him of "the difference between himself and myself, of the difference of color."

His predecessors in the White House had lived in a quaint and quiet past. Lincoln lived in the noisy modern world—with all its real-time news. He spent countless hours in the telegraph office, getting the latest news from the battlefield. Drowning in information, from battlefields and from hundreds of newspapers, he pioneered a version of the Presidential Daily Briefing.

He kept his attention on the mood of the American people too. It can be so easy for power and success to isolate—to create a bubble of reinforcing perceptions. "Though the tax on my time is heavy," he explained, "no hours of my day are better employed than those which thus bring me again within the direct contact of our whole people." He called his meetings with ordinary Americans, with office seekers, with favor askers, with quarrelsome people, with parents of soldiers, with critics and admirers, his "public-opinion baths," and he prioritized the practice, no matter how busy his schedule.

Being smart is common. Being an effective executive, especially at the highest level, is rare.

"In weaker hands such a Cabinet would have been a hot-bed of strife," his aides wrote; "under him it became a tower of strength." Lincoln himself was proudest of his ability to keep people together, the nation and his advisors. "I may not have made as great a President as some other men," he said, "but I believe I have kept these discordant elements together as well as anyone could." It wasn't simply that he surrounded himself with a diversity of input and voices, it was that he *used* these perspectives, expertly wielding the talents of his administration— he literally built the federal government, instilling in it the ethos and spirit that would enable it to invent the internet and land on the moon, to say nothing of creating Social Security and the modern university system.*

It was a time of immense passions, in a cabinet of vast differences of opinion, yet Lincoln ruled his cabinet, created order from the chaos around him, by first assuming command of

---

*Lincoln's Morrill Land Grant College Act is directly responsible for the creation of colleges like MIT, Cornell, Rutgers, and the entire University of California system, a remarkable feat for a man who received no traditional education and an incredible contribution to the sciences, humanities, and advancement of the human race.

what the Stoics called the greatest empire—himself. "Oftentimes, when men came to him in the rage and transport of a first indignation over some untoward incident," his secretaries wrote, "they were surprised to find him quiet, even serene—perhaps with a smile on his face and a jest on his lips . . . his own spirit had already been through the fiery trial of resentment."

Wisdom is not erratic. It is not impulsive or emotional. It is calm. It's cool. It's patient. It's kind. It is *philosophical.*

Without this equanimity, had Lincoln not had incredible mental self-control, he would have "lost—lost all, all," Herndon believed. And Herndon knew, firsthand, just how masterful Lincoln was at interpersonal relations, what command he had over his temper. The two of them had not fought once in their sixteen-year law practice.

Indeed, it's hard to find anyone who had cross words with Lincoln—the man was almost unbelievably agreeable.

He did not take things personally. He did not care about people's motives or past mistakes. He only wanted to get the job done. He only wanted to move forward.

He showed patience and forbearance, even in the darkest moments of the war. At Bull Run, at Fredericksburg, after Shiloh, after the second defeat at Bull Run, after the missed opportunities at Gettysburg, as the campaign in the Wilderness piled up unfathomable casualties, Lincoln could have pointed fingers. After each betrayal, each bungled opening that his generals threw away, as the country tired of the war, after the loss of so much life, Lincoln could have grown discouraged. He could have traded the country away.

He did not.

"I must save the government if possible," he told the governors of Louisiana and Arkansas. "What I cannot do, of course I will not do; but it may as well be understood, once for all, that I shall not surrender this game leaving any available card unplayed." It was his habit, Lincoln said, not to dwell on the past, but to "look to the present and future only." "No man resolved to make the most of himself can spare time for personal contention," Lincoln would write to an officer struggling with a far less acrimonious situation. He encouraged the man to yield on issues that didn't matter so that he might hold fast on those that did.

Again, just as opposing lawyers who underestimated Lincoln were destroyed in court, politicians who took his friendliness and compassion for weakness were outmaneuvered. "He handled and moved man *remotely* as we do pieces upon a chessboard," Leonard Swett, one of his advisers, observed. "It was by ignoring men, and ignoring all small causes, but by closely calculating the tendencies of events and the great forces which were producing logical results." Lincoln never seemed to forget that he was a politician. He was a savvy, almost Machiavellian master of people, persuasion, and politics.

"There was never a closer calculator of political probabilities than himself," his secretaries wrote. "He was completely at home among election figures . . . he was familiar with all the turning-points in contested counties and 'close' districts and knew by heart the value of each and every local loss or gain and its relation to the grand result." Lincoln's nickname in the White House was "the Tycoon," a nod to his inestimable shrewdness and leadership. Yet like the real-life Machiavelli, Lincoln's understanding of power was fused to his bedrock principles. "Nobody knew better how to turn things to advantage politically," Horace White, a journalist who had followed Lincoln since the Douglas debates, explained, "and nobody was readier to take such advantage, provided it did not involve dishonorable means. . . ."

Lincoln replaced anger, fear, resentment, and anxiety with compassion, faith, and what he called "cold, calculating, unimpassioned reason." "Happy day," Lincoln had said in a speech in 1842, "when, all appetites controlled, all passions subdued . . . *mind*, all conquering *mind*, shall live and move the monarch of the world. . . . Hail fall of Fury! Reign of Reason, all hail!"

Wise people quickly learn discipline. They know how easy it is to be wrong. They are not glib. They do not spout off. They try to look at everything as Washington, the first president, learned to: "in the calm light of mild-philosophy."

Lincoln didn't despair after every Union setback, in part because he was calm, but also because he saw the big picture. Unlike so many partisans, he understood the North's enormous strategic advantages—more manpower, more money, more industry, and, as he slowly turned the dial on emancipation, more moral legitimacy.

At the outset of the war, Lincoln knew next to nothing about military theory. From the White House, he sent for every book the Library of Congress could find him on military science, reading with great interest, for instance, a book on logistics that was written by the man who would become chief of staff for the army. He also understood which conventional wisdom to ignore (the nineteenth-century military focus on conquering cities) and which new theories to embrace (destroy the opponent's army and its will to fight).

"I have long held to the opinion that at the close of the war," General W. F. Smith said, "Mr. Lincoln was the superior of his generals in his comprehension of the effect of strategic movements and the proper method of following up victories to their legitimate conclusions." He became, in time, the era's wisest strategist, seeing as clearly as Ulysses S. Grant the path to triumph. Lincoln certainly understood the stakes better than his opponent, Jefferson Davis, though Davis had served as secretary of war and graduated at the top of his class at West Point.

War is an extension of politics by other means, Clausewitz had just recently written, and these ideas had made their way to the voracious, ever-curious mind of Lincoln. The Emancipation Proclamation was the greatest act of statesmanship of the century, if not the millennium. It was also Lincoln brilliantly extending politics into war and war into politics; Lincoln paired it with a battlefield victory, and presented it as a wartime measure, saying it would go into effect on January 1, the following year, only if the South did not immediately cease its unlawful rebellion.

"Surrounded by all sorts of conflicting claims, by traitors, by half-hearted, timid men, by Border States men and Free States men, by radical Abolitionists and Conservatives," Harriet Beecher Stowe said of Lincoln, "he has listened to all, weighed the words of all, waited, observed, yielded now here and now there, but in the main kept one inflexible, honed purpose, and drawn the national ship through."

He was traveling from point to point, always with a vision not just for winning the war but for securing a lasting peace, trying to save the Union and transform it into something *worth* saving. His plan for Reconstruction was anchored around reconciliation as well as justice. He intended to be merciful. He intended to move forward. He intended to keep the promises he had made in the Emancipation Proclamation. He would let the rebels go back to their homes; he would bind up the nation's wounds and take care of its widows and orphans. "It is due to the President to say," his secretary of state wrote, "that his magnanimity is almost superhuman."

Was that why they had to kill him? Because he was too good

for this world? An assassin's bullet—fired by a snowflake petrified of racial equality—struck Lincoln down on April 14, 1865, just days after Lincoln had successfully amended the Constitution and killed slavery in America forever.* He had waged four years of battles, but more important, he had transformed public opinion—moved humanity forward toward justice.

"There would never come a time when Abraham Lincoln abandoned the role of politician," his biographer William Lee Miller wrote; "what he did instead as a lifelong politician was to realize that role's fullest moral possibilities." Karl Marx, writing during the war, was struck by the incredible arc of the man's life—what a shining light in the dark it was. "The new world has never achieved a greater triumph than by this demonstration," he wrote, "that ordinary people of good will can accomplish feats which only heroes could accomplish in the old world!"

Lincoln was, it is not an exaggeration to say, the complete man. Disciplined. Courageous. Just. Most of all, wise. It has been said that no man is a hero to his valet, yet Lincoln's valets, who saw him in his most private moments, spent the rest of their lives trying to honor his memory. They, along with his

---

* "That means nigger citizenship," John Wilkes Booth said after hearing an impromptu speech where Lincoln had floated some of his plans for life after the war.

friends and even many of his enemies, believed he was one of the greatest men who ever lived.

What defined this man? What was his greatness? It was not flashy brilliance or ambition but a kind of moral wisdom, a *philosophical* ethos, that doesn't just sustain a person through immense personal tragedy but allows them to touch something deep in other people.

Lincoln was able to do the hardest thing there is to do: He brought that wisdom into the world. His greatness was used in pursuit of goodness; his ambition in service of virtue.

As he bled out in a room across the street from Ford's Theatre, laid diagonally across a bed he was too tall to fit in, it was Stanton—the man who had so misjudged him—who uttered the most fitting of benedictions: "Now he belongs to the ages."

Or, as scholars continue to debate, he may have said, "Now he belongs to the *angels*."

In any case, he belongs to *us*—whether we live in America or the Caucasus, now or decades in the future.

He is an example to follow. An ideal to live up to.

Lincoln had that rarest form of human wisdom—goodness and greatness—that was not some historical myth but real. It walked the earth. In a time of venality and violence, it survived a law career and politics, survived ambition and suffering and failure.

He was the four virtues embodied.

Brave. Strong. Good. Wise.

It's a heavenly combination, yet an attainable one.

Lincoln's example sits before us. Perhaps we shall never reach it, but we must never cease to try to approach.

Practice Empathy

~

It was only when she jumped in with the animals that she figured it out.

It was only because Temple Grandin cared enough to jump in with the cows that she saw.

The cattle were backing up and resisting entering the vaccination chute. The ranchers wanted to force them through, but she had another idea. "To me getting inside the chute was the obvious thing to do," she explained. "I knew I had to *see* things from the cow's point of view to understand and solve the problem."

It turns out a loose chain was banging against the metal gate, scaring the animals and causing needless suffering to the cows during a routine medical process.

Temple Grandin has autism. Yet she is famous for her empathy, especially for animals. It was Grandin who invented a restraining device that significantly reduced the stress on cows as they were processed in plants. It was Grandin who noticed all the unnecessary ways that light and noise and other previously ignored factors were contributing to the distress and agitation of animals in livestock-handling facilities. By reducing these issues, she made their lives better.

A German term, *umwelt*, means one's *sense of the world*—the experience of being a person or a polar bear or a pill bug. Everyone and every lived experience is different, yet most of the time we are totally ignorant of the other worlds that are someone or something's *whole world*.

It's basic curiosity. How could you not want to know about what it's like to be someone else?

A simple camera was how Grandin figured out what the cows were seeing. "What cattle and dogs and most of the animals are is they're dichromates," she explained. "They can see blue and they can see yellow and they're red colorblind. But they see contrast better than we do." By taking some black-and-white photographs, she got closer to the cows' *umwelt* and could suddenly see why something as ordinary as a hose on the ground or a shadow might seem terrifying.

"I was one of the first people to notice that the cattle were afraid of little things that we tend to not notice," she said with a shrug about this massive breakthrough in animal welfare. But again, it wasn't just that she noticed. It was that she *cared* enough to notice.

Empathy demands courage—whether it's jumping into a cattle pen or talking to someone you disagree with. Discipline— to keep your own emotions in check. Justice—to genuinely fight for someone's interests and not just your own. Wisdom—the curiosity to explore and then the sense to turn this information into understanding.

Perhaps Lincoln's greatest skill was his empathy. He detested slavery. Nearly his entire political career was based on his resistance to the expansion of the slave powers that had captured the country and betrayed the fundamental principles it had been founded on, and yet . . . he seemed to perfectly understand why slave owners thought and acted as they did.

He understood their guilt, their fear. He tried to think about what it would be like to have one's entire economy and identity based around an institution, to be bombarded with propaganda and lies from the press and pulpit your entire life. What would that do to a person? Slavery, he understood, was "highly seductive to the thoughtless and giddy headed young men"—a form of intoxicating power and indisputable evidence of your wealth. He understood that the benefits of this system distorted the very reality that Southerners lived in.

This empathy didn't mean he accepted their logic or forgave their crimes, for he also thought long and hard about what it must be like to be owned by another person, to have your labor stolen from you, only because of your skin color. "I used to be a slave," Lincoln said of his own miserable, backbreaking childhood, where his father had not spared the lash. He never had to fear being sold down the river, but he knew what *wrong* felt like.

During the war, Lincoln's interest in the experience of Black

Americans allowed him to unlock the lever of Black power—spiritually and physically. "Negroes, like other people, act upon motives," he said, explaining the logic of both the Emancipation Proclamation and the Thirteenth Amendment. "Why should they do anything for us, if we will do nothing for them? If they stake their lives for us, they must be prompted by the strongest motive—even the promise of freedom. And the promise being made, must be kept."

You can empathize without accepting or excusing. Lincoln certainly did.

So did James Baldwin when he tried to understand what made the Southern sheriff attack and beat protesters. "You know," he said, "no one can be dismissed as a total monster. I'm sure he loves his wife, his children. I'm sure, you know, he likes to get drunk. You know after all, one's got to assume he is visibly a man like me." What struck Baldwin was that the sheriffs themselves did not seem to understand what made them do what they did, what drove them to menace and persecution. "Something awful must have happened to a human being to be able to put a cattle prod against a woman's breasts," he said. "What happens to the woman is ghastly. What happens to the man who does it is in some ways much, much worse."

Replacing our anger with empathy doesn't lessen our commitment to justice. It just allows to us to actually see what's happening.

Yet here we have Elon Musk saying, with apparent real belief, that "the fundamental weakness of Western civilization is empathy." What?!

Empathy is as much a practical skill as it is a moral one. Temple Grandin was using it to solve a problem at work.

There was a famous diplomatic crisis during Lincoln's presidency. An American vessel had captured two Confederate "diplomats" aboard a British ship on their way to London. The British felt it was serious violation of international law, and they gave Lincoln seven days to apologize or risk war.

On Christmas Day, his cabinet convened to argue the case. Lincoln wanted to keep the prisoners, but instead of telling his cabinet what to do, he proposed an exercise: Secretary of State William Seward was to take a few hours to put together his best argument for the British position in writing, while Lincoln himself would articulate the American case.

To Seward's surprise, Lincoln conceded almost immediately after hearing Seward read his views aloud. Lincoln had tried to come up with a stronger argument than the British but found, as he tried it on for size, that he could not. "Presidents and kings are not apt to see flaws in their own arguments," one of the staffers who witnessed the exchange later wrote. "But fortunately for the Union, it had a President at this time who combined a logical intellect with an unselfish heart." This was a skill Lincoln had honed as a lawyer—how to understand the opponent's case as well as his own. And because of the unique character of frontier law, Lincoln had worked at different times as defense and prosecuting attorney, had tried cases for the railroads and against them—and thereby learned how to put himself in the shoes of a judge or a jury.

Empathy is about caring. It's also about savvy.

Too often we forget that there even *is* another point of view.

Self-awareness and empathy are an elite combination. They create lifesaving wisdom.

Are some of us naturally better at this than others? Sure, just as some have an aptitude for math or design. But that just means we have to work at it. Lincoln had to *learn* how to apply it in extremely trying situations, with his literal enemies. Elon Musk seems to be trying *not* to learn it, despite his incredible influence and responsibility.

There is no art without empathy. There is no long-term business success without empathy. There is no politics. No compromise, no collaboration, no creativity.

Empathy opens us to everything and everyone.

Be Humble

~

It was 2004, and the cracks in the case for the invasion of Iraq had begun to show. George W. Bush's "Mission Accomplished" speech was already aging poorly.

When pressed on the potential weaknesses of the administration's policies by the journalist Ron Suskind, a top adviser to Bush explained that these criticisms were the feeble understandings of what he dismissed as "the reality-based community," the experts, reporters, diplomats, historians, and academics with their pedantic and "judicious study of discernible reality." This was all naïve and antiquated, the man explained, because America was "an empire now, and when we act, we create our own reality. And while you're studying that reality—judiciously, as you will—we'll act again, creating other new realities, which you can study too, and that's how things will sort out. We're history's actors . . . and you, all of you, will be left to just study what we do."

It was the kind of thing that the Athenians could have said before they sent their ships to Syracuse. Napoleon could have said it before heading into Russia, or Japan's generals, on an island dependent on foreign imports before they started a world war.

The Iraq War, like so many other disasters—military or otherwise—had its roots in hubris.

If study does not result in humility, it's worthless. For the past is nothing if not a catalog of the enormous costs of ego, of impatience, of certainty, of rushing in, of wishful thinking. History is, as one historian said, "the record of unintended consequences." Even just the recent past reminds us: Be prepared. Slow down. Think this through.

Pride goeth before a fall . . .

Perhaps this is why wisdom, as a virtue, is sometimes rendered as *prudence.* Our own experience plus the store of experiences of the past should teach no lesson more clearly than that of our limitations, of human fallibility and the costs of arrogance.

In the run-up to another famous blunder, one of Lyndon Johnson's advisers wrote the president a memo. He began with a quote from Emerson: "Things are in the saddle, and ride mankind." Johnson's "most difficult continuing problem in South Viet-Nam," the aide explained, "is to prevent 'things' from getting into the saddle—or, in other words, to keep control of policy and prevent the momentum of events from taking command." This was hubris from the beginning; events were always in the saddle, and it was not just Johnson but a *chain* of American presidents and generals who believed they could create their own reality in Southeast Asia . . . decisions that were paid for in the blood of American soldiers and the civilians in Vietnam, Laos, and Cambodia.

If only someone could have grabbed any of these folks—from Napoleon to Kissinger to Bush—and said to them, as Oliver Cromwell had famously said, "I beseech you, in the bowels of Christ, think it possible you may be mistaken." The sad thing is that someone had. Many times. They were besieged with criticism, inundated with warnings. The powers that be had access to all sorts of information, but they proceeded anyway.

There was so much history that could have been learned from. So much that didn't need to be learned anew by painful trial . . . and catastrophic error.

Of the fifty-nine epigrams that adorned Montaigne's ceiling, a sizeable percentage address intellectual humility in some way. "If any man thinks he knows anything, he knows nothing," from Paul's letter to the Corinthians. From Ecclesiastes, "All things are too difficult for man to understand them." From Isaiah, "Woe unto them that are wise in their own eyes." From Socrates, "Impiety follows pride like a dog."

What you don't see in Montaigne's *Essays* are many expressions of certitude. No, he's only telling you what he *thinks*. He is supposing, guessing, pondering, etc. It's not that he's hedging, it's that he has the discipline to respect the discipline of learning; he's aware of his limitations, aware of human follies. This is what bothered him most about the bigotry and persecution of his time—the sheer arrogance and certainty of it. How did they *know*?

If your wisdom has not taken you down a peg, then you do not have wisdom.

A student once told Feynman a story about an ape that had fashioned a stick into a tool, discovering that it could be used to get treats that were outside of her cage. To the student, this was a metaphor about our ability to combine knowledge and technology to improve our condition. Feynman had a much more humbling—yet also empowering—slant on it. "What I would learn from your story," he said with a smile, "is that if an ape can make a discovery, so can you."

For all his power and his wisdom, Lincoln knew who was really in the saddle. "I claim not to have controlled events," he wrote in a letter in 1864, "but confess plainly that events have controlled me." He understood, at some level, that he couldn't move soldiers and politicians around like chess pieces. He couldn't snap his fingers and change public opinion or human nature. Many radicals on his own side were constantly frustrated by what they perceived to be his caution and his slowness. But Lincoln understood that transformation not only took time, but that he had to wait for the right opportunities and could not simply will them into existence.

Life had taught him that.

Have you learned that lesson?

It is so easy for knowledge to puff us up. It is so easy for success to make us stupid.

Fools are rarely humble, but brilliant people often are.

It's not that you're *always* wrong, but understand that you always *could* be. It's the irony of wisdom that the smarter you get, the less you need to feel like a smart person. The less you need to be right. The more comfortable you are with uncertainty and ambiguity and, of course, *humility*.

Experience should reduce ego, not enlarge it. Study should make us less certain, not more so.

That was the power of Montaigne's question *Que sais-je?* What do I know? The answer was usually, in fact, almost always: *Not much!* But by embracing humility, we learn. Because if we know little, it means there is lots to learn. Curiosity is an open window. Certainty is a closed door.

Stay open.

Stay humble.

It's the wiser path.

It may well save you from disaster.

Always Stay a Student

He was an old man.

He was the wisest leader of his time.

Yet there he was, leaving the palace, carrying his books.

Where are you off to, a friend asked.

"I'm off to see Sextus the Philosopher," Marcus Aurelius told him, "to learn that which I do not yet know."*

He didn't make the teacher come to him. It was a marvelous thing to see, the friend noted, the king still picking up his tablets and going off to school.

But this is what the wise do. They don't just learn when they're young, but all their lives. They identify *as a student*, not as a person who has attained wisdom. They don't see themselves as better or apart. They are just like everyone else, still learning, needing to be taught.

"Until when is a person obligated to study Torah?" Maimonides asked. "Until the day of one's death." "At no rank,"

---

* As it happens, Sextus was likely the grandson of Plutarch.

General Mattis likes to say, "is a marine excused from study." It doesn't matter if you're a private or a president, a CEO or a summer intern. It doesn't matter if you're young or old, your education is your responsibility. And it's something that continues, indefinitely, endlessly—for there are always new lands to discover, new lessons to learn and old ones to discover anew.

At age twenty, Martin Luther King Sr. (then known as Mike King) realized that segregated schooling had given him a fifth-grade-level education, so he humbled himself and went back and took what was rightfully his. Da Vinci taught himself Latin at age forty-two. At the same age, Neil Peart, then probably the greatest drummer in the world, started taking lessons from Freddie Gruber, a jazz teacher who had worked with many of his peers. "What is a master but a master student?" Peart said with a shrug. "And if that's true, then there's a responsibility on you to keep getting better and to explore avenues of your profession." For her sixtieth birthday, Angela Merkel attended a lecture on nineteenth-century Euro-Asian relations.

Stefan Zweig, unusual for such a well-read man, was not familiar with the works of Montaigne until he was in his late fifties. He found a copy of Montaigne's essays in a cellar while on the run from the Nazis. "Certain authors reveal themselves to us only at a certain age and in chosen moments," Zweig would say in his biography—his final work—of the man who found him at his lowest ebb.

This is why we must remain a student—we don't know what the future holds, what we will need to learn.

Will this sometimes be awkward? To be a beginner again? To have to ask basic questions? To sit in class like everyone else? To admit you were only now learning some classic idea or text? To still be striving when everyone else has given up? Perhaps. But Socrates's indifference to what other people thought of him is fitting here. "If anyone laughs at us for going to school at our age," he said, "I quote Homer: 'Modesty is not good for a needy man.'"

The most critical case of Lincoln's life was actually one where he was basically fired. Lincoln had been hired by McCormick Reaper for his patent expertise and local standing, but he was quickly outranked and outshined by the other lawyers (including Edwin Stanton, his future secretary of war).

Bumped from the case, Lincoln was told he could go home and would be paid anyway. Still, Lincoln decided to stay and observe, even though he was allowed to make no arguments and was deliberately ignored by the other lawyers, who refused even to speak to him, let alone inform him of developments on the case.

It could have been humiliating for a former Congressman, but Lincoln never complained. He just showed up and watched. At the end, he told a friend that he was going home to "study the law." "You stand at the head of the bar in Illinois now," his friend said in surprise. "What are you talking about?" "I do occupy a good position," Lincoln admitted, "and I think I can get along with the way things are going there now. But these college trained men who have devoted their whole lives to study are coming west, don't you see? They study on a single case perhaps for months, as we never do. I'm as good as any of them, and when they get out to Illinois, I will be ready for them!"*

Learning keeps you young, even as wisdom adds years to your life.

So what are you studying? What are you returning to as if you were a beginner?

Every new role, every new phase in life will require and demand new wisdom. Just as our prior success was built on the back of the work we did long ago, what future success are we sowing with our reading, our travels, our questions and deep dives?

It may be true that scientists tend to make their biggest discoveries when they are young. Musicians write most of their biggest hits when they are just starting out. The young are often brilliant, but they are rarely wise. It is only with time and expe-

---

*In 1860, a campaign biographer exaggerated Lincoln's education by claiming he was familiar with the works of Plutarch. When Lincoln saw this in print, he quickly made it true by picking Plutarch up at age fifty-one. Plutarch became one of his favorite authors and this episode one of his favorite funny anecdotes.

rience that one can become fully capable of *understanding* the ideas in their work.

The fact that you're old is not an excuse. After all, Diogenes points out, you're supposed to speed up, not slow down, as you approach the finish line of a race.

Besides, there are some things we can only begin to grasp now. Yusuf Islam/Cat Stevens's song "Father and Son" was originally recorded in 1970, when Yusef was himself just twenty-two years old. But in 2020, he rerecorded the song, pairing his twenty-two-year-old voice in a duet with his now seventy-two-year-old self. The same song, the same lyrics, sung by the same man . . . and yet it is something different and new and deeper. Because five decades of real-life experience, of raising his own children, of living the experiences of both characters, had helped Yusuf better understand his own work and the timeless struggle of one generation to connect with another.

This is why we return to the things we read long ago, why we travel back to places we've already been, why we reconsider the assumptions and beliefs we picked up when we were young.

Mastery.

Remastery.

Discovery.

Rediscovery.

It's still day one. We have still learned only a fraction of what it is possible to know. This should keep us humble. It should also get us excited.

Disce quasi semper victurus
Vive quasi cras moriturus

Learn as if you were going to live forever,
Live as if you were going to die tomorrow.

Stay curious. Stay hungry. Keep learning. Keep growing.

Be a Teacher

~

It was his first day of practice as a pro. Bill Russell walked onto the court as a Boston Celtic, a gangly six-foot-ten rookie on a perennial Eastern Conference powerhouse team, loaded with veteran All-Stars, coming off their tenth straight playoff appearance.

Knowing that playing time was nobody's right, Russell steeled himself for a long and lonely first season. But the first thing that Arnie Risen, the Celtics' four-time All-Star center, told him was, "After practice I have some things to show you."

Here, less than a decade after Jackie Robinson broke the color barrier in baseball, an established white player was taking the time to teach the rookie they both knew was there to take his job. Arnie explained to Russell how the league worked, what to expect from different players. He showed Russell a few moves on the court.

Had he given up? No, as Russell later reflected, it was the

opposite. Arnie Risen "wanted the team to win more than he wanted to hang on." Russell took the starting spot, but together, the two men would win a championship in 1957.

No great athlete is born fully formed. Coaches teach them. Teammates support them. Even rivals and critics, in their own way, help them get better. A debt comes with this, one that cannot be paid back, only forward. That's what Arnie Risen was doing.

It's what we must do too.

Each of us, in our time here, has managed to learn some things. We've read history. We've witnessed some of it. We've made mistakes. We've also had teachers and mentors and friends who have taught us.

Even if we were truly self-made, our knowledge confers responsibility. What we have is special and valuable. It can't be clutched tightly—it must be shared.

To not teach is an injustice!

This was the critical inflection point in the life of Siddhartha Gautama. It was his individual journey that brought him to enlightenment, but what made him the *Buddha* was his decision not to retreat into individual solitude and serenity and instead to try to teach and help others. For nearly half a century, he brought wisdom to men and women across India, and set in motion a tradition of teaching and a coaching tree that survives to this day.

It is also one of the most famous ideas in Western philosophy. We should imagine, Plato said, that we are all chained inside a deep cave, only able to see the shadows of what is happening outside. Now, say that one of us escapes and manages to discover what is happening out in the world. Are they not obligated to return to the cave to explain to the others what they know? To free them both literally and figuratively from their chains and illusions?

Of course they are.

What do you think Plato was doing but paying forward the truths he'd been shown by Socrates? And was not Aristotle paying forward the truths he'd been shown by Plato? This is what it means to be an apostle. Every one of us was taught . . . and now we must teach.

Even if that challenges our very self-interest, even if it sometimes feels like a burden.

Richard Feynman or Madame Curie, like all academics, accepted that their university privileges came with teaching obligations—paperwork, dissertation advising, grad students and their personal problems. They, like all professors, were training their future replacements, just as Gregg Popovich has mentored and advised coaches and executives who have beaten the Spurs and poached his players. Wally Pipp, whom Lou Gehrig replaced in 1925, was in the stands in Detroit the day that Gehrig's streak ended. And just as Pipp had made way for Gehrig, Gehrig was gracious and supportive of Babe Dahlgren, who took his place. "Go on, get out there and knock in some runs," he told him.

Antoninus became Hadrian's successor only on the condition that he train Marcus Aurelius to succeed him. Is that fair? Sure, in the sense that *all* of us will be succeeded by someone. But that doesn't mean he always liked it. Will our ego prevent us from doing our duty?

Wisdom cares about progress, not itself. Each of us is only a vessel—and not a permanent one. It is inevitable that we will all be replaced eventually.

Knowledge is power, as they say, but like the power given to Antoninus, it has strings attached. We owe something to our teachers. We owe something to someone else now too, to future generations. That debt, as Stockdale described it, is *teachership*.

But we are wrong to see this simply as charity, as some onerous moral obligation—we get something out of it. "The process is mutual," Seneca said of mentorship, "for men learn as they teach."

In helping others, we are forced to examine our own thinking, to reflect on our experiences. We sit down and write, putting what was previously intuition into knowledge. And in writing this for someone else, we practice empathy and understanding. Feynman would say that if someone *can't* do this, if they *can't* clearly and simply explain what they know to someone else in simple terms, it's because they themselves don't fully understand what they think they know.

We learn as we teach.

Someone was our mentor. Who are we mentoring? We've had our board of directors. But whose board are we on now?

That's what it's about now.

We have to go back into the cave.

We have to bring others out into the light with us.

Embrace the Mystery

~

The poet John Keats found that the more he learned about existence, the less he understood. The more he tried to grasp or explain the essence of something, the more it escaped him.

The artist's great skill, then, he said, was "negative capability," the ability to be "in uncertainties, mysteries, doubts, without any irritable reaching after fact and reason." He would explain that understanding was like entering a large "Mansion of Many Apartments." The first chambers are simple and bright. He called this "the infant or thoughtless Chamber." As long as we don't think too much, or question too much, we can pleasantly remain there. But the more we explore, the farther we get into the mansion, the more "We are in a Mist," he said. We lose our bearings. We find darkness and confusion. We feel, he said, the "burden of the Mystery."

This, of course, is the world of the artist—especially the poet. The unknown. The ineffable. The majestic. The vastness of human experience. For an artist there is no black and white—even when they paint or photograph in that form.

But wait, isn't wisdom the ability to make things simple? It is. And the simple truth is that *things are complicated*. It would be wonderful if study and mastery led to certainty.

But they most certainly do not.

"I have for some time," Admiral Rickover warned young people, "thought that a few of our present ills stem from this chiding faith in the existence of perfect answers. It requires a degree of maturity to realize that all solutions are partial ones." And that all conclusions are snapshots, estimations, and guesses.

Art, leadership, and enlightenment demand the ability to handle ambiguity. They require a strong tolerance for contradiction. You have to be able to deal with the mystery and the mist. Because they never go away.

When the physicist John Wheeler said that as our island of knowledge grows, so does the shoreline of ignorance, he wasn't just speaking of the endless possibilities of all the things we can learn. He was also speaking of the way that knowledge and bafflement seem to follow each other. Because we are pushing up against our upper limits. Because we are discovering new cases, new situations, new scenarios that demand a reevaluation of everything we thought we knew.

The Eastern philosophers understood this better than their Western counterparts. Who knows what some of those famous koans mean? What *is* the sound of one hand clapping? What *is* Buddha? Perhaps they didn't know either. But there was something about wrestling with koans that led to insight. Their minds were stronger for accepting that logic and paradox have their place.

Confucius once told a student that the secret to wisdom is patience. Later he told another student to stop waiting around and solve his problems quickly. An observant third student objected that the great master had contradicted himself. Surely, only one strategy was the proper one. Confucius shook this pedantry aside. "Ran Qiu is overcautious," he explained, "and so I wished to urge him on. Zilu, on the other hand, is too impetuous, and so I sought to hold him back."

Everybody is different. Every situation is different.

Wisdom is not rigid.

Montaigne said admiringly of Cato that if you struck one of his keys, you had struck them all. This was to say the man was a singular note, in a nice way. But what was so fascinating about Montaigne is that he was the opposite. In his own words, he was "bashful, insolent; chaste, lustful; prating, silent; laborious, delicate; ingenious, heavy; melancholic, pleasant; lying, knowing, ignorant; liberal, covetous, and prodigal." He was a free agent. He changed. He grew. He had flights of fancy. This is what made him intellectually curious in ways that Cato was not. That allowed Montaigne to survive civil strife and bring people together in ways Cato was constitutionally incapable. "If I speak diversely of myself, it is because I look diversely upon myself," he said of his contradictions and complications.

Centuries later, Whitman put it this way:

Do I contradict myself?

Very well then, I contradict myself,

(I am large, I contain multitudes.)

These multitudes cannot tie us up. "The test of a first-rate intelligence," F. Scott Fitzgerald reminds us, "is the ability to hold two opposed ideas in the mind at the same time, and still retain the ability to function."

This would make plenty of fools geniuses, though—believing a bunch of obviously contradictory ideas is also a test of a feeble mind. Naturally, it's a complicated balance.

How about this: If wisdom is not an end state but a process, then we will never actually arrive at full understanding. There will always be unresolved questions, since we are still in the middle of *working things out*. We will have variables for which we haven't yet accounted. We will have pieces that don't fit together.

Can we tolerate the mess?

If we can't, we're only going to make it so far.

A great negotiator once said that people who can't handle uncertainty will get their certainty . . . they just pay for it. Someone who wants and needs things to be simple will simplify things—often at the expense of all the things they could have learned.

The Buddhists spoke of inviting Mara, the god of anger, to tea. We must also sit down with Dionysus, the god of chaos and disorder, from time to time.

Uncertainty is a fact of life. So is contradiction.

Not only is the human heart often in conflict with itself, so is truth!

Don't be jealous of the people who have stripped nuance out of life, who have transcended doubt. They live in a dull, boring, and false world.

The artist revels in the indescribable. The physicist ponders the unseeable. The philosopher considers the unknowable.

This is an art we can practice: Spend some time mulling over complete nonsense. Consume fiction and art and fantasy and myth. Lincoln loved the exactness of Euclid in equal measure to the dark strangeness of the poems of Edgar Allan Poe. We don't know if Lincoln ever read Keats, but they shared a love of the beauty—and complexity—of poetry. It was said that Lincoln could recite nearly all of Robert Burns' by heart. He knew Byron and Shakespeare. He would give all the money he had in the world, he once said, to write something as good as William Knox's poem "Mortality."

Lincoln understood better than anyone the need for nuance— which is also why he staffed his cabinet with politicians who disagreed with him.

Talk to people whose ideas you don't understand. Take them seriously. A fool relies on straw man caricatures of their opponents' arguments so they never have to feel seriously challenged, so they are never faced with the confusing possibility of having to consider two things that might both be true.

A wise person, on the other hand, not only resists the straw man but *steel mans* the ideas they disagree with. They don't focus on the superficial but try to understand and articulate the substance—the strongest parts—of other opinions. They know what they think, but they also have the empathy and the confidence to understand and appreciate what someone else thinks. They can hold both views in their mind, and even if they ultimately favor one, they have the ability to understand the reasons (even if foolish) that someone else believes differently.

This is not just kind and fair . . . it also helps us understand our own views better and resolve the weakest points within them.

Embrace the immensity and the contradictions and the impossibility of knowing.

Be flexible.

Let your mind get comfortable having its boundaries pushed.

Grasp that you will never grasp it all.

Be Self-Aware

Montaigne, a brilliant man, could have been an important politician. He could have made breakthroughs in science or biology. He could have written amazing literature.

Although he dabbled in all these fields, he mostly chose to study . . . himself.

From boyhood, he had been trained, he said, "to see my life reflected in other people's," to really look at how someone lived and what made them tick, whether it was Socrates or some important dignitary in town to visit his father. He was looking at them critically . . . so that he could study himself critically.

This might seem a little pointless, but in the centuries since the Oracle at Delphi proclaimed, "Know thyself," how many people have actually tried? Of all the geniuses and powerhouses of history, how many had a shred of self-awareness? Who was the last person you met who really had it?

Self-awareness is one of the rarest things in the world!

It's a pursuit that takes a lifetime. "I, who make no other profession but getting to know myself," Montaigne said, "find in me such boundless depths and variety that my apprenticeship bears no other fruit than to make me know how much there remains to learn." It was not an egotistical pursuit, but an inherently humbling one; in years of thinking and writing Montaigne barely scratched the surface.

What are your strengths?

What are your flaws?

What do you like? What do you hate? What do you love?

What are the patterns you picked up in childhood?

How does your mind work? *Why* does it work that way?

Who are you, *really*?

These are essential questions, no less so than any of the existential and scientific questions for which we award famous prizes. "One must know oneself," the philosopher and mathematician Blaise Pascal reminds us. "Even if it does not help in finding truth, at least it helps in running one's life, and nothing is more proper."

The unexamined life is not much of a life, practically or otherwise.

To most people, it must not have seemed like Montaigne was working at all. Surely his wife and his friends and neighbors were confused about what he was doing up there in that tower, on those walks, on his rambling travels. Was there a point? Why wasn't he out making money? Or putting his energy into more productive pursuits?

Ambrose Bierce joked that everybody is a lunatic, but only

one who understands their delusions is a *philosopher*. Montaigne understood that philosophy wasn't just contemplating the heavens, it was also spending time contemplating this body we've been given, our consciousness, our lives, our own craziness. He was solving the equation of himself instead of any of the vexing math problems.

By the end of his life, he knew something of his virtues and his flaws, the monstrosities and the miracles and mundanities that he said were within him. He knew his favorite fruit (melon); he knew his favorite sexual position (lying down); he knew who he liked to spend time with (his Boétie, his daughter, his cat); he knew he had a tendency to be lazy; but he also knew that he was at his best when he wasn't overthinking or being too hard on himself.

Do you have the self-awareness to understand where your mastery begins and ends? Where your domain expertise begins and ends? Where your buttons are? What your Achilles' heel is? What makes you tick? What your flaws are?

One of the fascinating things about biographies is how obvious certain personality traits and patterns are in people. The way someone might be kind to their employees but cruel to their relatives. The way someone's downward spiral is clearly linked to a childhood trauma or the way their success was obviously driven by the need to prove something that could never be proved. *What were they thinking? How could they not see this?*

After a couple of hundred pages, you know them better than they seemed to know themselves!

Remarkably good at seeing the vulnerabilities of other powerful, ambitious people, Richard Nixon never seemed to be able to apply this skill to himself. "Ego is something we all have," Nixon once said, without a hint of self-awareness, "and then you either grow out of it or it takes you over. I've grown out of it."

Oh really?

Elon Musk has said he doesn't need to be liked. Come again? It doesn't take a psychologist to see that the man *desperately* wants to be liked. Who would tweet thousands of times a month if they weren't desperate for attention, affection, adulation. It's obvious to everyone . . . but him. And yet how sad it is that despite this need, he looks for that love in all the wrong places.

Even philosophers can be guilty of hypocrisy. Diogenes the Cynic thought Plato was pompous. Invited to a dinner party, Diogenes deliberately tracked dirt in on his shoes, saying that he was stomping on "the vanity of Plato" by soiling his carpets. But Plato, calmer and wiser at least in this instance, could see what was behind Diogenes's scorn for others, something that Diogenes himself so often missed. "How much pride you expose to view," Plato said as he watched this childish performance, "by seeming not to be proud."

We'd rather stare directly at the sun than in the mirror . . .

A person doesn't have to live to age eighty to realize that work is not the most important thing or that we're trying to fill a hole by pretending it is. You should not need to end up all alone, your accomplishments cold comfort, to finally grasp that there is little meaning in money, power, or fame. A little introspection should get you there.

And you probably don't need the "insights" that people credit to psychedelics or shamans. Um, yeah, these epiphanies were available the whole time. They were in literally every philosophy book ever written!

You could have been doing the work in your notebooks, day to day, as Montaigne and Marcus Aurelius had, and gotten there much sooner.

This is why Joan Didion was so reluctant to reduce her notebooks to just a professional tool. Even though she benefited immensely from her compulsion to write and record as an author, she came to see that there was something more profound about these pages she filled on so many mornings, afternoons, and late evenings.

Flipping through scraps of dialogue she had put down at a train station in Delaware, or recounting childhood experiences or facts about pollution in New York City, she wondered why she had bothered to write this all down. Was she ever going to use it? Was it important? Who was this person who had felt the need to record so many seemingly banal details?

Then she realized *that was the point.* "I think we are well advised to keep on nodding terms with the people we used to be," she later observed. "We forget all too soon the things we thought we could never forget." The pages of a journal or a common-place book are a kind of snapshot—of what we're observing or reading but also of ourselves. Long before the feature was available on smartphones, Didion noticed the photo she was taking in the form of her journals was not just showing the front-facing view but was also capturing herself at the same time. "Remember what it was to be me," she said of her journals; "that is always the point."

A journal is a means of self-awareness. Because knowing yourself isn't just about who you are right now (after all, who we are today is a product of all the selves we have been). We have to understand who we were *then* and why we did what we did—that's how we change, that's how we make different choices now, that's how we make amends to others and ourselves.

It would be a shame to spend your whole—your only—life in this body and barely know it. We cannot be strangers to ourselves. It's wonderful to visit foreign lands but not if it means our own interior remains unexplored. Our mind does not need to be a black box. If we wish to free ourselves from habits and biases, we must find a way to see ourselves with perspective, to get to what's underneath, to make sense of the complications and multitudes we contain.

So much wisdom is lost to us because we are ourselves lost . . . and lost to ourselves.

We need empathy for others . . . and empathy for ourselves.

Who we are.

Why we are who we are.

Who we are trying to be.

Know thyself.

Free Yourself

~

Epictetus would have shuddered at the cliché that *knowledge is power*. Especially if he heard it uttered by some aristocrat or a tenured academic—which, sadly, far too many philosophers have been.

Epictetus was born into slavery. His thirty years in bondage left him with a limp for the rest of his life, courtesy of a sadistic owner who tortured him.

Having known *real* powerlessness, he would not have been so glib about freedom or power.

But this is not to say he did not believe, deep in his soul, in the power of wisdom.

At the time, in Rome, many people believed that only freedmen were capable of being educated. In fact, Epictetus said, it was the opposite. Only the educated, he said, *were free*.

Wisdom is freedom.

Someone who doesn't know what's what is slave to impulses, ignorance, and illusions . . . even if they possess incredible worldly power and wealth.

This was an indisputable truth that Epictetus saw every day in the moral disorder and dysfunction of Nero's court, where his master served as a high-profile secretary. There were many things that Epictetus could not legally do, but he managed to direct his own education within the restrictions and in the process freed himself of the self-imposed forms of slavery he saw among the ambitious millionaires and power-hungry schemers around him.

The things he learned, the wisdom he acquired—no one could take this away from him. It was the one thing that was exclusively his. And it was indeed the most priceless and powerful thing in the world.

Even after he was granted his legal freedom, Epictetus lived in a world that was largely out of control. He would be exiled by a paranoid emperor. He would be robbed by a petty criminal. He would be attacked and criticized by people who didn't like what he taught. But Epictetus knew that what he carried in his mind was his forever—no one could take that from him. He was a precious, vulnerable human being, as we all are . . . yet philosophy and wisdom also made him invincible and unconquerable.

And so it goes for us. Study is not just a path to wisdom, it is the path to freedom. And it is, ultimately, its own form of power—even a *higher* power.

There is something poetic about Hadrian, then the emperor, stopping in Nicopolis on his travels through Greece, to attend one of Epictetus's lectures. Was the slave not then the master? Was that not the powerless conquering the powerful?

Hadrian had everything. He could do anything. Yet there he was, after a possession that only Epictetus seemed to have. Marcus Aurelius, a lifelong student of Epictetus and the adopted grandson of Hadrian, contrasted the great conquerors against the great wise men of history, and believed that the thinkers came out the better. Because, he explained, "the philosophers knew the what, the why, and the how. Their minds were their own." It was their example that he sought to follow . . . and so must we.

We are all born equal, with the same flaws, the same anxieties, the same ignorance, the same death sentence—but some of us, through hard work, manage to transcend these limitations. We free ourselves.

From the things that have enslaved and controlled and directed people for all time.

From desires and delusions.

From our impulses and emotions.

From bitterness and frustration and resentment.

We should become *philosophical*, which is to say calm and patient and relaxed.

In 1859, before he was president, before he suffered through the harrowing train ride to Washington on his way to the office where many thought he would be killed on arrival, before the carnage and the violence of the war, Lincoln gave a speech at the Wisconsin State Fair. The subject of the speech was supposed to be agriculture, but Lincoln decided to go a little deeper.

He told the story of an Eastern king who asked his wisest philosophers to provide for him a sentence that would be not just true in each and every situation, but always worth hearing too. "They presented him the words," Lincoln said, "'And this, too, shall pass away.' How much it expresses! How chastening in the hour of pride! How consoling in the depths of affliction! 'And this, too, shall pass away.'"

Did Lincoln know that this story was a core teaching in Buddhist philosophy? Did he know the incredible triumphs and fiery trials that lay ahead? Could he have been morbid enough to sense that it applied to his brief existence on this planet—that he had less than six years left to live, in which to do his work, before he too would pass away?

Marcus Aurelius understood this, writing that we must "keep in mind how fast things pass by and are gone—those that are now, and those to come." The events of the world—good and bad, beautiful or tragic or terrifying—flow past us quickly. None of them is stable; each of them disappears with due time into the rush of the water, and is never seen again. "It would take an idiot," Marcus wrote, "to feel distress or arrogance or anger."

In the immediacy of events, without the perspective of history, an understanding of the nature of things, we are not free. We are overwhelmed. We are subjugated by our fears, by our anxieties, by the zeitgeist.

Overcoming this doesn't just happen. It is incredibly hard work.

Nor is freedom always fun.

"I've had to struggle all my life against my own misapprehensions, my own false ideas, my own distorted perceptions," Joan Didion would say in a famous speech of her own. "I've had to work very hard, make myself unhappy, give up ideas that made me comfortable, trying to apprehend social reality. . . . And that's not easy, it takes work. You have to keep stripping yourself down, examining everything you see, getting rid of whatever is blinding you."

But the inward struggle she is talking about is very different from the one that too many of us engage in—fighting, raging, arguing with the world around us. Like Elon Musk, we wake up and choose violence, plunging, as Seneca said, "headlong into the middle of the flood" of noise and distraction and turbulence. Wisdom, then, is the freedom, we could say, to be at peace instead of war. Do we have it?

We have to free ourselves from mental slavery, for we are the only ones who can do it.

We have to free ourselves from provocation and prejudice and pointless trivialities.

There is no freedom without wisdom, there is no wisdom without freedom.

"The closer people are to the truth, the more tolerant they are of the mistakes of others," Tolstoy once said. Confucius, hearing someone criticize one of his students, replied that the man must be perfect if he had the time to attack someone else. "I," he said, "do not have this much leisure."

After a lifetime, after all our success, after all the blessings that have come our way, if we are still stressed, still harnessed to the same vices, still upset by the same things, still chasing the same things, how free are we?

If wisdom doesn't free us from the prison of delusion and from the addictions that enslave most of humankind, doesn't help us deal with our fellow flawed humans, doesn't help us deal with our own issues, what good is it?

It must give us back our own minds. It must give us power over ourselves.

Be Happy

Elon Musk has money.

He has power.

He has fame.

He has achieved mastery of many subjects.

But would you actually want to be him?

"Being in a big empty house, and the footsteps echoing through the hallway, no one there," Elon Musk described his life in 2017, "and no one on the pillow next to you. Fuck. How do you make yourself happy in a situation like that?"

Instead of working on himself, Elon Musk did what so many brilliant but miserable people do: He just *worked*. Worked and worked and worked. He made billions more dollars, but no lasting relationships. He had a shocking number of children, none of whom he could possibly have much time for. He spent more time picking fights on social media than a teenager, more time than a man with his gifts and his responsibilities could ever justify.

"There were times when I didn't leave the factory for three

or four days—days when I didn't go outside," Musk told a reporter the following year, after a rough period at Tesla. "This has really come at the expense of seeing my kids. And seeing friends."

Not surprisingly, his mental health deteriorated. His relationships suffered. His heart hardened. His worst impulses ran wild. Anything resembling peace or happiness eluded his grasp.

He has described his life as "difficult" and "excruciating." He once compared running a company to "chewing glass and staring into the abyss." With time, he said, the staring is no longer so terrible, but the chewing never ends. This was probably why he told the same reporter that although some of the business problems were easing, "from a personal pain standpoint, the worst is yet to come."

Asked if the storm in his mind was a "happy storm," by another reporter, he lamented that it was not. "No," Musk said. "I can remember even in happy moments when I was a kid that it just feels like there's just a rage of forces in my mind constantly."

Here is a man who can solve every imaginable technical problem, but can't fix his own life, still dealing with the same unaddressed issues from childhood. He has all the money in the world, only to find it can't buy the one thing that's worth the most. His work may be miraculous, but his day-to-day existence is misery.

If self-awareness is rare among the greats, true happiness is rarer still.

Which is strange . . . considering it's sort of the whole point of life.

Aristotle's word for happiness was *eudaimonia*, and it is, he said, the highest expression of human flourishing. "Wisdom produces happiness," he said, "not in the way that medical science produces health, but in the way health produces health."

Wisdom is happiness. Happiness is wisdom. This is not a tautology. No one would be happy not fulfilling their potential, and yet, can one *flourish* without joy and happiness?

In one jaw-dropping exchange, the disgraced investor Sam Bankman-Fried wrote a memo to his girlfriend about why they should not be together. "I make people sad," he explained. "Even people who I inspire, I don't really make happy. And people who I date—it's really harrowing. It really fucking sucks, to be with someone who (a) can't make you happy, (b) doesn't really respect anyone else, (c) is constantly thinking really offensive things, (d) doesn't have time for you, and (e) wants to be alone half the time."

In recovery circles they call such expositions "taking fearless moral inventory," but Bankman-Fried was simply stating facts, not engaging in actual self-awareness. Because someone with real self-awareness could not have seen these observations as anything other than a five-alarm fire—something that needed to be addressed *immediately*. Bankman-Fried's ego (and what seems like profound depression) normalized his attitude, accepting it as a feature and not a bug of his mental powers and lifestyle.

"I asked him once how he can be happy," a friend and early employee asked him. He replied, "Happiness does not matter."

The ancients were suspicious of happiness that was contingent on external factors. They thought that true happiness—happiness based on virtue—could be found in any situation. And while it would be tough to spend years in exile or to deal with a painful illness, they thought that a wise and disciplined person would be able to flourish there too, to find contentment, humor, and love.

For too many people and far too often, happiness is conditional. We think we'll be happy if we can just achieve enough, accomplish enough, acquire enough, be respected enough, meet the right person, live long enough. We feel dread and anxiety and fear because we worry that if certain things happen—or don't happen—then we *can't* be happy.

Remember: The basis of Stoicism is focusing on what you control. A happiness that is dependent on things outside your control is a recipe for unhappiness.

You might not control what other people do or what happens in the world, but you control your disposition in response. Voltaire said that our most important choice is to be in a good mood. We can choose to smile. We can choose hope. We can choose perspective. We can choose a good mood not because everything is going our way, not because the sun is out and the weather is fine, but because we are wise and strong enough to make good of any situation.

The great basketball coach George Raveling, now in his late 80s, has talked about what active work this is. He wakes up each morning, sits on the side of the bed, and gives himself two choices. "George," he says to himself, "you can either be happy or you can be very happy."

"The primary indication of a well-ordered mind," Seneca said, "is a man's ability to remain in one place and linger in his own company." Seneca was not a perfect Stoic or a perfect human being. But his understanding and sympathy for Epicureanism instilled in his work but most importantly in his *life* a happiness that is not always there in the other Stoics. "Of all the things that wisdom provides to help live one's entire life in happiness," Epicurus said, "the greatest by far is the possession of friendship."

By directing your thoughts properly, you can gain not only resilience, but the ability to experience joy, love, and contentment. Seneca had friends. He had fun. He made the best of life, both adversity and achievement. He came to see that the purpose of self-improvement was to be a good friend to others . . . and to yourself.

Peace, like an education, is not something the world gives you, it's something you give yourself. It's possible anywhere, anytime. If what you learn does not give you the tools to achieve this peace, what good is it?

Lincoln experienced depression. He lived through a fiery trial. Humor helped him live through it. So did his philosophical disposition, his sense that these difficulties, like all things, would one day pass. Somehow, still, it's accurate to say that even though Lincoln lived through poverty, through grief, through war, through stress, through a troubled marriage, he was on the whole a happy man—a man content and calm within himself, in the midst of extraordinary circumstances. Indeed, that's one of his most impressive accomplishments, that he was able to be happy *despite it all.*

Leonardo da Vinci had a painful childhood. He didn't always love the politics of the art world, but he was fun to be around. He took great joy in the beauty of the world and infinite folds of the mind. De Gaulle's life was enriched by his selfless love for his disabled daughter. "Life is a school in which we live all our days," Eleanor Roosevelt once wrote, "and by 45, we should know that happiness does not come from the seeking, that it is never ours by right, but that we earn it through giving of ourselves." "The surest way to be happy," she wrote many years earlier in a school essay, "is to seek happiness for others."

When John Stuart Mill had his mental breakdown, he found himself questioning everything: the assumptions he got from his father, the primacy he had put on ideas and rationality. Despite being shaken to the core, he said, "I never, indeed, wavered in the conviction that happiness is the test of all rules of conduct, and the end of life." He was onto something when he realized that it was his intention, his intense desire to be happy and wise, that was the problem. "But I now thought," he said, coming out of his stupor, "that this end was only to be attained by not making it the direct end." You can't attain happiness or wisdom by making it a bull's-eye.

We can create happiness in ourselves by thinking of ourselves less and thinking of others more. We must embrace the paradox that happiness is essential but not something we can *aim* at. We get it indirectly by living well and doing good.

Like wisdom itself, happiness is the result of a process, of doing the right things in the right way. It's something that *ensues* as opposed to something we *pursue*. Instead of trying to *get* it, we're better when we try to *give* it.

Happiness matters. Everyone deserves it.

Suffer into Truth

~

It had been a grueling campaign. It had been a painful few years. Robert Kennedy was about to give a speech in inner-city Indianapolis when he got the news that Martin Luther King Jr. had been shot on a balcony in Memphis.

Another murder. Another light extinguished.

Kennedy was the one who had to break the news to the milling crowds that King, their leader, whom he had known and worked so closely with, was dead. The crowd roiled with anger and despair. He knew what they wanted to do, Kennedy explained, holding back tears. His own brother had been struck down the same way just five years earlier. They wanted to burn and hate and punish. But he also knew personally what a dark and empty road that was.

His prepared remarks woefully insufficient for the moment, Kennedy began to riff, largely inspired by his own grief and a book he had been reading by the classicist Edith Hamilton. "My favorite poet was Aeschylus," Kennedy explained, and then quoted the poet from memory: "'In our sleep, pain, which cannot forget, falls drop by drop upon the heart until, in our own despair, against our will, comes wisdom through the awful grace of god.'"

He urged the attendants to return home and to pray, and offered them an alternative, a chance to take meaning from this terrible experience. "Let us dedicate ourselves to what the Greeks wrote so many years ago," he said, "to tame the savageness of man and to make gentle the life of this world."

All over the country similar crowds turned into mobs, which turned into deadly riots. But not in Indianapolis.

The wisdom that Kennedy drew on in this moment had not come cheap. Kennedy had suffered immensely for it, precisely as Aeschylus had said.

> *Zeus has led us on to know,*
> *the Helmsman lays it down as law*
> *that we must suffer, suffer into truth.*

Learning through experience is more than just getting our hands on things, as important as that is. It's going to mean suffering, failure, heartbreak, loss, sacrifice.

Drip by drip. Disaster to disaster. Moment after moment.

They won't always be lessons we want to learn.

"I've aged from all this wisdom I've never wanted," Volodymyr Zelenskyy said as the criminal invasion of his country dragged on into its third year. "It's the wisdom tied to the number of people who have died, and the torture the Russian soldiers perpetrated. To be honest, I never had the goal of attaining knowledge like that."

Who would?

Yet where would we be if these lessons were not learned?

Not that suffering is always going to be physically painful. Thankfully, it will not always be punctuated with funerals or grief. Darwin was tortured for years, first as he attempted to make sense of the theory he had begun to form and second by its enormous implications.

Two decades passed between Darwin's voyage on the *Beagle* and the publication of *On the Origin of Species*, and while this period was hardly a prison sentence, it was an exhausting ordeal for him. The same went for Katalin Karikó, who toiled away in the bowels of academia as she developed her groundbreaking mRNA research. It took much longer than she expected, required much more sacrifice and struggle than she would have guessed.

Wisdom is never free.

Without someone to codify and communicate the painful lessons of tragedies, of failures, of injustices, we can't prevent them from happening again. This is partly the definition of leadership, to channel the sum of one's life and personal sufferings in a moment of crisis to help other people through it. It is also the definition of art. "A writer—and I believe, generally all persons," Borges reminds us, "must think that whatever happens to him or her is a resource. All things have been given to use for a purpose, and an artist must feel this more intensely. All that happens to us, including our humiliations, our misfortunes, our embarrassments, all is given to us as raw material, as clay, so that we may shape our art."

Everything that happens to us is practice. Everything is a potential insight into the human experience.

Lincoln was not destined for an easy life. His pain and struggle affected him profoundly and never left him. Friends noted that even during a joyous occasion, Lincoln could not help but return to a melancholic state; "his features would at once bespeak a kind of sadness as indescribable as it was deep." Melancholy, they said, *dripped from him as he walked.*

But this sadness, born from suffering, gave him something that he never could have found in books. In fact, it was a piece he came to see as missing from all his readings, the way that biographers smoothed over the struggle and setbacks of great men, "never once hinting at failures or blunders." His disposition may have been shaped by immense suffering, but it was also what gave him the ability to see when all was dark, continue when all was bleak, and avoid sectarianism and hatred. And this was not only to save the republic, but to bring it ever closer to the true meaning of its creed.

The young think that life is all rainbows and sunrises. The old know that it is full of pain and suffering. There is freedom in this understanding, and power in the experience. When Lincoln ran for office for the first time, he told voters that defeat was not something he feared, having been "too familiar with disappointments to be very much chagrined." Churchill also understood that this pain was power, saying that each of us must go into the wilderness if we hope to create *psychic dynamite*.

But it's also true that knowledge can be what sends us into the wilderness; it can isolate us and cause us suffering. It's hard being a prophet. It's painful, sometimes, to be right. Ignorance is a kind of bliss. Wisdom, then, is intertwined with suffering.

We have to remember that all suffering is relative. Viktor Frankl, who survived Theresienstadt, Auschwitz, Dachau, and Türkheim, took pains to acknowledge this. Suffering is like a gas, he said; it expands to evenly fill the room it is in. This means that it is unavoidable and consumes a person, whether we're talking about a gruesome injury or a childhood memory, a failed relationship, a long apprenticeship, or a failed political campaign. Whatever it is, it's happened to us, and we feel it deeply.

The only consolation is the wisdom that it creates and the lessons it teaches.

"Progress is to be measured by the amount of suffering undergone," Gandhi said. "The purer the suffering, the greater is the progress." Through suffering, we are exposed to truth—truths about the world, about ourselves, about what we're capable of. The key word here, though, is *exposed*.

Because nothing says we *have* to learn from our suffering. Plenty of people don't.

They deny. They blame. They resent.

Ego doesn't learn. That's not what it does. It protects the self from *having* to learn.

This is why plenty of suffering leads to nothing, becomes nothing, is made meaningless and destructive . . . by choice.

The critical question of life is: What will we take from our experiences? Will our suffering make us better or worse? Wiser or more cynical? Will we prove ourselves worthy of it?

We don't have to like adversity.

We don't need to glamorize it.

If we can prevent it, we should. It is not something we need to seek out.

But certainly we should never be surprised by it.

When suffering finds us—and it will—we have to take what it gives us.

We just have to survive it, endure it, understand it.

We suffer, that's unavoidable. Whether truth comes from it, that's on us.

Laugh

~

It was another moment when it seemed like the war would be lost. It had been one string of disasters after another.

When Lincoln called his cabinet together in the fall of 1862, they probably expected more bad news. Or another round of arguments about the slavery question, on which his cabinet remained divided. Each had something serious they needed to talk to the president about, their own agenda with which they intended to steer the meeting.

Instead, as they filed into the office, they found Lincoln reading. Looking up at them and smiling, Lincoln asked if they knew the work of the humorist Artemus Ward. "Let me read you a chapter that is very funny," Lincoln said.

The cabinet was not amused, nor did any of them enjoy the juvenile jokes in the chapter that Lincoln read aloud. But Lincoln—whose laugh, it was once said, resembled the neigh of a wild horse—enjoyed it so much that he continued, reading a second chapter. "Gentlemen, why don't you laugh?" Lincoln asked them. "With the fearful strain that is upon me, day and night, if I did not laugh I should die, and you need this medicine as much as I do."

Then, having amused himself a little and—as intended—caught his cabinet off guard, he moved to his real purpose and proposed what would become the Emancipation Proclamation, one of the most serious and significant policy ideas in human history.

Seneca, for his part, actually said laughter was the central part of wisdom, and to make his point he contrasted the examples of two famous ancient philosophers, Democritus and Heraclitus. "For the latter," Seneca explained, "whenever he went forth into public, used to weep, the former to laugh; to the one all human doings seemed to be miseries, to the other follies. And so we ought to adopt a lighter view of things, and put up with them in an indulgent spirit; it is more humane to laugh at life than to lament over it."

Will our understanding of the world break us or make us shake our head? Will we laugh or cry?

Lincoln understood that humor was a powerful tool. That it not only relieved tension, but was an effective way of making a point.

Before the outset of the Civil War, when a politician advised Lincoln to cede various forts to the South to avoid provoking a conflict, he told a funny story from Aesop, about a woman who wanted to marry a lion. Her parents were concerned the lion would hurt her, so in exchange for their consent, they asked the lion to remove his claws and teeth. When he did, they promptly killed him. The politician laughed at Lincoln's story but insisted that this was "not altogether a satisfactory answer."

In fact, it was.

Lincoln had pointed out the absurdity of appeasement indirectly—using humor as a tool. Whether that politician understood was irrelevant, because everyone else got it. For Lincoln this was a well-honed technique. As a congressman, when political dinners would get heated, Lincoln was known to set down his silverware, say, "That reminds me," and begin one of his silly stories. His friends knew to prepare for "explosions" of laughter, and that rarely would the conversation return to the contentious topic. In the political environment of the day, Lincoln was constantly prodded to parrot racist beliefs. He was quite adept at dodging these traps, and often buried incredibly subversive beliefs within his remarks.

"If a white man wants to marry a negro woman," Lincoln joked to a reporter, "let them do it—if the negro woman can stand it." He was almost vicious in using humor to mock his racist opponent, Stephen Douglas, joking that while he had never been inclined to marry a Black woman, "Douglas and his friends seem to be in great apprehension that they might, if there were no law to keep them from it." And when he was asked outright to condemn "miscegenation" during the war, Lincoln explained with a smile that he could not because it was "a democratic mode of producing good Union men, and I don't propose to infringe on the patent."

A laugh helps the truth land better. It's disarming. It often goes over the heads of the people you didn't want to offend anyway. That's the art of the jester, isn't it?

People didn't always get Lincoln's sense of humor or appreciate his stories. Fools are rarely funny, not on purpose, anyway. In 1864, some opponents of Lincoln actually held up signs at the convention that said, "No More Vulgar Jokes." There's something tragic about this—hundreds of thousands of people were dying on the battlefield and they were upset by dirty jokes? These were fragile, foolish people.

And some of his stories actually were pretty filthy, as he himself admitted. A book of his humor, he once said, "would stink like a thousand privies." In one story, Lincoln told of a prank where he tried to shit in a sleeping friend's hat . . . only to find that his friend, anticipating it, had switched out his hat for Lincoln's own.* Did he actually do this? Lincoln stole like an artist when it came to jokes, grabbing from all sorts of sources, putting his own spin on them, changing them to fit the purposes of the moment.

---

*In *Meditations*, Marcus Aurelius tells a joke about a rich man who filled his house with so many valuables "that he had no place to shit." Scatological jokes (and curse words) have always been funny.

His cabinet was often annoyed by his stories, finding them unseemly or unimportant. They missed the point—not just of what he was doing, but of life in general too. But "What's so funny? I don't get it" is a much more revealing thing to say than the person thinks.

It takes intelligence to understand a situation, wisdom to see what's humorous about it.

These days, most poetry is very serious and emotional, but a lot of the ancient stuff was filthy and funny. Shakespeare wrote seventeen comedies, and even his dark plays all have laugh lines. Seneca wrote a whole analogical essay lampooning the emperor who had banished him. Its title, *Apocolocyntosis*, seems serious, but translation—*The Pumpkinification of (the Divine) Claudius*—reveals the biting and hilarious satire that it was. Churchill was, of course, hilarious, famous as much for his bons mots as for his soaring oratory.

It takes a mastery of language and emotion and even empathy to be able to communicate the truth while bringing out laughter or a smile in another person on command. And what a valuable skill this is, essential to leadership and to friendship. To be able to cheer someone up. To be able to make them feel better about something. To help them calm down.

Funny people are phosphorescent. They light up the world.

We know that power corrupts, we know that it distorts. This is why a good sense of humor about *oneself* is important too. Asked for a blood sample, Churchill told his doctor, "You can use my finger, or my ear, and, of course, I have an almost infinite expanse of arse." No one was quicker to point out his gangly or unusual appearance sooner than Lincoln himself. He liked to tell a joke about an ugly man on a mission to find and kill someone worse off than himself. When the man found the future president, Lincoln said, busting up, Lincoln tore open his shirt and said, "If I am uglier than you, then blaze away."

At the absolute height of his power, literally as the Confederate capital at last fell to the Union army, Lincoln was still joking about his own limitations. Pointing out the humbling nature of the soldiers' travel delays as they attempted to rush Richmond, Lincoln told one of his final jokes about a man who had come seeking an appointment to some high-ranking foreign position. When Lincoln turned him down, the man asked for a lower position, and when he turned him down again, he asked to be made a customs officer. Turned down for a third time, the man finally asked Lincoln if he could have a pair of pants that were lying over a chair in the office. "Ah," Lincoln said with a laugh. "It is well to be humble."

Life will humble us. Frustrate us. Confuse us. Confound us. We can get angry about this. We can rail against it. Or we can find it funny.

Life is painful and absurd.

It's also laughable and ridiculous.

How we choose to see it is everything.

Don't Lose the Wonder

There was one question that mattered more than others, Feynman once told a struggling postgrad. A matter of first principles that the student—trying to decide if a life in theoretical physics was for him—needed to get to.

"Go look at an electron microscope photograph of an atom," he told him. "Don't just glance at it. It is very important that you examine it very closely. Think about what it means."

"Okay," the student said.

"And then answer this question," Feynman went on. "Does it make your heart flutter?"

"Does it make my heart flutter?" the student asked, confused.

It's a yes or no question, Feynman said, as he concluded the lesson. *Don't overthink it.*

Why does it matter if an atom makes your heart flutter? Because as Aristotle had said, philosophy *begins in wonder.* No one can accomplish greatness in any field if they are not driven by love and fascination and genuine reverence. Nor can anyone continue in their pursuit of wisdom if, with the knowledge they acquire, they become jaded and cynical.

Curiosity is the desire to know what's on the other side of the hill. Wonder is the highest form of that curiosity, what propels us to understand the universe, to produce poetry and art, to explore the depths of human knowledge, to seek answers to the fundamental questions of existence. Wonder is what lifts us up, keeps us going, makes life worth living.

A sunset. A leaf. A bug that's evolved over millions of years to *look* like a leaf. The smell of rain on concrete. The pyramids. A passage in a book or a scene in a play that gives you goose bumps.

The world is filled with wonders, filled with almost unimaginable, almost absurd things.

Imagine the first time a European laid eyes on a kangaroo! Imagine the first time a native person saw a European step onto a beach wearing a suit of armor!

One of the most transcendent experiences of Lincoln's life was a brief trip to Niagara Falls in 1848. "It calls up the indefinite past," he wrote rapturously. "The eyes of that species of extinct giants, whose bones fill the mounds of America, have gazed on Niagara, as ours do now. Co[n]temporary with the whole race of men, and older than the first man, Niagara is strong, and fresh to-day as ten thousand years ago. The Mammoth and Mastodon—now so long dead, that fragments of their monstrous bones, alone testify, that they ever lived, have gazed on Niagara."

Lincoln was equally fascinated by our relationship to and with nature. "Every blade of grass is a study," he marveled. "And not grass alone; but soils, seeds, and seasons—hedges, ditches, and fences, draining, droughts, and irrigation—plowing, hoeing, and harrowing—reaping, mowing, and threshing—saving crops, pests of crops, diseases of crops, and what will prevent or cure them—implements, utensils, and machines, their relative merits, and [how] to improve them—hogs, horses, and cattle—sheep, goats, and poultry—trees, shrubs, fruits, plants, and flowers—the thousand things of which these are specimens—each a world of study within itself."

It was this fascination that spurred his earliest political efforts. He envisioned an America linked together by canals, railroads, and navigable rivers. The wonder of man was his ability not just to labor but to improve at his labors, and to improve the world around him in so doing. Nature, to Lincoln, wasn't just something to look at, but something that could teach, something whose power could be directed, something that, ultimately, could be mastered.

It should not surprise us then that Lincoln not only created the Department of Agriculture, but also created what was effectively the first national park in the world, protecting Yosemite "for public use, resort and recreation . . . inalienable for all time."

The process of play, exploration, going to beauty, is an essential part of science, Feynman held. Talking to students about

Descartes's discoveries about rainbows, Feynman would remind them that it was very easy to miss the most important part of Descartes's breakthrough—what allowed him to get to the bottom of the phenomenon. "I would say his inspiration," Feynman said with a smile, "was that he thought rainbows were beautiful."

Yet the sad feature of intelligence and study, for many people, is actually a collapse of wonder. "For in much wisdom is much grief," the unnamed author of Ecclesiastes tells us. "He that increaseth knowledge increaseth sorrow."

We figure stuff out. We dispel myths. We solve mysteries. We find that there was, in fact, nothing at the end of the rainbow. Slowly, steadily, we poke holes in every truth that we were handed down, we dismantle every understanding that came before us, until what is left? We learn that what we were told as children wasn't true. Much of the history we were taught was a lie. Naturally, we become cynical.

A fool does this when they study the past, missing the subtle but always present reality *that things could have gone differently.* The unlimited possibilities of the past and the future should make our hearts flutter. They should fill us with wonder and gratitude, hope and determination.

Sartre talked about the temptation to confuse disenchantment with truth. Without a steady sense of wonder, we can easily slip into a kind of nihilism. It's good to be skeptical, but Goethe writes pityingly in *The Sorrows of Young Werther* of the person who "imagines everything to be so small, because you are yourself so small."

We cannot allow ourselves to be disillusioned . . . even though the very purpose of education is to disabuse us of our illusions.

Beginning in wonder is in some ways the easy part. The hard part is *maintaining* that wonder as we go through the work of a lifetime.

The world is hardly all rainbows and waterfalls. It takes immense courage and strength to continue to find beauty in a world where so many ugly things happen, when they have happened *to* you. Maya Angelou was subjected to such horrible sexual violence as a small child that she lost her ability to speak.

"Out of this evil," she said, "which was a dire kind of evil, because rape on the body of a young person more often than not introduces cynicism, and there is nothing quite so tragic as a young cynic, because it means the person has gone from knowing nothing to believing nothing. In my case I was saved in that muteness, you see, in the sordida, I was saved. And I was able to draw from human thought, human disappointments and triumphs, enough to triumph myself."

It was ultimately poetry and the beauty of art that brought her out of this darkness, along with the teacher who pushed her to begin reciting it. "You do not love poetry," they told her, "not until you speak it." Her own poems and fiction would not shy away from discussing the painful realities of the human experience. Yet still she rose, yet still her work possessed a hopefulness and light.

In her most famous poem, which she read at the presidential inauguration in 1993, she echoed the same wonder and images that Lincoln had used:

> A Rock, A River, A Tree
> Hosts to species long since departed,
> Marked the mastodon,
> The dinosaur, who left dried tokens
> Of their sojourn here
> On our planet floor

Still, her heart fluttered. Still, she could look at each new day and say, "Good morning," and mean it.

You cannot allow the events of life to destroy your hope. Nor can you allow knowledge and facts to do it either.

"Let me ask you something," Feynman said to that student considering his future. "Think back to when you were a kid. When you were a kid, did you love science? Was it your passion?"

"As long as I can remember," the student replied.

"Me too," Feynman said. "Remember, it's supposed to be fun."

So is life. Not always, not every minute, but as a whole, it must be.

Grasp the Essence

~

In 1863, one of America's most famous men stood up to address the thousands of mourners gathered at Gettysburg. There on hallowed ground this worthy peer of Demosthenes spoke of the battle that had taken place not far from where they stood, memorializing the heroes who had died there.

The audience was spellbound and deeply moved—many to tears.

But you have never heard this speech.

It was actually after Edward Everett, the day's main speaker, had finished his two-hour address that Lincoln rose, a ceremonial afterthought, put on his spectacles, and, removing a scrap of paper from his pocket, gave a quiet speech that he believed no one would remember. It was just 271 words—and not many big ones.

The crowd was caught off guard. Lincoln's speech was shorter even than the prayer that had opened the morning, and so when he turned to finish, they weren't quite sure if more was to come. But then the applause came, and when it did, according to one diary, it was "no cold, faint, shadow of a kind reception—it was a tumultuous outpouring of exultation, from true and loving hearts. . . ."

Everett knew greatness when he heard it. "I should be glad," he told Lincoln, "if I could flatter myself that I came as near to the central idea of the occasion, in two hours, as you did in two minutes."

The success of the Gettysburg Address is not rooted in the fact that it was short, though it was. On that battlefield, and on battlefields across the country, from Vicksburg to Shiloh to Hampton Roads, Americans had been fighting a war whose purpose was not quite clear. For four score and seven years—in fact much longer than that—American political parties had been clashing in an endless series of debates and decisions: Nullification. Popular sovereignty. The Fugitive Slave Act. Dred Scott. States' rights.

All this struggle. Then all this death.

Why? What was this for? Why did it matter?

Lincoln got his arms around it in a few beautiful sentences that made it all very clear: America was a *nation*—he used that word five times—and it should not be torn apart. That nation had been "conceived in liberty, and dedicated to the proposition that all men are created equal." Slavery was anathema to that. On some level, every American knew this. The war was a test of whether they really believed it.

Lincoln had chosen not so much to commemorate the

cemetery that they had come to open, but to use the occasion to redefine what America was and every citizen's role in it. In those 271 words, he made no references to generals or topography, and did not say the name of the place they were at—he did not even specifically mention slavery or secession.

Instead, he sought to explain the national project in transcendent moral terms, thus consecrating a constitutional disagreement and a bloody conflict as a cause worthy of the full measure of one's devotion, toward a "new birth of freedom" so that "government of the people, by the people, for the people, shall not perish from the earth."*

This was not an easy task. In fact, it was the kind of "hostile act" that Joan Didion was referring to when she talked about great writing. Few Americans at the outset of the war believed that they were fighting for the freedom of Black people, most of the soldiers who died at Gettysburg would not have said they wanted racial equality. Lincoln was changing what the war was about right beneath their noses.

---

*In 1861, Alexander Stephens, vice president of the Confederacy, gave a longer speech but, to his horrible credit, did manage to express the essence of the Southern position with clarity that a century and a half of Lost Cause mythology has not been able to erase: "Our new government['s] . . . foundations are laid, its cornerstone rests upon the great truth, that the negro is not equal to the white man; that slavery—subordination to the superior race— is his natural and normal condition. This, our new government, is the first, in the history of the world, based upon this great physical, philosophical, and moral truth."

And he had been practicing for this moment his entire life—his fascination with languages, those words he had written onto boards as a child, with a pen made out of buzzard feathers, the love for the Declaration of Independence, which he knew all but by heart. "For the simplicity on this side of complexity, I wouldn't give you a fig," Oliver Wendell Holmes Jr., who fought for that cause that Lincoln evoked and was grievously wounded at Antietam and Chancellorsville, said. "But for the simplicity on the other side of complexity, for that I would give you anything I have."

The simplicity and clarity of the Gettysburg Address were not singular, nor an accident. Lincoln worked on the speech for months, and it was the descendant of the countless speeches he'd been giving since the 1850s as well as the Euclidean proofs he had worked out in his notebooks. As late as the morning of, he was still revising and refining. When it came time to speak, he had it perfect—there was not one word out of place, nothing to add, or subtract.

But more than just the language, the Gettysburg Address was an expression of Lincoln's genius, his ability to get to the "nub" of a subject, as his law partner had said—and more impressively, to be able to *explain* it.

Most Americans had not understood why the Kansas-Nebraska Act, as rammed through by Lincoln's political rival Stephen Douglas, mattered. But Lincoln knew in an instant that it transformed slavery from an institution in decline into a growth industry, a political flashpoint that would bring the nation to a crisis. This is what Lincoln hammered at over and over again in his famous debates with Douglas, which, while far longer than his Gettysburg Address, had the effect of galvanizing the Republican Party into a force that could take the presidency.

Throughout the war, Lincoln was continually exasperated by the inability of otherwise smart people to grasp the central issues of the war and win it. "He whose wisdom surpasses that of all philosophers," he had said, quoting the Bible, "has declared that 'a house divided against itself cannot stand.'" "Union is strength," he said before the war. And when war finally did come, he saw it for what it was and refused to accept the framing of the radicalized, fratricidal slave interests.

This was a *rebellion*, he said hundreds of times in speeches and letters. There was no such thing as "the South," he reminded them. The "so-called Confederate States of America," as he referred to it, did not exist and had no legal status. The "Union" was not some temporary thing but a sacred, unbreakable pact from which America the *nation* was formed.

In fact, just a few days after the victories at Gettysburg and Vicksburg, Lincoln had given an extemporaneous speech to a crowd that had gathered outside the White House. "How long ago is it?—eighty odd years—since on the Fourth of July for the first time in the history of the world a nation by its representatives, assembled and declared as a self-evident truth that 'all men are created equal,'" he said, clearly presaging the more famous remarks he would make four months later. "Now, on this last Fourth of July just passed . . . we have a gigantic Rebellion, at the bottom of which is an effort to overthrow the principle that all men were created equal."

That was his frustration with General George Meade in the aftermath of the great victory at Gettysburg. Meade had wired that he had repelled Lee from Maryland and thus driven the enemy "from our soil." Lincoln was stupefied. "Will our generals never get that idea out of their heads?" Lincoln said in frustration. "The whole country is our soil."

People miss the point. They miss the forest for the trees. Their preconceived notions blind them, their minds are too full to take on the right information. They *can't tell what's what.* "To see what is in front of one's nose needs a constant struggle," Orwell said. One of the reasons we keep notebooks, he said, is that it helps us keep track of things—it helps us hold on to truth when we are surrounded by lies, by chaos, by conflicting opinions.

"*Lee's* Army, and not *Richmond*, is your true objective point," Lincoln reminded his generals when they came to him repeatedly with plans to take the enemy's capital. They were crushing a rebellion, not trying to acquire territory. If we press Lee, Sheridan said to Lincoln in 1865, he'll surrender. *Let the thing be pressed*, Lincoln wired back.

The purpose of wisdom is not to be able to hold an enormous catalog of facts in your head. It's to be able to distill these facts to decipher what they mean. To get to the essence of an issue, a problem, or a story. *To see the here and now, the only thing that accounts.*

Lincoln's second inaugural address was another short one—the shortest in American history.* In it, he explains the cause of the war clearer than anyone has, before or since.

Four years ago, he told the country, we stood here dreading the specter of a civil war. "Both parties deprecated war, but one of them would make war rather than let the nation survive," he said, "and the other would accept war rather than let it perish." Why did one side want war? "One eighth of the whole population were colored slaves, not distributed generally over the Union, but localized in the southern part of it," he explained. "These slaves constituted a peculiar and powerful interest. All knew that this interest was somehow the cause of the war."

How many people have tried to make it more complicated since!

Lincoln would not dance around what had caused the war, but he also knew that blame was different than guilt. The North had once participated in slavery, had sold slaves south, had profited via its banking and shipping interests, had avoided the

---

* The fact that both the Gettysburg Address and his second inaugural address can fit on panels in the Lincoln Memorial is a testament to their distillation.

political problem as inconvenient and not worth the trouble. All were responsible. All were implicated. If the suffering and the scourge of war must continue for a little longer as repayment for their sins, that was out of their control. But what was before them, as the war came to its inevitable close, was this:

> With malice toward none, with charity for all, with firmness in the right as God gives us to see the right, let us strive on to finish the work we are in, to bind up the nation's wounds, to care for him who shall have borne the battle and for his widow and his orphan, to do all which may achieve and cherish a just and lasting peace among ourselves and with all nations.

And with that address, unlike at Gettysburg, he knew his speech had done his job, believing it would hold up better than anything else he had ever said. "Lots of wisdom in that document, I suspect," he said of it.

And simple wisdom too, hard won but clear enough for a schoolchild . . . deep enough that we are still wrestling with his meaning and his call today.

Our job is to make things clear. To find what is important and discard the rest. We must do the work to make the complex simple . . . and keep what's simple, simple . . . but no simpler.

Nietzsche was half joking but completely right when he said that the Stoics were sometimes superficial *out of profundity*.

But he's right.

We need to see what's in front of us.

It's the rarest thing.

It is the only thing.

Pass the Final Test

~

As a philosopher and a playwright, Seneca knew.

He knew that he'd messed up. He knew he'd been hypocritical. He knew he had stayed too long in Nero's service and that in so doing, he had undermined his philosophy. He knew he had debased himself as he enriched himself.

Yet he also knew that audiences will forgive a flawed character—indeed, flaws in the plot itself—if there is redemption. "Life is like a play," he tells Lucilius in one of their letters; "just give it a good ending."

Seneca was late in walking away from Nero. He was late in turning on the deranged emperor. But it was also what set up the final act. And when the goons came to kill him, as they had for Cicero, he was ready with the performance of a lifetime.

"Who knew not Nero's cruelty?" he said to his weeping friends, who were surprised by the death sentence. Seneca didn't try to run. He stepped forward bravely. He had the perfect wisdom. Why weep over this part of life, he said to his wife with a smile, thinking of that contrast between Heraclitus and Democritus, if the whole thing calls for tears?

But what of the sadness that death leaves behind? Seneca, who had buried a child and many friends, had written some of his best work on grief. Who would want their memory to torture their friends and loved ones after they were gone? We want them to think of us and smile. We want them to think of us and do good. *I leave you my example,* he said to his friends, *as my final gift.*

Why wasn't he afraid? Why didn't he tremble as each flawed method of execution failed—first the slitting of his veins, then the poison? Practice had steeled the man for the moment. *To philosophize,* Cicero—who himself was put to death by assassins on a dusty road outside Rome—had written, *is to learn how to die.*

In fact, philosophy had taught Seneca the most important lesson about our mortality: Death is not something we do once, at the end of life. In fact, Seneca knew that *life is death.* We are dying every day, Seneca understood, for every moment that ticks by on the clock is dead and gone. So is the person we were in that moment. He understood that he had been in this situation before, as we all are, for we don't die once but countless times, with a shrug. The death to be worried about is not the one you meet as an old man in exile, but the one you refused to see when you were young and thought you had all the time in the world.

When the end for him finally came in the steam bath, where he was sent to be suffocated, Seneca never complained, never wavered. And then soon enough he was gone.

The example he left to his friends would live on far after him.

It would outshine the flaws of his middle age, soften his hypocrisy, and cover the holes in his story.

We can mess up so much in life . . . but we should try to get this last thing right.

It is the final test of all wisdom.

Feynman. Lincoln. Montaigne. Joan Didion. Socrates. Da Vinci. The Wright brothers.

What do they all have in common?

They all died. They all saw death up close. Not just at the end, either. Feynman buried his wife at age twenty-seven. Cicero's beloved daughter, Tullia, died giving birth in the prime of her life.

Joan Didion, who grew up chanting, as many Christians do, that "in the midst of life we are in death," would watch her husband drop dead mid-sentence in front of her and attend her daughter's funeral only two years later.

Lincoln lost his mother, his sister, and then two sons. Just a week before his own death, before he too would be embalmed and shipped home by rail, like countless soldiers who had given the last full measure of devotion on those great battlefields, Lincoln had recited from memory for his guests Longfellow's poem "By the Fireside":

> There is no flock, however watched and tended,
> But one dead lamb is there!
> There is no fireside, howsoe'er defended,
> But has one vacant chair!

Life comes at you fast. It will break you open.

What use is wisdom if not to help us here?

To give us perspective, to give us strength, to give us understanding about the hardest thing that we alone among the animals are given to contemplate.

"Premeditation of death is a premeditation of freedom," Montaigne wrote. "He who has learned how to die has unlearned how to be a slave. Knowing how to die frees us from all subjection and constraint."

Think of how many people feel a daily dread about death. What scares them the most is the thing they know the least about. *I don't want to think about it* . . . and yet they do, and it's never good thoughts. Nor are they the only ones whose lives are warped by their ignorance about death. Think of the people who, because they are afraid of dying, because they want to live forever, will do *anything* to stay alive. They thus degrade and make worthless the life they have. Or they miss out on so much life because they refuse to risk losing it. They miss out on life because they are chasing immortal fame.

If philosophy cannot free us from this prison of anxiety and fear, if it cannot give us back the gift of the present moment, what good is it?

We can see the freedom that Montaigne was talking about in the final moments of Epicurus, which were profoundly happy despite his serious illness. Today we think of Epicurus as a pleasure lover, but in truth, he was someone who worked to free himself from self-inflicted pain—that is, the *spiritual* pain we add on top of our symptoms. Death is not terrible, he came to understand from his considerable thinking on the topic, it is *the opinion that death is terrible that is the terrible thing*. He didn't control that life would cease, but suffering in existential fear about it was up to him.

After all, what would be so bad about *not* being alive? It didn't bother you before you were born!

Again, this is why we turn to philosophy—to help us make sense of the human condition, to help us resolve the most nagging and painful of thoughts. Lucretius, a poet very much influenced by Epicurus, found himself saddened, constantly, at the thought of dying and leaving behind his children. "Never again will your dear children race for the prize of your first kisses," he wrote, summarizing the joy that all parents feel, "and touch your heart with pleasure too profound for words." It was a little insight from Epicurus's teachings that helped him transcend this pain that could have easily paralyzed him: "You will not care, because you will not exist."

Our death is not a loss, for we lose ourselves along with it.

Memento mori.

Remember, you are mortal.

Which means you must master the *ars moriendi*, the art of dying.

All the wisdom of the past was aimed, in some way, at this

final lesson. All of it, ultimately, provides us with examples of how to do it.

Cicero, resigned but not afraid, resting his hand on his chin as he often did while lost in thought, looked his killers in the eye. "There is nothing proper about what you are doing," he said to them, "but do try to kill me properly."

Montaigne lost his brother in an accident (playing tennis of all things), was deeply affected by the death of his best friend, Étienne de La Boétie, at age thirty-two, and had his own near-death experience. At age fifty-nine, the death that had first danced on Montaigne's lips after his accident would return. Montaigne had written about the fear of death. Was he afraid? He had not lived in fear. He had not been afraid to question. He had not been afraid of himself. He had plunged himself into the unknown. He had made nothing off limits. "Let us deprive death of its strangeness," he had written; "let us frequent it, let us get used to it . . . at every instant, let us evoke it in our imagination under all its aspects."

Indeed, he was no stranger to death. An accident that ultimately changed his life had nearly cut it short. Montaigne had lived through terrible outbreaks of the plague, the worst of which had claimed a third of the population of Bordeaux. He had seen massacres and executions. He had buried all but one of his beloved children. He knew there was no place or time that death could not find a person, that it hung over him and all of us like the sword of Damocles.

From these meditations on death, he had come away with a sense of urgency. He left nothing undone, he said, put off nothing until tomorrow. He said his goodbyes when he could. He wanted, he said, for death to find him planting his cabbages, not worrying about mortality or the state of his garden, simply enjoying the moment he was in.

He had retreated from the dissolution and chaos of his time and found stability and strength . . . in himself. That's what this had all been for, all been leading up to—as it is for every mortal being. With equanimity and poise.

Montaigne had always admired those who could joke about death, who could meet it with a laugh. Now, as the quinsy was killing him, paralyzing his tongue, he would need to make every word count. Did he appreciate the irony that one of history's great talkers was finally being silenced? Could he make light of it?

If we know Montaigne at all, we must think yes, he went to his death curious and in good humor. Deprived of being able to tell a joke, he would have laughed to himself.

On September 13, 1592, he called for mass one final time and then departed this earth, bringing a good life to a good close—the best and rarest of feats.

May we follow in his wise footsteps.

Wisdom Is Virtue.
Virtue Is Wisdom.

~

The virtues are like music. They vibrate at a higher, nobler pitch.

STEVEN PRESSFIELD

In the beginning," Goethe opens his play *Faust,* "was the Word." Then he corrects himself. No, in the beginning there was the *deed.*

This has been a book about wisdom, the fourth and final in a series about the cardinal virtues. Here at the end of it, it's worth once again pointing out: Words don't matter. *Deeds do.*

This might seem strange to say that about something as ethereal and cerebral as wisdom, but as much as any of the other virtues, wisdom about *action.* One must *do* the reading, the listening, the questioning, the searching, the experimenting, the living, the learning. Wisdom is *work,* a lot of it . . . and it never stops.

Wisdom is also the work that precedes the other virtues.

Without contemplation first, courage, self-discipline, or justice are impossible . . . and probably worthless. Edmund Burke, a member of that famous scene that Samuel Johnson curated, said that wisdom—or *prudence*, as he rendered it—was not just the first in rank of all the virtues but "the director, the regulator, the standard of them all." This is why we say that wisdom is the mother of virtue. It tells us the what, the when, the where, the who.

"Wisdom is one thing:" Heraclitus said, "to grasp the knowledge of how all things are steered through all." In practice, it is that steering that makes the virtues so inseparable. Wisdom is worthless without the will and the determination to bring it into the world, to bring it to bear on our problems and opportunities.

Talking about wisdom is easy. Celebrating the great minds of history is inspiring. Putting up their choices and mistakes for review is simple. It fills many pages, here buttressed by centuries of poetry and literature and memories. But the purpose of writing this book, and the hours you spent reading it, was not mere entertainment. That's not what philosophy is about.

We are here trying to actually get better, to become wiser ourselves. Trying to do our own work, to make that Herculean choice ourselves. Today. Tomorrow. At every moment.

What good will any virtue be if it exists only on paper? What's the point if you don't have the courage to live it? The strength to pursue it? The integrity to insist on it even with so many rewards accruing to a life moving in the opposite direction?

Sure, there is a relationship between study and practice, but at some point the rubber meets the road. We contemplate truth and then we have to act on it.

The four virtues are about instilling character—good character—so that at the critical point, a person's true nature kicks in. Wisdom is not something that just happens to you, and no one is born with it. But the good news is that once you learn something—as the great John Lewis's mother used to tell her son—no one can take it away from you. It's ours forever, if we choose to use it.

The people we have followed, from Montaigne to Marcus Aurelius, Abraham Lincoln, Maya Angelou, Joan Didion, George Patton, Plutarch, Thomas Merton, Monet, Da Vinci, Zeno, and Temple Grandin—they were not perfect and certainly not perfectly wise. At times, they exhibited the exact opposite of the virtues we are studying, and that must be noted. Still, it cannot be denied that at key, critical moments, their *character* kicked in and they did something profoundly great. Not just then, for the people they helped or the cause they furthered, but also today, for us, in the inspiration their achievements provide.

This is also true for the brilliant figures who served as cautionary tales. It wasn't their words that mattered. It was what they did because of who they were.

That's what Lincoln expressed at Gettysburg: It doesn't

matter what we say here, it matters what *they did there.* Yet what he did would not have been possible without the unique education that preceded it, he could not have given that speech without his years as a lawyer and a politician, he could not have written it without all his reading, and he could not have conceived of the moral thrust of his argument without his profound understanding and love for his fellow human beings.

And to be sure, the words he said did matter and were not forgotten. The wisdom contained in them—because it was sincere and lived—has echoed down in the century and a half since, effectively redefining the purpose of a free government, and inspiring people to *do* their own good, called as they were, to action by his words.

That is the loop of wisdom: Learn. Apply. Repeat. Not just in our own lives, but collectively as a society, learning from those that came before us, learning from our own lives, "leaving footprints behind us in the sands of time."

Virtue shines.

We cannot consecrate it. It stands eternal on its own.

There is only one way we can honor it.

By adding to it our own deeds, by picking up their "unfinished work." We must continue the tradition we are now a part of, whether we know it or not. We must use the shoulders of the giants who came before us to see further, to help more people, to live better.

We're not talking about showing off how smart we are. We're not talking about virtue signaling, but virtuous *living*.

We can learn about virtue all we want, but when we get to the crossroads, there we will have to make a choice.

We opened this series with the Bible and with John Steinbeck. Let us close by bringing them together. In *East of Eden,* Steinbeck concludes that the most powerful phrase in Christianity is *timshel*. When we read the commandments translated into English, they are rendered as just that, *commandments*. But Steinbeck thinks the Hebrew rendering is more accurate, not "Thou shalt" but "Thou mayest."

"Here is individual responsibility and the invention of conscience," he reflected to his editor as he wrote those pages. "You can if you will but it is up to you. This little story turns out to be one of the most profound in the world. I always felt it was, but now I know it is."

Whether it's from the Bible or from Hercules or *East of Eden* or *Faust,* the parable's message is the same: *We have a choice.* We *choose* between wisdom and ignorance, cowardice and courage, discipline and excess, right and wrong, virtue and vice.

We take up our tablets and begin our own unique education. We avoid the traps of fools and lies—especially the lies and foolishness that success and intelligence can engender. We keep carrying those tablets until the day we die. Learning, always, forever, for life, not school. That's the job.

No one is grading us. No one is checking our progress. No one hands us a diploma. Wisdom will always, forever, elude our full grasp.

Will we keep reaching anyway?

Will we keep learning every day?

Will we stay hungry and humble?

Curious and kind?

Wisdom takes work.

Will you do it?

Afterword

~

I don't know why I thought it was a good idea, but I wrote my college admissions essay on the distinction between *schooling* and *education*. While Socrates might have appreciated the sentiment, it was unlikely that the academics who held my fate in their hands felt the same way. I thought I was being clever, but needless to say, acceptances did not come rolling in.

I have no complaints, however. I ended up with a scholarship to the University of California, Riverside, where I would meet my wife and the mother of my children.

I was not long for the classroom anyway. I dropped out at the end of my second year to work in Hollywood. A music and movie producer had offered me a job, and as I considered the opportunity—scared that if it didn't work, I'd end up living under a bridge somewhere—he asked me a question that changed my life: "How are you going to feel sitting on campus reading about people doing stuff you could have been a part of?"

Disscepolo della sperientia. So I became a disciple of experience.

Within a few months of that conversation, I was in a room for a pitch that poached the band Linkin Park in a multimillion-dollar deal. In fact, it was my new media strategy the managers were pitching. But as a young *anteambulo*, I'd been assigned to set up the speakers and the projector.

I would be there for the rise and fall of American Apparel, running the marketing for a publicly traded company before I could legally rent a car. I saw chaos and dysfunction, as well as creative genius. I oversaw budgets of many millions of dollars and my campaigns made news all over the world. I had a reputation as a bit of a wunderkind, and while I was definitely young and decently talented, I don't think people fully appreciated what I was actually doing, which was just soaking in everything I could possibly learn, mainlining experience and knowledge and advice . . . and getting paid for it?

It was crazy and I loved it.

On top of everything else I was doing, at night, I was learning to write. I had attached myself as an apprentice to the great Robert Greene, who slowly, patiently, taught me the craft of writing. I transcribed interviews. I read obscure books he didn't want to waste time on. I wrote reports. I worked on his website. I asked questions. I listened. I watched. I absorbed his research and note card system, which I continue to use to this day (including for this book).

Here was one of the great writers of our time, who, in addition to telling me what to do, was also *showing*. He lived and worked like a monk. His focus was legendary. And beneath his Machiavellian reputation, there was kindness, patience, decency, generosity, wisdom.

I worked for and with a lot of different people in that period, working multiple jobs and then starting my own company. Some of the work was glamorous, some exciting, some of it shameful and inexcusable. I am not proud of all of it, and it nearly wrecked me (as I discussed in *Ego Is the Enemy* and the afterword to *Courage Is Calling*), but painful experiences—and our many mistakes—should not be wasted. I came to understand people; I saw power up close. I was inspired; I was horrified. In the wreckage of it, I slowly came to understand myself better too—the various motivations and demons that swirled within my ambitious younger self and why that inner child in me seemed to be drawn so often to monstrous men.

I had talked about the distinction between schooling and education in that college admissions essay, but I did not really know the difference. Yet it is clear to me now that my education began the day I walked into the registrar's office and asked for the paperwork to drop out.*

When my parents found out, they basically disowned me. The night I moved to Los Angeles, my car was towed, and the apartment that had looked so nice in daylight turned out to be

---

* As it happens, they charged me $40 for the privilege. It was the best money I ever spent.

disgusting after dark. I showed up for work in Beverly Hills, having burned the boats behind me, only to find that my boss—the one who had inspired me with his question about reading versus doing—was missing. He'd checked into rehab and would be gone for who knows how long. In his absence, his business partner renegotiated my salary significantly downward. Oh, and there was still a person in the job I was supposed to have, still sitting in my chair.

Ah, so this is what the messy real world is like.

We are the accumulation of lessons we've learned. Little ones stand out to me more than some of the big ones.

I remember sitting in some important meeting that I probably didn't deserve to be in. At some point, I interjected and said something, you know, just to contribute. My boss took me aside after and asked, "Did you really need to say that, or did you just feel like you wanted to have something to say?" I think about that question almost every day. Of course, it also appeared as the fourth law in *The 48 Laws of Power*—always say less than necessary—but it is classic Zeno too. Two ears, one mouth . . . for a reason. This is the mark not just of a self-disciplined person, but also a wise one.

I still struggle with this. Just last week I left a dinner with George Raveling—a guy who was there for the March on Washington, who met John Wooden and Kareem and Ali and Jordan and has spent nearly nine decades on this planet—and in my car on the way home, I thought, *You talked more than he did!*

We are the product of our little habits.

Was it from Montaigne that I got the idea to start a commonplace book? Possibly. Or maybe it was Emerson and his savings bank? Was it Joan Didion, whose old chair I write in each day? The best ideas are common property. I stole it from someone and everyone and have kept the habit for nearly two decades. Just as much, it has kept me—the thousands of note cards and journal pages I have filled have not just allowed me to produce my books, they've helped me as a husband and a father, and kept me sane in these deranged times.

In any case, my time *at* school didn't exactly end either. I'm pretty sure the first time I entered the college library came *after* I dropped out. There was some obscure book I noticed in the bibliography of something I was reading and, given that it cost hundreds of dollars on Amazon, I went back to see my girlfriend and tracked the book down. I would spend countless hours in the stacks at the UCR library—as well as the libraries at UCLA, Tulane, and the University of Texas—in the years since, researching for Robert Greene, and later when I was writing my own books.

Oh to be young again—how many great books then lay ahead. How many big ideas sat between those covers, of every shape and size. To get to read those classics, those incredible works of art for the first time. How much there was left to discover and learn, how many turns of phrase to delight over . . .

I love my life, and that period was incredibly stressful, but I am jealous of that kid sometimes.

I must remind myself: It is not only the young on whom this incredible gift is wasted. Five thousand years of literature precede us, with new books published every day. We are all teenagers in the face of this wellspring of human knowledge. There is an unfathomable number of books that you haven't even heard of, let alone read yet. There remain so many books to reread, at your new age, as a new person, to get something new out of.

At the beginning of this project, I would have told you I'd read all I needed to read on Lincoln . . . but as I sat down to tackle part three of this book, I came up short. So I read Michael Gerhardt's 496-page book on Lincoln's mentors. I read Hay and Nicolay. I read Doris Kearns Goodwin's 944-page *Team of Rivals*. Still there was more to know. So I read David S. Reynolds's 1088-page *Abe*. David Herbert Donald's 720-page *Lincoln*. My eight-year-old has the Gettysburg Address memorized, but I needed to read Garry Wills's Pulitzer Prize–winning book specifically about the address (his book has many more pages than the address has words). I spoke with Ken Burns about him, and Doris too. I went back through the books I'd already read (William Lee Miller, especially, but also Harold Holzer, Joshua Wolf Shenk, and Carl Sandburg). I read Lincoln's own writings, his letters and his speeches. I reviewed my pictures (and journals) from trips to Gettysburg, Antietam, and Ford's Theatre. I stood, multiple times in the course of this writing, and looked up at the Lincoln Memorial. I stood spellbound at Krzysztof Wodiczko's art piece, which projected the faces and experiences of American veterans on the face of Lincoln's statue in Union Square Park in New York. And even now—thousands of miles and at least ten thousand pages deep into the man—I suspect there's more I don't know than I do.

Patton, when he finished a book, would put a little R inside the front cover to confirm that he'd read it. It's obvious if I've read something. The book is beat up. The pages are folded to mark things I wanted to transfer to my commonplace book. The margins are filled with writing—in pen, in pencil, in a crayon I snatched away from one of my children coloring nearby. There are stains and water damage, memorializing whatever I ate while I read. Some books are signed by the author, whom I like to track down to ask questions.

What a joy it was to return to some of these books again. To pick up my old friend Montaigne. To see what struck me about Lincoln a decade ago. To see what I'd noted about Didion in her essay about notebooks. It was like traveling through time and to different worlds.

I say "like," because of course nothing can ever quite match the power of actual travel. I still want to see Lincoln's birthplace. As he said in one of his last conversations before he died, I too want to see Jerusalem. I've been to many places and have so many left to go.

There's something about travel, something about walking on hallowed ground: Here a great man gave a speech. Here a soldier gave the last full measure. Here a woman walked, carrying a toddler, leaving footsteps preserved in the sand for the next twenty thousand years. I've seen the streets of Aquincum, where Marcus Aurelius wrote some of *Meditations*. There is a tree, near some property I own in California, is one of the oldest living things on the planet, which was alive and old while Alexander the Great was conquering. Here's the agora where Zeno talked to the dead. Here's da Vinci's *Last Supper*. Here, at Waverley, on the cliffs at Bronte, is the most beautiful cemetery in the world . . . filled with once-famous people who probably did not expect to be forgotten so soon.

Each of us has a calling, the task of our lives is to listen to it . . . and be brave enough to follow.

I suppose I could have kept going professionally. I could have jumped from one fashion brand to the next; I could have built a start-up, as many of my friends did. I could have done more investing, and I watched my friends make many millions doing exactly that. I could have made a lot more money doing basically anything besides writing about an obscure school of ancient philosophy.

I spent my early twenties trying to help people sell stuff. Businesses, brands, personalities. I did very well doing so. There were a lot worse things I could have been doing—certainly in worse ways—but at some point I realized, this was not what one ought to spend one's life on. "Towering genius disdains a beaten path," Lincoln said in a speech in 1838. "It thirsts and burns for distinction; and, if possible, it will have it, whether at the expense of emancipating slaves, or enslaving men."

We can apply this logic to much more humdrum intelligence and ambition too. Ultimately, wisdom—like all the virtues—is hallowed or degraded by what it's used *for*. Do you use your brain to make the world better or worse? That's the question.

I also, you know, wanted to be happy. I have had many mentors in my life, but the woman I met at that party in 2007—my wife, Samantha—taught me as much as any of them. I've never been a king, but she has prevented me from going king-crazy more times than I can count. And she was the one who pushed me to leave behind the career I had built to become a writer.

It was her encouragement . . . and the history and literature I read had led to my first book.

I still have my copy of Budd Schulberg's *The Harder They Fall*. Almost all the final pages are marked in a now-fading neon-yellow highlighter. But it's mainly the lines about the illusion that one can deal in filth without becoming the thing they touch that led me to begin the walk away from publicity and publish what I intended to be a kind of whistleblowing account of the modern media system.

Still, it was always philosophy that I wanted to write about. My introduction to the Stoics came not long before my traditional education ended—a book recommendation changed the course of my life.

As it happens, Marcus Aurelius notes in the opening pages of *Meditations* his gratitude to Rusticus "for introducing me to Epictetus's lectures—and loaning me his own copy." The wisdom of a Greek slave, hard won through slavery and exile, would shape the mind of a king by way of a thoughtful teacher.

He was, as I am and hopefully you are too, part of a centuries-long chain of people being let in on the secret of Stoicism, this philosophy of wisdom. There, at the table in my college apartment in Riverside, vast differences in technology and culture disappeared. Suddenly, I was talking to the dead. Suddenly, I was sitting down with a great mind, engaged not in logic-chopping or philosophical paradoxes but in, as Brand Blanshard would observe of *Meditations*, "something of far more permanent interest, the ideals and aspirations that a rare spirit lived by."

I remember reading it and thinking, *How does everyone not know about this?* I remember thinking, *This—this is what I want to do.*

It took a while, but eventually I came back to it. There was something crazy, I admit, about writing a book about philosophy at twenty-five. I had no degree ... and still don't. I can't read Greek or Latin. Even now, doing this book on wisdom in my late thirties intimidates me. As far as courage goes, it hardly ranks, but the book nevertheless felt like a big swing. Who am I to speak of wisdom?

Certainly I don't claim to have it. But I can say I am a student of it.

I also reject the notion that virtue is inaccessible or inalterable. Or that the conversation belongs to Greece or Rome or people with PhDs.

"We always picture Plato and Aristotle wearing long academic gowns," Blaise Pascal wrote, "but they were ordinary decent people like everyone else, who enjoyed a laugh with their friends. And when they amused themselves [with their philosophical work] they did it for fun. It was the least philosophical and least serious part of their lives: the most philosophical was living simply and without fuss." The "schools" of the classical world weren't formal institutions. Zeno set up shop on the stoa, a porch not far from that bookshop that had changed his life. Montaigne, you could argue, learned as much from that peasant family he lived with as all the books in his library.

We can look to the past with reverence ... we should also not be afraid to challenge it. Emerson pointed out the absurdity of young men and women meekly accepting the thoughts of the ancients when "Cicero, Locke, and Bacon were only young men in libraries when they wrote their books."

My life's work has been writing and teaching about the Stoics. I hope I have added a few ideas of my own in the process.

Anyway, the real reason to write a book is that *you* will get better for having written it. My time with Stoic philosophy has made me a better person—just as writing *The Daily Dad* (and the *Daily Dad* email) has made me a better parent.

Why?

Because writing is a contemplative act.

These last six years have been spent almost entirely focused on the four cardinal virtues. And what a half decade it's been: Pandemics and fires. Floods and freezes. Demagogues and wars. Market crashes and inflation. Technological disruption. My kids growing up. My hair turning gray.

How do you stay sane in a world gone crazy?

By returning to the same truths over and over and over. In one of his letters, Seneca said that this is the path to wisdom, picking a theme or a thought to digest each day—something that fortifies you against poverty or death or adversity or whatever else life throws at you, and putting it up for consideration.

Daily Stoic's daily email, which I began in 2016, is both a great privilege to produce and also the kind of penance that Thomas Merton spoke of. Over four thousand emails now. Seven hundred thousand words. Eighty million sends. My writings in the virtue series alone amount to nearly three hundred thousand words—perhaps more if I counted what discipline demanded I methodically cut in the editing process (nearly twenty thousand words from this book, for one).

Has this made me wise? No, but *wiser* than I might have been otherwise!

And that I get paid to do it? To popularize applied philosophy as I learn it? It's the same hustle I discovered as a kid. Plus, it's a joy. It's a debt I am paying forward.

I finish this book as the world begins to grapple with the existence of functional forms of artificial intelligence. As I write this line, not only does software make suggestions on spelling and help me eliminate errors, it suggests how I might finish sentences or word them better. If I want, I could simply click over to other software and ask it to write the draft for me.

Would I do this?

No, because once again, Seneca's warning from nearly two thousand years ago still holds up. Wisdom is work. Writing is supposed to be hard. It's supposed to force you to think. I am instead writing these chapters with a stack of note cards, some of which date back fifteen years or more, just as chapters in this book draw on books that I read nearly twenty years ago (Herodotus springs to mind).

At the same time, there is something fundamentally foolish about being a Luddite—and I refuse to be one. Of course, I look things up on Wikipedia. I search things on Google Books. Of course, I listen to podcasts. The ancients would have been lucky to have such magic at their fingertips. The Library of Alexandria? Each of us has some version of that in our pocket now, and we're lucky for it . . . as long as we use this access to make us *more* effective and to learn more, not to be lazy.

I have spent many hours trying to figure out AI tools and large language models, seeing where they can make me better, where they might help me. In some cases, they have. In other cases, they reminded me of the value of the old techniques, like when I tried to confirm a quote about Abraham Lincoln. ChatGPT first told me it was Tolstoy speaking of Dickens . . . and then tried to tell me it was from Hay and Nicolay, and then told me it didn't actually exist. Only when I went back through, page by page, an eight-hundred-page prizewinning biography was I able to confirm it that my handwritten note card had in fact been correct.*

This is the kind of work we have to be willing to do . . . and that too many of us think technology can spare us from.

I write this at a time when millions around the world have given themselves over to demagogues, when we are awash in disinformation and noise. In a time of complex problems, perhaps it makes sense that we'd be seduced by simple solutions and seductive speakers.

---

* This is something AI is particularly terrible at—saying, "I don't know" and "I'm not sure." It wants to please you . . . so it often ends up *misleading* you.

This is the tragedy of Elon Musk, I think, and why he serves as such a focal point in this book. You never know what your experiences will someday help you to understand, but given what I saw firsthand with Dov Charney at American Apparel— a similarly brilliant but erratic person—I think I was well suited to grasp what too many other smart people I know are obviously missing. Writing about such a brilliant and important person so critically was not a decision I made lightly— after all, back in 2017, I wrote a book about a different billionaire who spent a decade and tens of millions of dollars to destroy a media outlet he disliked. Elon Musk is not just the richest man in the world, with a president in his pocket and an army of followers at his command; he happened to move his factories and his businesses into the little town where I live and where my bookstore is. He is a thin-skinned, impulsive person. He could make things very painful for me.

We also have many mutual friends. I've been invited to his house. I'm a fan. It would have been much easier and safer to write about almost anyone else. I'm sure a significant portion of my readers will disagree with my take entirely.

But this is what we're talking about, isn't it? You gotta do what you think is right. You speak the truth as you see it.

It's also a reminder: You can be very smart and very powerful and indeed even very brilliant, but none of this can purchase conscience or decency or happiness.

There is an interesting passage in *Meditations* that I have been thinking a lot about these days. In it, Marcus recalls a time he was up on the rostrum, really working the crowd. For a man usually so controlled and wise, this must have been a strange but exhilarating experience. But after the rush of the pandering wore off, he was racked with guilt, ashamed of what he had said. He notes that the audience didn't mind, didn't catch his low techniques. "And so you have to be an idiot as well?" he says, challenging his rationalization, letting the choice hang there.

I've been wrong about a lot, but as far as the great con of our time is concerned? I can proudly say I didn't fall for it for a minute. Even when it might have worked out better for me. Even when smart people I know managed to outsmart themselves about it.

Just because the world seems to be cruel and stupid these days doesn't mean we have to be. Just because some people seem to revel in the fantasy world they have created, preferring fictions to complicated reality, doesn't mean we should. That was the whole point of philosophy, Chrysippus said, to not be part of the mob and rabble.

We must soldier on, even if it's a little lonely, even if we doubt ourselves sometimes.

I refuse to despair. I refuse to become cynical.

I know history. I know human beings. Or rather, I know *something* of it.

Still, my heart flutters.

In any case, here I am now, though, coming to the end of this series. Gibbon, when he finished *The Decline and Fall of the Roman Empire*, noted his sadness at taking "everlasting leave of an old and agreeable companion." I don't feel exactly that way, because virtue isn't something you take leave of—but there is something bittersweet about drawing these books to a close.

I am better now for having done them, not just as a person but as a writer. Sure, I think of all the things I'd do differently if I was starting over, the things I've learned since I published the first book in 2021. But again, isn't this the point? To get better as you go. Our job is to learn from our time here. The aim is to be able to put our past selves to shame—even if our notebooks are a way of keeping in touch with who we used to be.

Mostly, though, I am proud of what I have put to the page. I am grateful that you, the reader, made it this far. Thank you.

How is a person supposed to know if they're making progress if wisdom is so elusive? The same way it works with the horizon. We're never actually getting closer to it, but we can look behind us and see that we are at least covering serious distance— we can see how far we've come from where we started.

One thing I've noticed? I am calmer. I am quieter. I argue less. I get upset less. I admit I am wrong more often.

This is wisdom, Epictetus said. Getting in fewer fights, letting more things go, focusing more on what you control. *A smooth flow of life.*

There's still a long way to go, but I'm proud of the progress I've made.

Self-awareness is not common—not in presidents or local pooh-bahs, or even among writers. It takes work to hold yourself up for review. In therapy. In conversations with your spouse. Alone in the pages of a journal.

But it's the only way. The only way to heal that wounded inner child. To learn from your mistakes. To figure out what's what and what matters.

I close this series here, but I remain committed to the work.

Day by day. Page by page. Trial by trial.

Wis*er*, not wise.

Miramar Beach, FL
January 2025

What To Read Next?

~

For most people, bibliographies are boring. For those who love to read, it's the best part. In the case of this book, which relied on so many wonderful authors and thinkers, I could not possibly fit the entire bibliography in the book. Instead, I've prepared a full list not only of all the great books that influenced the ideas you've just read, but also what I got out of them and why you might like to read them. To get this list, please just email **books@wisdomtakeswork.com** or go to **wisdomtakeswork.com/books**.

CAN I GET EVEN MORE BOOK RECOMMENDATIONS?

YES. You can also sign up for my list of monthly book recommendations (now in its second decade). The list has grown to include more than two hundred thousand people all over the world and recommended thousands of life-changing books. **RyanHoliday.net/readingnewsletter**. I'll start you off with ten awesome books, I know you'll love.

Acknowledgments

~

Like everyone in this book, I am a product of all the wisdom that came before me and the mentors and teachers who guided me. I will never forget the booming sound of Ms. Whitaker in fourth grade: *What are you doing?!* She had caught me hiding something underneath my partially opened desk. She marched over to fetch it. It was a Louis L'Amour book I had been sneakily reading. *You can understand this?* she asked. Yeah, I said, it's really good. Instead of getting mad, she got me accepted to a gifted and talented program. I am indebted to Mr. Dell'Orto and Mrs. Kars, who opened my eyes to real history and encouraged me to be a writer, respectively. A teacher can change the course of someone's life—if anyone's life has been changed by my work, it is only possible because those three teachers (and others, to be sure) first changed my life. I am grateful to General James Mattis, not only for his example but for a few of the stories that appear throughout this series. Robert Greene, who not only mentored me but taught me how to be a writer. There are few people whose wisdom and advice I value more. I thank the great George Raveling for his mentorship. Dolores Molina, I'm so lucky you came back into my life. I must acknowledge my two boys here, whom I was hiking with (one in tow and the other in a backpack) in Bastrop State Park when the idea for this series first popped into my head in 2019. That was the start of my being half-consumed and distracted by this project, and I appreciate your indulgence . . . as well as all you have taught me. I'd say it's over now, but you know I'm already starting on the next one. Thanks to Billy Oppenheimer for all his research. Hristo Vassilev, I've lost track of how many books and articles you've helped me get right. The team at *Daily Stoic* and the Painted Porch, thank you—Dena Beattie, Brendan Bures, Jessica Davidson, Chelsea Debrot, Eric Empson, Jordan Gracey, Claire Hooker, Liz Shear, Ashley Weldon, Trysten Tinajero, Peyton White—for making everything work and for putting up with me. Thank you to my agent, Stephen Hanselman, and to Julia Serebrinsky, whose rigorous edit helped me cut those twenty thousand words. Thanks to the entire staff at Portfolio, who despite being a business imprint took a chance not just on a twenty-four-year-old interested in ancient philosophy but supported and funded this multiyear, multibook series on *virtue*. And of course, Samantha, thanks for showing me what most of this virtue stuff looks like in practice . . . and for holding me accountable to things I am blasé enough to put in writing.